Forests, Woods & Groves

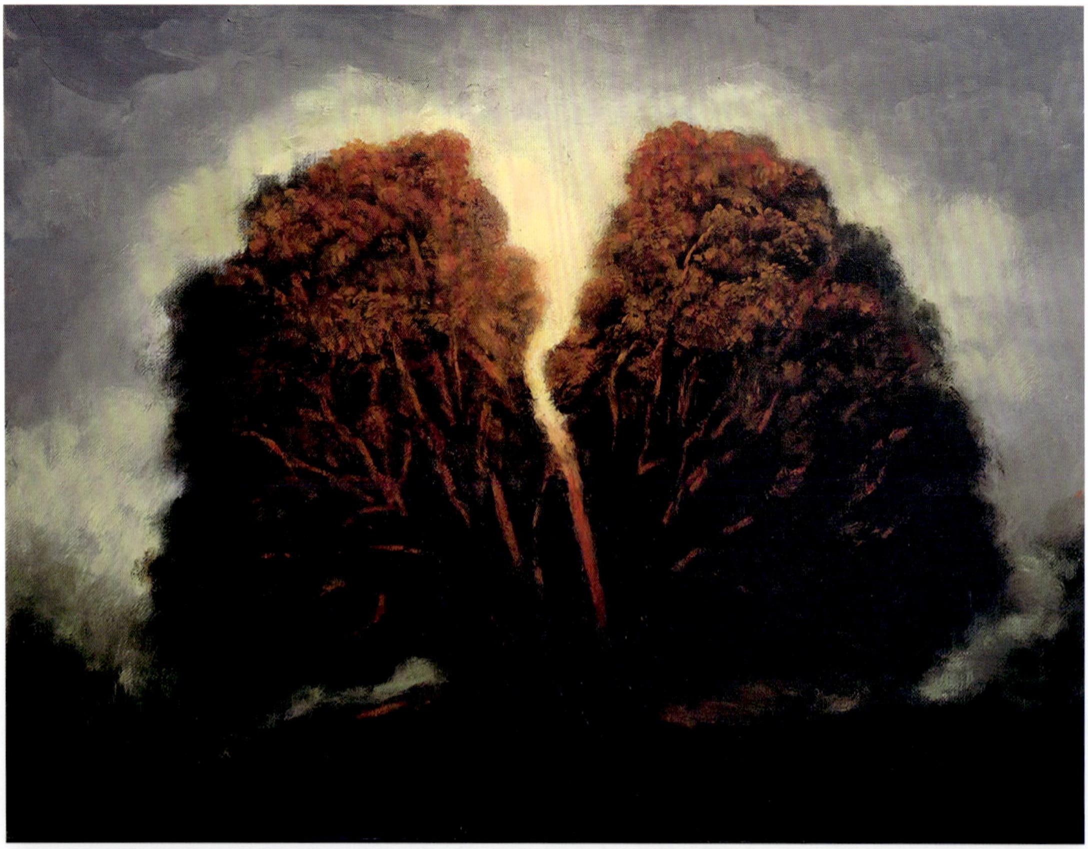

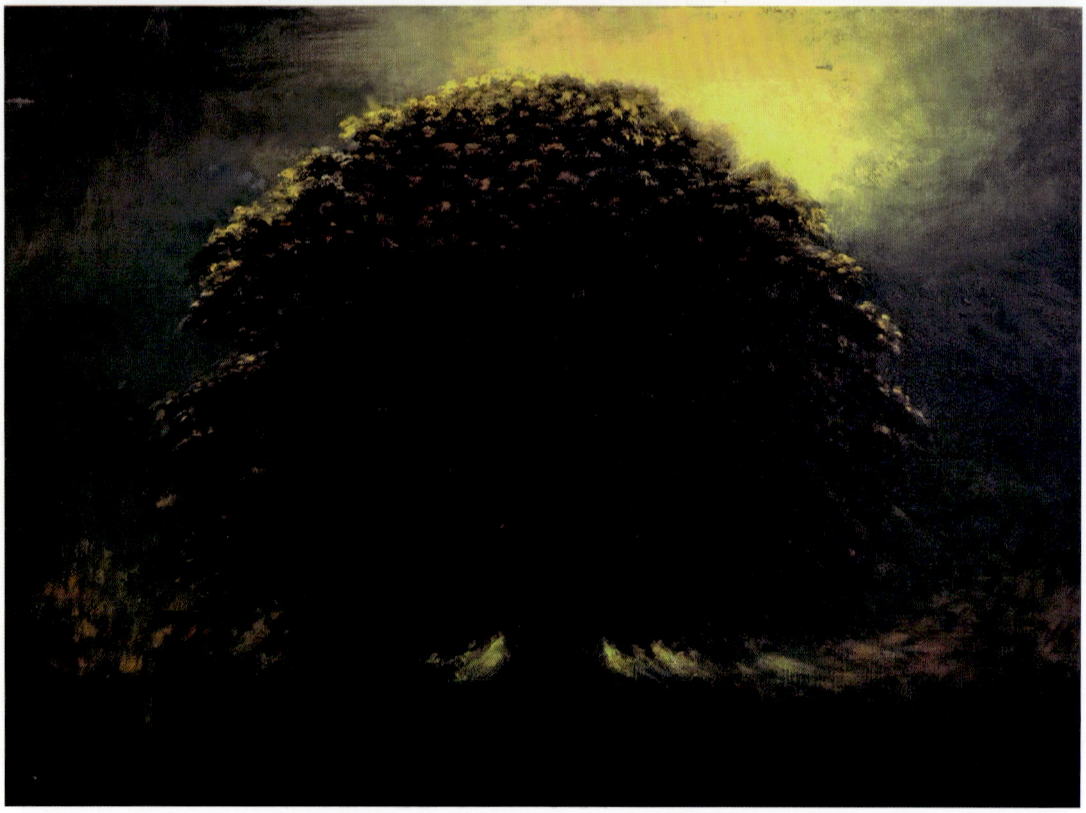

Dedicated to the memory of Lesley Slight,
a founding member of the Arborealists
1939–2024

Forests, Woods & Groves

ART FROM THE ARBOREALISTS

BATSFORD

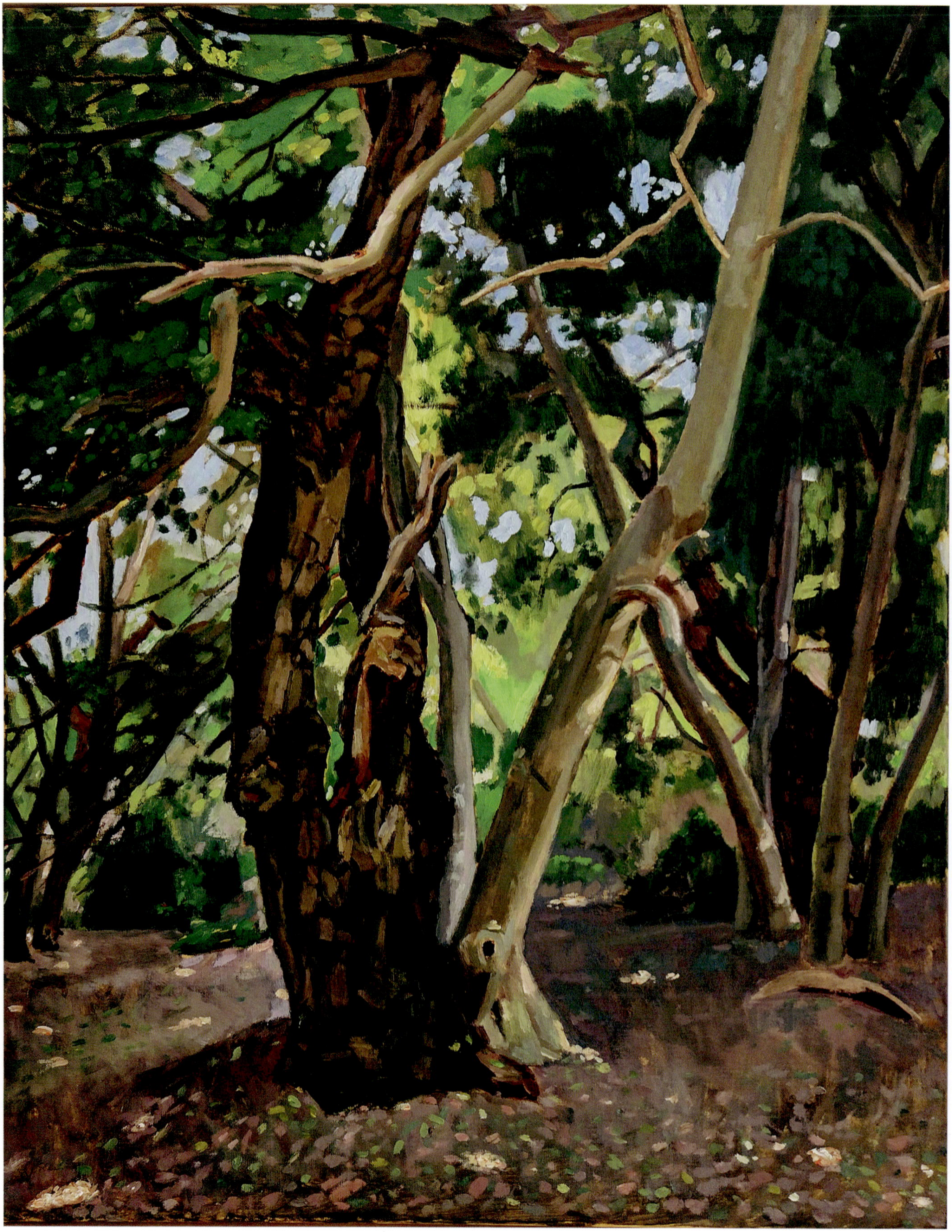

Contents

OPPOSITE Nahem Shoa, *Staverton Ancient Oaks*, 2023

Foreword

Philippa Beale – Artist/Curator
Chloe Hughes RCA – Curator

This book is published for the tenth anniversary of the Arborealists, a group of professional artists who feature trees as an important aspect of their practice. Since their formation by Tim Craven in 2014, they have had 38 exhibitions, establishing a strong international profile. The Arborealists have always been involved in site-specific projects, and in 2016, George Peterken OBE, forester, ecologist and author, invited the group to respond to Lady Park Wood near Monmouth, the only scientifically monitored unmanaged woodland in the UK. The film *Lady Park Wood*, produced by founding member Fiona McIntyre and screened throughout Europe, shows the artists collecting site-specific information. Since 2018, the Arborealists, in partnership with Katrina Munro (Sustainable Economy Officer at Exmoor National Park Authority), have worked on a project at Dartmoor and Exmoor. This project culminated in a major travelling exhibition in 2020, starting at the Somerset Museum and Art Gallery, before continuing to different venues throughout Somerset and Devon during 2021 and 2022. As part of the HM Queen Elizabeth II Green Canopy Project, the group has chronicled the ancient trees of England in association with Julian Hight, presenter and judge of the *Tree of the Year* for Channel 4 and Chair of the Ancient Tree Forum. This has resulted in an ongoing exhibiting partnership, 'From Ancient Trees', at Nature in Art Gallery in Gloucestershire. A current project is to survey Staverton Park in Suffolk, one of the oldest sites in the UK, to create another major exhibition (2025) at The Minories Gallery, Colchester, Essex. Other ongoing exhibitions include 'The Quietness of Feeling: An Exploration of Trees Through the Art of Benjamin Haughton' and 'The Arborealists' from October 2024 to September 2025 at Portsmouth Museum and Art Gallery, as well as 'Forests, Woods and Groves' at Batsford Gallery, London from November to December 2024.

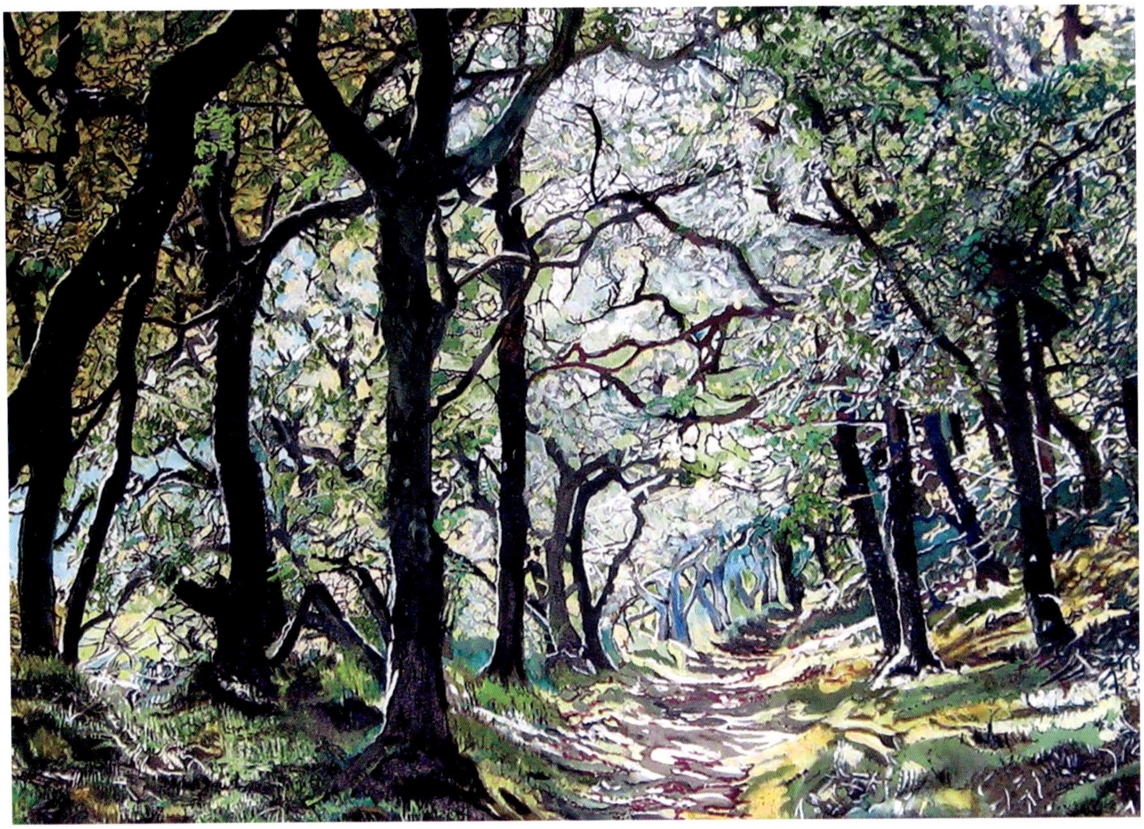

ABOVE Philippa Beale, *Bageworthy Ancient Woodland, Exmoor*

It is the first time Chloe Hughes has worked with the Arborealists, discovering a group of highly skilled artists who feature trees, forests and woodlands as their most vital subjects. The Arborealists' diverse and influential practices, involving over forty members, have highlighted these protected woodlands' history and changing landscapes, as well as expressing new perspectives on how art can illuminate the enchantment of ancient trees. Each member has developed their artistic language, showcasing manifold applications in everything from scale and medium to style and philosophical approach. In the last ten years, their many successful exhibitions have carved a strong national profile for the Arborealists and garnered widespread critical acclaim. Their first publication in 2016, *The Arborealists: The Art of the Tree*, sold out within the year; their second in 2017, *The Arborealists, The Art of Trees*, was published in both English and French. Chloe has found great pleasure working with such an extraordinary and contrastive group of artists, and looks forward to continuing supporting their endeavours in the future.

The Arborealists: site-specific projects 2017–2024

Tim Craven, President of the Arborealists

A chance glance in Lymington High Street serendipitously kickstarted the Arborealists' first site-specific project that would reap rewards and open doors. In the summer of 2016, George Peterken OBE, celebrated expert and author on trees and natural woodland, was on holiday in the New Forest, where he had spent much of his youth. That day, he was cycling through Lymington when he was stopped by a traffic light. Glancing around, he spotted a tiny advert tied with string round the pole of a Belisha Beacon. It announced that the St Barbe Museum & Art Gallery was staging an exhibition on 'The Art of the Tree' by the Arborealists, a group he knew about because he had bought a copy of *Under the Greenwood* the year before, when visiting Chichester Art Gallery with his wife, Susan. Trees being his subject, he instantly knew he should check it out. If the lights had been green, he would not have stopped. If he had stopped at any other position, he would not have been by the post and seen the advert. Of such moments are collaborations made.

Impressed with the show, he hit upon the idea of inviting the group to Lady Park Wood to engage in an art project. George enjoyed reproductions of historic woodland paintings, often using them to front his book jackets, though he found it challenging to find any without a trace of human activity; he was aware of the importance of art as his wife was an artist. Owned by Forestry England, Lady Park Wood is on the banks of the River Wye, near Monmouth, and is the only scientifically monitored, unmanaged wood in the country. Parts of it have remained untouched for over 150 years and George, living nearby, knew it intimately. Indeed, he knew the stories and behaviour of many of the individual trees over decades. They are measured and documented every ten years; students and interested parties are taken there and told that 'this is what happens when you leave nature to its own devices'. Without hesitation, we were there like a shot, and we met George in the woods to discuss possibilities. We were immediately on board to engage in an exciting project – with an opportunity to learn much from a distinguished ecologist. A group of 18 Arborealists duly met the following spring for a first focus weekend, and after a fascinating briefing tour from George, members went off in search of suitable motifs for their art. Wye Valley Area of Outstanding Natural Beauty (AONB) staff had been alerted to our gathering and generously arrived with cake at lunchtime to introduce themselves, and to see what was going on. Their Spring Festival the following year was serendipitously to be themed 'On Woodland', so some form of connection was evident to all. An autumn weekend for a different season, colours and atmosphere was subsequently planned, and the pub-supper get-togethers arranged for the evenings would become a feature of all future site projects. Fellowship and mutual support are a major part of the group's ethos.

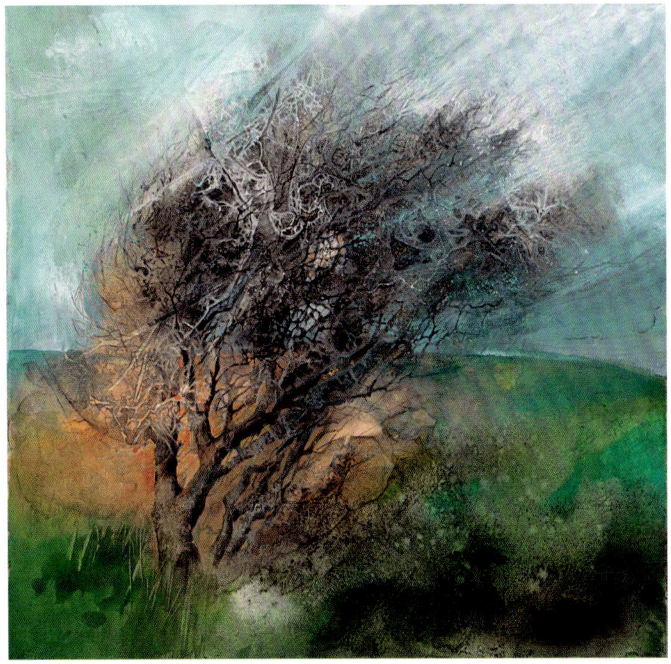

ABOVE Ann Blockley, *Wind-Blown Hawthorn*

I now needed a venue for an exhibition of all the works generated. The obvious choice was the Nelson Museum, Monmouth, the central county venue. I eventually contacted Curator Annie Rainsbury and paid a visit to pitch the idea of showcasing the fascinating story of this unique woodland through an exhibition of our artworks. The main exhibition space was already programmed for the AONB 2018 Spring Festival; additionally, Annie generously gave us the mezzanine floor above for a pop-up show the following year, promising an extended exhibition. Arborealist Fiona McIntyre had the great idea of commissioning a short film to document the project and secured the services of celebrated eco filmmakers Kashfi Halford and Manuel Valcarce, who joined the group for the autumn weekend. The film, sponsored by Forestry England, as well as various organisations and numerous artists, was premiered to acclaim at the festival in Monmouth's Shire Hall. Wye Valley AONB duly won an award for the varied and rich content of their superb festival.

George announced that he would like to write about what the works of art had revealed to him as a scientist. Connecting art and science is not new, but this was a fascinating and innovative angle, and we were subsequently successful in securing a grant for a publication entitled *Art Meets Ecology* from the AONB, published in 2021 by Sansom & Company. A second grant funded a reprint when the first batch of 500 sold out. George grouped the subjects for his observations using titles such as: Looking Down, Edges, Slopes, Woodland Space and Lost in the Woods. Art Historian Dr Christiana Payne of Oxford Brookes University contributed a superb end-piece essay entitled 'Roots in the Past'. A requirement of the grant was to organise a related educational outreach event in the region, which we successfully achieved with Hereford College of Art. This pilot project was a triumph on several levels and a valuable learning curve for the group. The collaboration with George has proved particularly fruitful and is ongoing. The notion of working with partner organisations to enhance projects and their impact was immediately embedded into the Arborealists' *modus operandi*. We have since worked to mutual advantage with National Park Authorities (NPA), other AONBs, the Woodland Trust, the National Trust and others. Local knowledge and expertise, increased marketing and audience enhancement have been hugely beneficial for the success of multiple exhibition projects and have added attractive leverage to secure first-class gallery venues. Each project is promoted with a detailed written proposal and backed up with track record. Early on, some of us shared the delights of the unique and historic Wistman's Wood on Dartmoor, and I had the idea of an exhibition project on the subject. Then, through Fiona, we were given a direct link to the outgoing Chief Executive of Exmoor National Park Authority, an opportunity not to be missed.

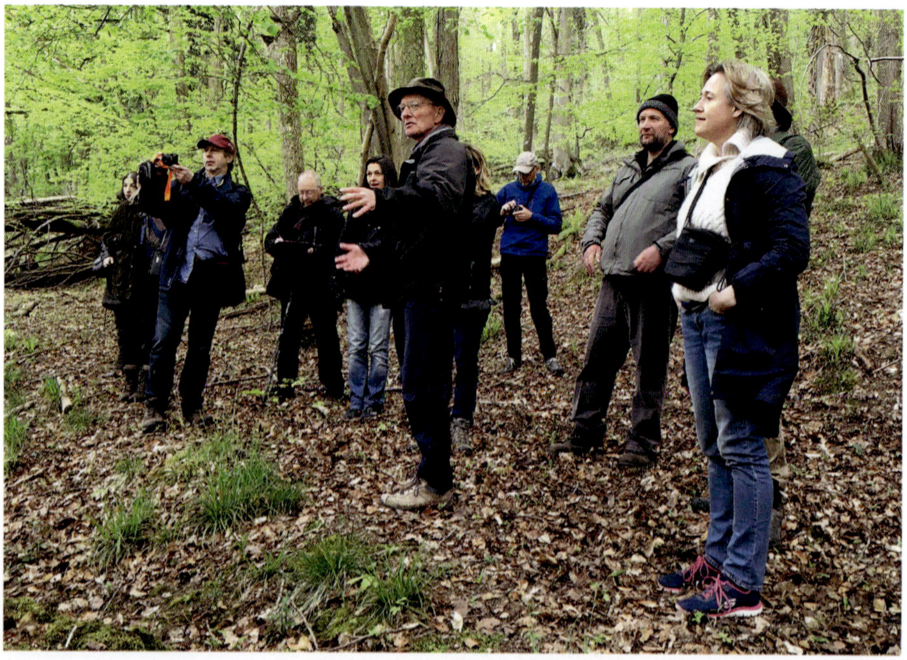

ABOVE The Arborealists with George Peterken, surveying Lady Park Wood

Therefore, the project was instantly expanded to trees and woodland on Exmoor and Dartmoor (including Wistman's Wood) in partnership with both National Park Authorities (would they collaborate or were they rivals? An interesting conundrum). Successful meetings with NPA staff at both HQs, in Dulverton and Bovey Tracy, initiated the two-year project for a spring 2018 start. Experts at the NPAs would each identify six trees and woodland sites of diverse and special ecological, social, economic and historic significance on their respective moors, at which the participating Arborealists (and a few local guest artists) would make work according to choice. The exhibition, benefitting all parties, would promote the excellent work and objectives of the NPAs. Considerable research, exploration and selection made this a rewarding project for participants, and we all learnt much about both moors and their varied environments, which was one of the project's aims.

I thought the ideal Gallery for the resulting exhibition would be in Taunton – the big city between the two moors. The impressive Somerset Museum was the obvious favourite. With perseverance and thanks to Arborealist Paul Newman (local connections again), we secured a slot for autumn 2021, the only physical exhibition we staged in the pandemic years. With a designer on the team, the show was beautifully presented, and the works were hung in the twelve site groups alongside interpretive texts supplied by the NPAs. Smaller, subsidiary shows were later staged on Exmoor at Lanacre Barn and on Dartmoor at Artmill Gallery, Plymouth.

Having enjoyed the Lady Park Wood art, George suggested another site project at Staverton Park near Woodbridge in Suffolk, with which he could assist us. He had worked at the privately owned site early in his career and could introduce us to the family. It is one of the oldest oak woodlands in Europe, an almost unique environment, with a rich and fascinating history. After the Second World War, the government had offered a grant to have it levelled for new crops, but the family rightly and indignantly refused, fully aware of its significance. The innumerably pollarded trees are quite extraordinary specimens and the park, though not large and now employed as cattle pasture, is ecologically somewhat different from the adjacent Staverton Thicks, having experienced a different history of use.

I pitched the idea along with our track record to the owner, Kate, and won permission to proceed. The autumn focus weekend in 2023 for 16 artists kicked off with a fascinating 4-hour briefing tour with George and Gary Battell, Suffolk county's Tree Officer, who also brought along his arborist. Their combined knowledge, love and enthusiasm for the park and even individual trees was truly revelatory and was the perfect inspirational introduction to make art. Our promotional and expertise partner is Suffolk & Essex Coasts & Heaths National Landscape (AONB rebranded), and exhibitions are planned for The Minories, Colchester and Gallery East in Woodbridge.

While the Ancient Trees project has a specific theme, it will incorporate multiple sites across the UK. At our 2018 Black Swan Arts exhibition opening in Frome, I was introduced to Julian Hight, who lives in the town and had published several books on British and world ancient trees. I had no hesitation in asking him if he would like to collaborate with the Arborealists on a future ancient trees-themed exhibition – a double subject encompassing the historic and mythological, with botanical stories. Ancient trees are invariably of extraordinary and seductive shapes, with strong personalities. Julian was enthusiastic and agreed to produce a list of 15 ancient trees, with suitable species and geological spread across the south of the country, and to provide interpretive texts.

The premise agreed was that participating artists would choose one tree from his list and another, presumably local, researched and selected by themselves. Texts on the stories uncovered would accompany the works and the different interpretations of a particular tree, such as the Tortworth Chestnut, would hang together in a small group. Unfortunately, momentum was severely interrupted by the COVID-19 pandemic and has had to be regenerated. Some artists dropped by the wayside and others needed to be recruited, some of whom would only be able to produce one work for either category in time for the exhibition at Nature in Art Gallery, Twigworth near Gloucester, in September 2024.

The tree as a subject for art is almost endlessly versatile in application, and the group's diversity of approach lends itself to visually rich interpretations. Site projects, where a distilled focus can be shared and considered over time, are a strong and valued strand of the Arborealists' ethos.

Staverton Park, Suffolk: imagination and reality

George Peterken OBE

The Arborealists have recently worked as a group in woods that are not only artistically rewarding, but also significant for ecological studies and wildlife conservation. The first of these, Lady Park Wood, is an ancient woodland in the gorge of the lower Wye Valley that has been used for 80 years to study natural woodland processes. This has been followed by a project in Dartmoor and Exmoor, including the renowned Wistman's Wood, and a new project in the Suffolk Sandlings in Staverton Thicks and the Park. Lady Park Wood generated a book – *Art meets Ecology*[1] – which featured the artworks created in the wood and linked them to commentaries setting out the understandings gained from 80 years of ecological research.

All these woods seem natural. Their wild surroundings and lack of management easily convince casual visitors that they are thoroughly wild, for they feel the freedom and hint of danger that accompanies wild and seemingly remote places and see manifestly old trees and no signs of management. Some ecologists, too, have come to regard them as expressions of natural forces, largely unaffected by the works of people, past and present. Artistically they bring out the exuberance of untamed nature and the endurance of individual trees. Whatever their particular interest, most visitors would like to think these woods have 'always been like this', unchanging places that contrast starkly with the rectilinearity of urban environments and the intensely cultivated character of most farmland.

These perceptions and impressions, however, are wrong. Not entirely, but mostly. Ecological research and historical records have combined to show that all these woods were different in the distant past and have been greatly influenced by the actions of people. Lady Park Wood was, until 1870, an ancient wood that, like so many others, had been managed as coppice-with-standards, supplying charcoal and much else to the local economy. It only looks like it does today because parts have not been touched since coppicing ended in 1870 and the wood was set aside in 1944 as a place to study unfettered growth of native woodland. Wistman's Wood, far from being an astonishing remnant of primaeval Britain, has been revealed by pollen to be changed so little over the years that it would still be recognisable to those who emparked it

1. Peterken, G., Craven T. and Payne, C. (2020). *Art meets Ecology. The Arborealists in Lady Park Wood.* Sansom & Company, Bristol.

RIGHT
Photograph of Staverton Park by Philippa Beale

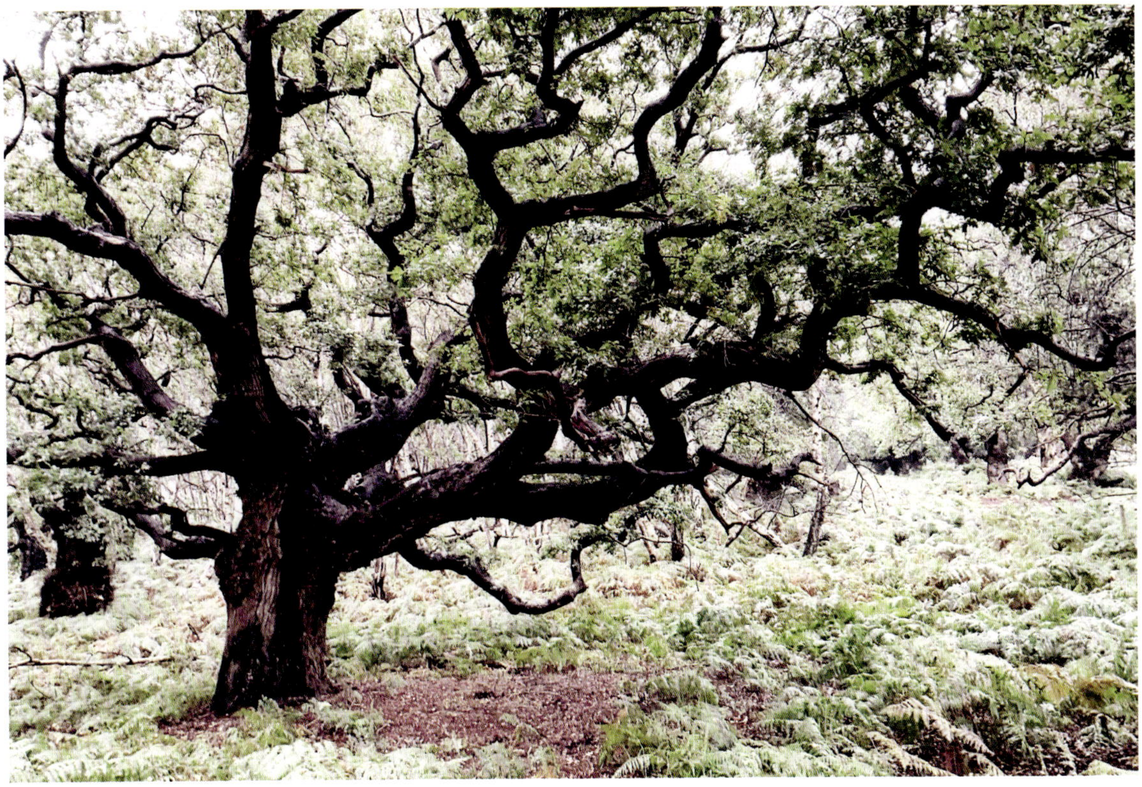

from the wooded waste 800 years ago or the nobility who chased foxes on horseback under its oaks shortly before the monasteries were dissolved. These mismatches between perception and reality are heartening in many ways. Among other things, they show that nature in general and woodland in particular can, given time, restore itself after profound alteration by people.

The story of Lady Park Wood has been set out in a book[2] and numerous articles. Wistman's Wood was recognised as one of the seven wonders of Devon in the nineteenth century and justly celebrated in both early and recent ecological literature[3]. Staverton Thicks and the Park are less well-known, but their origins and history have been clear since my own studies in 1967–69[4]. All three illustrate forms of both stability and long-term change. Here, I have chosen to concentrate on Staverton, the place where the Arborealists are currently working, to show that they are semi-natural, the product of both nature and people.

Staverton Park is unique. That's easy to say, for every place is different from every other place at some level of detail, but Staverton is unique in more profound ways. Hidden behind a thick, seemingly impenetrable wood in a world of pine plantations, ploughed fields and

2. Peterken, G. and Mountford, E. (2017). *Woodland Development: A long-term study of Lady Park.* CABI, Wallingford.
3. Mountford, E.P., Backmeroff, C.E. and Peterken, G.F. (2001). 'Long-term patterns of growth, mortality, regeneration and natural disturbance in Wistman's Wood, a high altitude oakwood on Dartmoor.' Report and Transactions of the Devon Association for the Advancement of Science, 133, 227–262. This built on earlier studies by Malcolm Spooner, Molly Spooner and Michael Proctor. Wistman's Wood was also featured in the classic early text by Sir Arthur Tansley, 1939. *The British Islands and their Vegetation*, Cambridge University Press.
4. Peterken, G.F. (1969). *Development of vegetation in Staverton Park, Suffolk.* 'Field Studies', 3, 1–39.

abandoned airfields, it is an open wood consisting of literally hundreds of ancient oaks that once formed part of a medieval park.

Ecologists know Staverton as an ancient, oak-dominated wood-pasture. Wood-pastures were common and widespread in the medieval countryside and all would have had many oaks, but most of these open, grazed woodlands included other trees, such as ash, field maple, small-leaved lime, large-leaved lime, wych elm and beech, along with a leavening of smaller trees, such as rowan and hawthorn, and ephemeral trees, such as birch. Staverton is unusual in having only old oaks and a modicum of birch and rowan, a reflection of the sandy, infertile, strongly acid soils on which it grows.

In prehistory, wood-pastures must have been widespread in the unclaimed land beyond the boundaries of early settlements. They survived after the Norman conquest on common lands, in forests and within deer parks. In recent centuries, most made way for farmland, and the rest were either stripped of their timber, leaving grass – heath commons, or were incorporated into landscaped parks around great country mansions and embellished with ornamental trees. Staverton escaped all this, sailing quietly through history into the turbulence of modern times. Its nearest surviving counterparts must be Dalkeith Old Wood, Midlothian; the ancient parkland of Wychwood Forest that was incorporated within Blenheim Park, Oxfordshire; and perhaps Gregynog Great Wood, Powys.

The wood behind which Staverton Park hides is the Thicks. Driving along the road from Woodbridge towards Orford one passes a dense wall of holly, thicker than the wall of pines opposite, but with much the same visual impact. Penetrate to the interior, however, and one immediately enters a world of ancient oaks embedded in a thicket of great hollies. Historically, this is just another portion of Staverton Park, but 200 or so years ago it was fenced off from the rest of the park. Hollies subsequently regenerated in droves. So tall and thick did they grow that the oaks suffered in their shade, leaving many dead and others in advanced states of decay. If anywhere evoked the supposed darkness and disorientation of primaeval forests, the pre-1987 Thicks was the place. The hollies grew so tall that one became the tallest holly in the country, but with age and height came vulnerability to wind and heavy snow falls. In October 1987, the Thicks was shattered by a great storm across south-east England. Now it is a disorientating mass of fallen, leaning and still upright hollies, mixed with regrowth from the fallen and leaning trees and a scatter of dead and degenerating oaks in all states of decay, grotesque monuments to both the passage of time and resilience in the face of adversity.

I first heard about the Thicks when studying holly in the New Forest. When I first read about remarkable holly woods on Dungeness shingle in Kent and in the Sandling district of Suffolk, my first thought was that these must be ancient hollins, the 'holly orchards' where hollies were once lopped for winter fodder, but I was wrong on both counts. At Dungeness, the Holmstone Wood proved to be an ancient shrubland that once furnished plump herons to the authorities of Lydd and their friends. In the Sandlings, the Thicks proved to be natural growth that had become the tallest and densest holly wood I had ever seen.

My first opportunity to visit Staverton came when I was helping with a field course at Flatford Mill. Noting my enthusiasm, Jim Bingley, the warden, asked if I would write an article for *Field Studies*, the journal of the Field Studies Council, and I agreed partly because it gave me an excuse for fieldwork while working in the Biological Records Centre at Monks Wood Experimental Station. During 1967–68 I explored, described and mapped the Thicks and the Park and spent an inordinate amount of time looking for historical references in the record office in Bury St Edmunds and working my way through calendars of medieval manuscripts in the main library in Cambridge. At the same time, I met Norman Scarfe, the author of the Suffolk volume in the *Making of the English Landscape* series, and corresponded with Hugh Farmar, who used to hire the Sheppard's Cottage in the Park and who had published *The Cottage in the Forest*, a small book about the park and its wildlife in the immediate post-war period[5]. Sadly, I never met Hugh: he wrote to me from Drapers' Hall, London. My account of the Park's history and ecology, published in *Field Studies* in 1969, was relentlessly factual: this was not a journal where authors could wax lyrical.

At the time, I was in regular contact with Oliver Rackham and sometimes chauffeured him to woods in East Anglia, but we never visited Staverton together. He did, however, subsequently find a valuable medieval reference to the park which I had missed, which is mentioned in his *History of the Countryside* and his *Ancient Woodlands*[6]. My account, and this extra source, concluded that Staverton Park originated in the thirteenth century on what must at the time have been a great tract of unenclosed heathland pastures with scattered woods and trees. Most likely this was common ground, for even today the neighbouring parish boundaries are distorted in order to share the land that became the park.

By 1967, the park had been managed, then owned, for 22 years by Mr Jack Kemble of Wantisden Hall Farm and his family remains the owner. It was a game preserve, presided over by George Boast and his wife, who lived in the cottage within the Thicks. Despite being in his 90s, George walked fast on what I remember were short bandy legs, and could still climb trees. He regaled me with tales of shooting parties at Staverton involving King Edward VII.

Today, the park is surrounded by arable fields, pig cabins and plantations, but in 1945 it lay among heathland, populated by stone curlews, nightjars and woodlarks, with marshland by the Butley River along the northern flank supporting snipe, redshank and yellow wagtails. Aerial photographs taken in 1945 show a rectilinear patchwork of different forms of heathland,

5. Hugh Farmar, 1949. *The Cottage in the Forest*. Hutchinson, London.
6. Oliver Rackham, 1986. *The History of the Countryside*. Dent, London, p.143. Oliver Rackham, 2003. *Ancient Woodland, its history, vegetation and uses in England*. 2nd edition. Castlepoint Press, Dalbeattie.

the fading sign of cultivation that had temporarily brought the heaths under cultivation. As Hugh Farmar described it in *A Cottage in the Forest*, 'Staverton Park is probably the oldest living survival in East Anglia, a strange place, history and tradition apart, with a character all its own. On a still midsummer night when the nightjars churn, and the roding woodcock croak overhead, in deep winter when the snow under the hollies is crimsoned by the berries dropped by ravenous birds, or at autumn dusk when the mist rises wraithlike from the stream and the rusty wailing of the stone curlew sounds across the trees, it has a magical beauty.'

However, Jack Kemble and the Ministry of Agriculture wanted a productive, modern farm, so gorse was rooted out and the heaths were ploughed deep enough to break up the iron pan layer and fertilised until they became productive arable fields. At the same time, large quantities of fallen wood were cleared from under the oaks. Fortunately, the oaks were spared.

Staverton Park and the Thicks are surrounded by an almost complete medieval park bank, but when was the Park emparked? Two national land surveys give an indication. The Domesday Book of 1086 records a few parks elsewhere in Suffolk, but not in the manor of Staverton[7]. The Hundred Rolls of 1275 do mention the park, which indicates emparking in the thirteenth century. Its early condition is indicated in some accounts from 1268, which record income from herbage, bracken, bark and pannage, a sure sign that the park was then, as now, an open oak woodland. The park bank forms an almost circular enclosure, so there was no other enclosed land in the immediate vicinity. Medieval parks were valuable as pasture and sources of timber and they were often created to keep deer, but there has never been any sign that Staverton was a deer park.

The medieval character of the Park was confirmed in 1362. After the owner of the manor of Staverton died, his possessions were tallied in an Inquisitions Post Mortem, thereby leaving us an unparalleled insight into the landscape as it was 660 years ago. At that time he held 240 acres of arable, and 240 acres of fallow land ('*terre frisce*'), so half his cultivated land had to be fallowed at any one time to maintain fertility. Some 140 acres were breck heath ('*bruer*'), which must have been used as rough pasture. Much the most valuable land was the 6.5 acres of meadow, which fed farm stock through the winter, and 3 acres of pasture, which sounds like a paddock by the farm. Finally, he owned profit of rabbits, but no warren, and one park with valuable letting for grazing ('*agistment*'). This is Staverton Park, evidently regarded as a pasture but seemingly overrun with rabbits, just as it was until 1952.

In 1528, just seven years before the monastery was dissolved, the Chronicle of Butley Priory recorded that '*Regina et Dux cum suis generosis et generosibus vulpes apud parcum de Staverton venati sunt et ibidem Padium suum sub Quercubus sumpsere cum Joco at Ludo satis Jacundis*'. This was a party. The monks entertained the Duke of Suffolk and his wife, formerly the Queen of France, by staging

7. For historical references, see Peterken, G.F. (1969).

a fox hunt under the oaks accompanied by fun and games and a picnic. The monks and their guests could not have galloped on horseback after foxes through a thick woodland.

Most illuminating of all is a map made by John Norden in 1600–01 of Sir Michael Stanhope's estate. This was a careful survey of the district by one of the leading surveyors of the time presented in maps that are remarkably free of decorative detail. Norden shows the park boundaries, the elongated meadows along the valley north of the park and the distribution of trees within the park. The dense woodland is where it is now, but it was fringed by scattered trees and there were also scattered trees in a belt all around the margins. Thus, the trees have retreated a little from the periphery in the last 420 years and the core woodland has been shaved back, but the main concentration of trees has survived. The medieval boundary bank shown by Norden can be followed without interruption to this day.

The Park has long been a Suffolk celebrity. This has encouraged visitors from way back to record what they saw and these descriptions allow us to consider whether the oaks we see today are those mapped by John Norden. For example, in 1732, John Kirby in *The Suffolk Traveller* recorded that 'An immense tract of ground commonly called Staveng park is [near Rendlesham], it has thousands of polled oaks growing on it and a vast quantity of holly'. Then again, in 1898, the annual excursion of the Suffolk Institute of Archaeology walked through 'the ancient manorial park of Staverton' and found that 'grand old oaks, some of them many centuries old, abound, most of them surrounded by holly trees of great age, grouped about in the most curious fashion. In some parts of the park tree grows within tree, birch upon oak. Beautiful green glades run through the wood, carpeted with sward and heather, and bordered by a profusion of bracken'.

This picture of astonishing long-term survival is slightly complicated by changes during the last 200 years. From 1820 onwards a series of maps shows that Staverton Park was divided by straight boundaries into eight main parcels, three of which were wooded: the Park, the Thicks and Little Staverton, the only survival of the fringing woodland mapped by John Norden. The unwooded parcels became a fluctuating mixture of heathland and cultivation, whose final state is recorded in low altitude, oblique aerial photos of February 1946 and the writings of Hugh Farmar.

The Thicks must have been separated from what is now the Park around 1820. It was evidently solidly fenced against grazing animals, for holly regenerated prolifically and grew into a dense holly wood almost overtopping the oaks, while the park remained as oak parkland. During the Second World War a flare path was cut across it (now untraceable), American servicemen camped in the western margins (still fairly open woodland) and a bomber crashed on the Thicks, leaving a clearing that was still obvious 25 years after the event. The Thicks remained a dense holly–oak wood when I first saw it in 1967, a truly dark and eerie place, but in October 1987 the great storm blew down many hollies and opened the woodland. Remarkably the oaks remained intact while the nearby pine plantations were levelled. Inevitably, the Thicks lost some of its gloom and mystery, but the leaning and fallen hollies have regrown, creating a more complex structure and restoring some of the gloom. No reason has ever been found for separating what became the Thicks from the Park, but the density of oaks is, or was, greater in the Thicks, so perhaps it was seen as real woodland.

The Arborealists are not the first artists to be attracted to Staverton and its like. It brings to life the dark woods painted as *Forest Landscape* in about 1600 by Gillis van Coninxloo. Centuries later, it fired the imagination of John Nash, who drew an image within the Thicks for the programme of the 9th Aldeburgh Festival (1956) featuring an ancient, but dead oak[8]. Nash went there with Ronald Blythe[9], the author of *Akenfield*, for whom Staverton Thicks also played 'a large part in my imagination. I took all my friends there, the poet James Turner, John Nash, the Garretts, Richard Mabey. "Yes," said Benjamin Britten, "I know it well." John Nash had told me that when he was painting he "liked to have a dead tree in the landscape". Nash "sat drawing in this not-quite-dead wood for hours, while I wandered about, ducking the liana-like ivies that fell from on high, sloshing my feet through the skeletal leaves that filled the ruts, and listening hard for perhaps a nightingale. It was dreadful how the trees mounted one another, and strange how, in what seemed their last moments, they reached for the sky.' For Blythe, 'the Thicks has a partly thwarted Phoenix ambition, to die yet live. It is grotesque, part a wood from Gormenghast, part a lecture on death, part a ruin of miscegenation. Holly propping up oak; ivy alone flourishes. Wild creatures for the most part avoid it. It is botany as departure – yet neither root nor leaf ever goes'. Incidentally, Nash's biography[10] quotes a description of the Thicks by Nash which ends with him saying it gives him the creeps.

Sarah Maitland featured Staverton Thicks in *Gossip from the Forest*[11]. For her, 'The oak woods at Staverton are the forests of childhood … Here more than anywhere else I have ever been, the forest of the imagination materialises … [it] opens into the world of magic, the place of fairy story that we inhabited as children and lost, I had thought, forever.' Entering the Thicks she was 'in fairyland'. As one walks from the Park ever deeper and deeper into the Thicks, one even finds a Hansel and Gretel cottage – flint clad, not made of bread, cake and sugar – where one might be at the mercy of a cannibalistic witch. Sarah was well versed in the scientific ecology of Staverton, but she chose to see it as a place to realise ancient imaginations.

The Thicks is likewise both a place for nature and an inspiration to spirituality. Robert Macfarlane in *The Wild Places*[12] remembered a visit with Roger Deakin, author of *Waterlog*

8. Reproduced in Blythe (2016).

9. The quotes come from Ronald Blythe's *The Time by the Sea*. (Faber and Faber, London, 2013) and his *Stour Seasons* (Canterbury Press, Norwich, 2016, pp. 88–90).

10. Andrew Lambirth, 2019. *John Nash: Artist and Countryman*, Unicorn Press, London.

11. Sarah Maitland, 2012. *Gossip from the Forest*. Granta, London. Chapter 6, Staverton Thicks, pp. 145–169.

12. Robert Macfarlane, 2007. *The Wild Places*. Granta, London.

and *Wildwood*. First a lesson in ecology: 'Roger had explained to me how essential this decaying matter was to the health of a woodland, that the benign influence of trees continued long after their death. He had stopped by a big prostrate oak limb, and prised off a curved gule of bark; beneath it teemed hundreds of insects: woodlice, ants and other species I could not recognise. Then a reflection on other people's beliefs and spirituality: We had forged on deeper into the wood, to a cleared circle where Roger said he knew local Wiccan enthusiasts came to worship, sometimes naked. I wasn't sure I believed him, but he held to his line. Talismans were hung by wool and string from oak branches; feathers, rags, fragments of text, spinning and swinging.'

Even ecologists have been moved by the otherworldly character of Staverton Thicks and the Park. Oliver Rackham (1986) was moved to describe it as '... a famous and awesome place of Tolkienesque wonder and beauty', despite being objectively fully aware of its history and ecological significance. He knew as well as anyone that Staverton Thicks, far from being a fragment of primaeval woodland, as some have supposed, is largely a creation of the last two centuries. It is the Park that is the remarkable survival, yet it is not primaeval woodland, but a relic of the wood-pasture management system that was familiar 800 years ago and possibly just as familiar to Raedwald, the Viking prince who was buried at Sutton Hoo, just up the road. Norman Scarfe[13], having read my Staverton article, was happy to summarise how he saw it: 'in looking at the historic landscape, one gets a rare sense of the prehistoric landscape', and I think that puts it very well.

Both the Park and the Thicks are ancient woodland, formed by the same trees that one supposes were dominant in the prehistoric woodland that stood where the park now stands. The soils reinforce this verdict and suggest that this is primary woodland, for they are brown earths, not the leached podzols they would have been if the land had ever been heathland. The park oaks were preserved because they were pollarded by local people to make wattle sticks, which were used with mud to make the walls of cottages. No doubt, too, some of the loppings were used as firewood. Staverton Park was not the only fragment of ancient woodland that survived on the Sandlings: there were old oaks on the heath at Iken. Sudbourne Great Wood contained old oaks that were cleared in the 1960s. Luckily Jack Kemball, kept Staverton Park intact at a time when the Ministry of Agriculture was urging him to turn it into carrots.

As for the general question raised by the three sites that have featured in Arborealist projects, there should be no difficulty in simultaneously knowing these woods to have changed under usage while appreciating them imaginatively as expressions of natural processes, tantamount to natural, prehistoric woodland. Insofar as we can know, entering Staverton must feel much the same as roaming into a Sandlings forest before Neolithic farmers got to work.

13. Norman Scarfe, 1972. *The Making of the Suffolk Landscape*. Hodder and Stoughton, London, pp. 44–47.

The Arborealists and their work

Philippa Beale

You may wonder why the Arborealists came into being, beyond wanting to exhibit together. Their reasons were political – all art is political! From Banksy engaging the 'man in the street' to the Black Paintings of Goya, professional artists always have something to say. For the Arborealists, their way is to contribute to the preservation of our planet and fight to address deteriorating ecosystems; while exhibiting art showing trees to raise public awareness. More trees create habitats and biodiversity for everything from birds to fungi. Planting native trees and plants offers shelter to native species. By creating images of these environments, individual artists contribute to improving areas degraded by human activity.

Arborealist exhibitions aim to create a ripple effect, inspiring communities to engage in conservation. This new book features work by the Arborealists, a group of British artists interested in painting trees and woodland. Founder Tim Craven and the rest of the group follow the precepts of Richard Buckminster-Fuller, an American architect, philosopher and systems theorist who said that rather than wasting energy on existing systems that do not work, instead create a new one that does. Following Fuller's precepts, we have sought opportunities for artists, building a compendium of original artworks that mainly emerged from studying natural woodlands, and we have created a successful exhibiting platform for these works.

Formed in 2014, the Arborealists are now a group of artists of diverse practices from across the United Kingdom. There are currently 43 members, including artists of national and international reputation. Between them, they have had 40 exhibitions to date, establishing a strong profile and wide critical acclaim. The Arborealists have shown in museums in France, Gibraltar and across the United Kingdom. Their first publication in 2016, *The Arborealists: The Art of the Tree*, sold out within the year.

One of their main activities is to participate in ongoing site-specific projects. In 2016, George Peterken OBE, forester, ecologist and author, invited the Arborealists to respond to the environment of Lady Park Wood near Monmouth, the only scientifically monitored unmanaged woodland in the UK. The film *Lady Park Wood*, which has been screened throughout Europe and the UK, shows the artists collecting specific information for paintings.

In 2018, the Arborealists began working on Exmoor and Dartmoor in partnership with both National Park Authorities. By 2020, this research had culminated in a major exhibition at the Somerset Museum and Art Gallery. This exhibition travelled to different venues across Somerset and Devon until 2022. In partnership with Katrina Munro, Sustainable Economy Officer for the Exmoor National Park Authority, these exhibitions encouraged the public to buy and plant trees for the National Parks.

The Arborealists have recently documented ancient trees across Britain for Julian Hight (presenter and judge of Tree of the Year for Channel 4 and chair of the Ancient Tree Forum). In 2022 as part of the Queen's Green Canopy Project, the Arborealists curated another travelling exhibition called 'Regeneration' which started at Nature in Art Gallery and Museum in Gloucestershire and resulted in a joint exhibition from September 2024. The Arborealists are now the chroniclers of Staverton Park in Suffolk, documenting the completeness, abundance and distribution of species of trees and regional flora at one of the oldest sites in the UK. The work produced from this study will form a major exhibition at the Minories Gallery in Colchester, Essex in 2025. A year-long exhibition is 'The Quietness of Feeling: An Exploration of Trees Through the Art of Benjamin Haughton and the Arborealists', at Portsmouth Museum and Art Gallery, from October 2024; and 'Forests, Woods and Groves' at the BT Batsford Gallery in London, from November 2024.

There is a consensus that fostering a personal connection to nature is vital to awaken and mobilise a predominantly urban population. As we become separated from our primordial roots, our instincts, particularly in times of war, and crisis, are soothed by images, which mitigate, assuage or allay, the pain, grief and doubt we experience at times of conflict. While much of the population shares the same concerns, they feel disconnected from nature due to the daily constraints of modern living. There is no simple solution to this problem, but hopefully the Arborealists, through their activities, can provide the public with visual experiences that enable them to feel connected to trees and their love of nature.

Through their ongoing research, the Arborealists know that depleted woodlands lead to a diminution of biodiversity. Both artists and ecologists intimately observe trees but express their understanding of woodland in totally different forms. The existence of the Arborealists enables these two interest groups to deepen their understanding of each other's perspectives. Such collaborations promote a broader interest in native woodlands. Elm and ash disease, the great drought of 1976, storms, flooding and snow have taken their toll on the ageing beech, oak, lime, ash, yew and hazel, many of which now lie prone in great heaps of dead wood, which also provides inspiration for some Arborealists.

Paul Finn (page 78) says that in the Blackdown Hills in Devon, he saw groups of trees acting as a barrier in front of a beautiful landscape, obscuring it while providing strong vertical elements. When painting in ancient woodlands such as Staverton Thicks, artists are offered complex interwoven branches of oak and holly, which can often develop into abstract paintings.

Abi Kremer's (page 92) neo-surreal abstracts enable her to enter woodland and experience a magical feeling and an energy that captivates her. She has been enthralled by Dorset woodland sites, as well as travelling all over France, the Welsh borders, Exmoor and Dartmoor searching for ancient trees.

Alex Faulkner (page 72) is drawn to the pastoral, as much as an image of loss and longing as an image of paradise. His work is about storytelling: 'myths are rooted in the groves of the past… the mind finds a home in the garden, woods and valleys'.

Ursula Leach (page 95) makes abstract images of trees as part of the landscape in which she is immersed, which is mainly agricultural where trees are scattered or solitary. As a colourist, trees offer a broad range of colours as seasons change. Colour is used to evoke a parallel between the atmosphere and the subject, and space is manipulated to imply distance, height and mass. The edge of an image indicates disappearance or fragmentation. Ursula's response to trees is as a formal artist; her main concerns are the subject, the colour and the liminal area between abstract and figurative.

The works of **David Wiseman** (page 133) are a playful, poetic response to the many contrasting elements of the landscape, such as the beautiful, complicated pattern of a closeup tree trunk with a flash of distant light and colour. Calligraphic brush marks, stains and shapes made with a wide variety of brushes, rollers and sponges become the landscape. The tree takes on many guises and is often used in contrast to the rivers and streams that have recently dominated his work. He wants his paintings to be intriguing and ambiguous, held between all the wonderful qualities of illusion and evocations of the depiction of nature.

Angela Rumble's (page 119) abstract work finds that trees have all the qualities she looks for in a subject, such as layering, light and shadow, linearity and texture. She aspires to create an atmosphere that is either unsettling or calm by turn.

Fiona McIntyre (page 104) recently spent seven weeks in Clifford Chambers on the River Stour, observing and drawing ancient willows, significantly affecting her understanding of the time continuum and how reality is perceived. This perception of Fiona's relates to the small Tudor hamlet mentioned in the Domesday Book, where the willows and surrounding countryside have barely been touched for centuries and have metamorphosed into mythological creatures.

While these artists' works are bordering on the abstract, **Lara Cobden**'s (page 54) super figuration recreates both stillness and fluidity, producing a sense of reverence. She likes to inhabit an in-between place and collect that residue of experience, grasping at the gossamer, waking from a dream. Both interior and exterior offer refuge and unease, for untold stories and portals into another world.

Crispin Heesom (page 84) moved to a small rural village and was attracted by the remnants of an eighteenth-century quarry known locally as the 'Hills & Holes'. Roots burrowing into a knotted surface, tissued, woven branches and the rotted, discarded wood have all become participants in the creation of a very different type of landscape. The age and decay of the Bowthorpe Oak gives it the impression of four trees, resembling an array of dark towers.

Ann Blockley (page 42) grew up near forest and woodland, and today she keeps watch over two old ash trees in her woodland garden. She paints them to cherish and relish in their abstract tangles and textures and tries to capture some of the old-fashioned magic all trees imbue. She experiments with paint and different mediums, adding recycled collage, sometimes incorporating photographic elements as a reminder of the underlying realities behind imagined, whimsical interpretations.

Julie Held (page 86) looks out at the world in awe and delight, observing changes that happen in her garden, sometimes within an hour. Each tree chronicles a history within its trunk; the vital complex underground network of their roots traces the past and also documents earlier climate catastrophes. The thin early morning light and the crepuscular light of dusk create a more nuanced abstract landscape.

Although many of the group produce quite abstract work, the Arborealists can neither be seen as illustrators nor landscape painters and generally adhere to the vertical rather than the horizontal. Some are devotees of Realism and **Kevin Tole** (page 128) believes that a good drawing, like a good book, has to take you beyond the immediate expression into some contemplation beyond the text or graphic work. He is uninterested in the romantic view of trees and landscape, though his images often capture some essence of beauty, destruction or death.

Tom Genders (page 81) paints trees because they are a necessity to his very being. The beautiful natives, hazel, hornbeam, oak and hawthorn are particular favourites. These species are the backbone of the history of this island, interwoven with everything humans have done since the last ice age.

Tim Craven (page 57) explores the dichotomy and long relationship between painting and photography and is attracted to complex and rhythmic imagery when flattened and abstracted by photography. His paintings are often monochrome or in muted colour, evoking memory and nostalgia, contrasting a deadpan and anonymous photorealism with English Romanticism. Tim

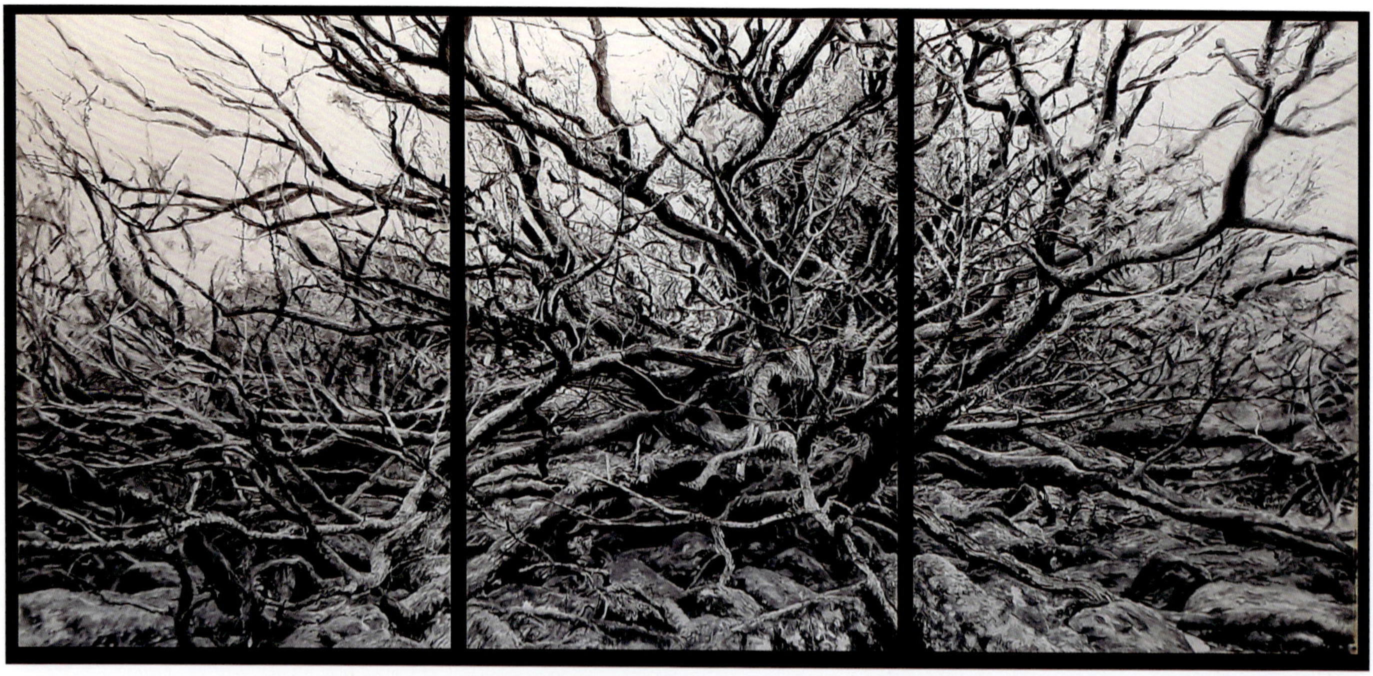

ABOVE Kevin Tole, *Burrator Oak Triptych II*

is drawn to the solid and dynamic verticals, spatial drama and abstract qualities that tree forms can provide.

Jemma Appleby's (page 31) photographic and highly skilled charcoal drawings are investigations into the complex relationship between architecture and landscape. The forest landscape is used as a haven for solitude and calmness, where the slightest change can result in phenomenological moments and twist the already sublime environment into moments of questioning.

Blaze Cyan's (page 63) interest is in ecology and the plight of trees, but this is not the sole reason she makes trees her subject. It's their beauty and structure, elemental and complex, their simple dignity and sense of presence that are of structural importance to her and essential in creating her etchings and aquatints.

Mike Dodd (page 66) regards trees as sentinels and witnesses to the comparatively brief span of human life and of human history in general. He is especially drawn to trees like Kett's Oak and the Glastonbury Thorn, which have a specific link to a particular historical time or event, whether actual or mythological.

Howard Phipps (page 113) is concerned with landscape, in particular the chalk downs of Wiltshire and Dorset, close to where he lives. Drawings or paintings created in situ become the basis for wood engravings, a method of relief printmaking where the polished surface of a block of end grain boxwood is engraved using traditional tools with names such as spitsticker and graver. Ancient trackways and striking hill forms, those timeless places on which earlier generations have left their mark, attract him; the fall of light reveals strong sculptural forms, such as ancient trees as seen in his *On Drove Roads* series, or the extraordinarily stunted oaks of Wistman's Wood, Dartmoor.

Paul Newman (page 110) lives and works on the Dorset and Somerset border, and is a graphic fine artist intrigued by nature. Working almost exclusively in graphite, he documents detail, texture and tone, inspired by elements of the ancient landscape and stories of Wessex. The history, geology, ecology and the interaction with human activity are all part of his working process, as well as understanding the distinctive atmosphere of a certain area, which Paul Nash called the 'genius loci'. Newman explores places that have significance, creating links between the places and the authors, geologists and folklore that fashioned them.

Annabel Cullen (page 60) paints the human figure and her connection with trees arises in part from their anthropomorphic and emotive qualities, and the correlation between their sinuous, jointed limbs and that of human anatomy. She finds the physical presence of great ancient trees sometimes overwhelming: they are powerful and poignant protagonists of the human condition.

Claire Cansick (page 45) uses Realism to document how the loss of trees negatively transforms a landscape. In the 1970s, the trees which lined the road where she grew up succumbed to Dutch Elm disease, which inspired her to explore the plight of all trees amid climate change, and their fight to survive against fire and flood.

Richard Bavin (page 34) is motivated by a deep and abiding love for trees and woodland, kindled in early childhood by his mother. Bavin's love for trees has increasingly turned into positive action, including surveys and conservation. His latest art project is about our native black poplar, close to extinction but with many champions striving to save it. He focuses on long-term projects about specific woodland and nature reserves, often partnering with the Herefordshire Wildlife Trust.

Władysław Mirecki's (page 107) paintings are still and silent. While painting and focusing on capturing each tree species perfectly, he also becomes still and silent, creating an atmosphere that emanates this silence in the colour, shape, texture and composition of the work. The context is also important, such as the leaf mould at the base and the other creatures and life forms that live upon the trees.

Moving from Realism to Romanticism and to another group of Arborealists, **Nahem Shoa** (page 125), celebrated for his larger-than life-size portraits, never paints from photographs, needing to relate in person with the tree or the sitter before him. The inner and outer parallels affect his work profoundly and can only be discovered through the act of seeing. Avoiding Realism, he has over the years developed his painting, enabling him to work from imagination as well as from life. His friend and colleague, **Natasha Lien** (page 98), is similarly passionate about visiting sites all over the world, drawing and painting in situ, creating compositions that relate to the individual textures of particular trees, and allowing the atmosphere of the site to influence the whole composition.

Stephanie Fawbert (page 75) works similarly, avoiding Realism by allowing the paint to drip and blur, creating a sense of light emerging through branches and leaves. Figures are included to give a sense of the scale of forests and our experience of being within them.

Celia de Serra (page 122) works in black and white in her search for atmospheric beauty within her landscapes, where trees are the central characters. Her woodlands, crammed with visual ideas, are dynamic spaces, broken by chaotic forms and shifting light. She gets to know the view intimately, so it becomes a personal experience and her works preserve the moment.

Stella Carr's (page 51) paintings focus on trees as a locus for pattern and energy, honouring deep ecology and exploring the tensions between man-made landscapes and wildness. Carr's work dramatises the mutual vulnerability of the artist and environment, both in her process, which often involves a somatic response to her subject, and in the finished work.

Jacqueline Wedlake Hatton (page 130) has long appreciated trees as a dynamic part of the landscape. They punctuate the environment in which they grow, reflecting her understanding that we are merely part of a magnificent whole. Jacqueline says that, for her, tree's growth patterns are just as visible and as telling as the postural habits and facial creases of human beings. Her approach, therefore, is to select a tree in the way the portraitist seeks an interesting face or a striking character.

Alan Rankle's (page 116) interest and inspiration in landscape art and depicting trees began after seeing paintings by Jacob van Ruisdael and Salvator Rosa. Landscape paintings of the seventeenth century seemed to represent the beginning of modern art times when the influence of religion in Europe had begun to wane and an existential enquiry into our relationship with the natural world became the crucial art subject.

Often working in collaboration with scientists, **Andrew Carnie**'s (page 48) main concern is to target the interface between art and science. His approach is agnostic, using all methodologies and media to create environments around subjects such as heart transplants and metabolic or neurological conditions. The web of life is what intrigues him and he is particularly interested in the tree-like forms within our bodies.

The earlier work of **Rosemary Mafrici** (page 101) focused on traditional media such as watercolours and oil paint. After working in community settings, where students and the general public were able to collaborate on creating a wide range of public art, her work emerged as intensely photographic, detailed and on a much larger scale than before.

John Blandy (page 40) follows a single tree through the seasons to build up a longitudinal portrait. Working in pastel on paper, *en plein air*, each work is completed on the spot. Timed and dated, they stand alone or can be viewed as part of a sequence. Each overall portrait has its own sequence and time intervals.

Tilia Holmes (page 89) uses wood as her main material, using the ancient art from of 'pyrography' to burn marks and textures into sustainably sourced wood. Working with the grain, she allows each image to emerge through the process of burning and scorching.

Alex Egan's (page 69) sense of purpose was awoken when searching for personal memories and realising that, for her, these existed in trees. Her memories then embedded themselves in the drawings and paintings she produced of these serene life forms.

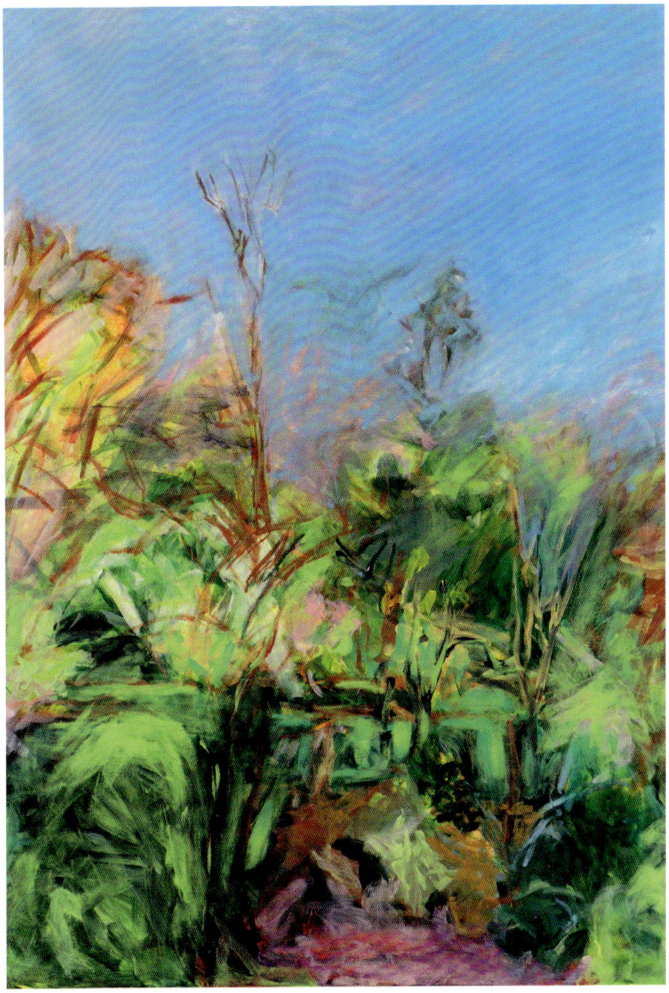

ABOVE Julie Held, *Late Summer 2022*

Influenced mainly by Euston Road and artists like Patrick George and Euan Uglow, **Robert Amesbury Brooks** (page 28) has over the years created a methodology which conveys the shapes in compositions in certain aspects of colour and the structure. This chiaroscuro fascinates him and encourages him to capture the volume and beauty that exists in his work.

Robert Amesbury Brooks

Over the years, I have constantly endeavoured to reflect on how nature creates drama. I capture this unique language and find my interpretation. I have always found it challenging to represent nature, as its sheer beauty is very difficult to capture, but this challenge spurs me on. There are so many different ways that artists can perceive what is before them. For me, there is no clear solution, and this becomes my continual journey, whether the change in seasons, the colour or the atmosphere.

I endeavour to be as true to my passion as possible, and the processes by which I make art. As an ageing artist, I have found myself tackling many highs and lows in pursuit of my dreams; it can be a lonely pursuit, inward-thinking and often misunderstood aspiration. I have enjoyed exhibiting alongside many dedicated artists over the years, which continues to motivate me with an unrelenting urgency. I have always had a fascination with landscape painting, focusing on nature and specifically trees, which allows me to keep developing as an observational painter.

The focus of my art is to draw the viewer into the physical aspects of nature and allow them a moment to feel in place. I am interested in the energies and drama that come from how colour works in harmony with other stimuli within a compositional structure. I use a methodology to convey the expressive shapes in composition, be it softness, playing off the roughness/hardness beside it, or warmth in the colour and structure next to natural darkness. These contrasts create volume and beauty within the frame of the painting. I aim to capture the essence of the sheer beauty within something I cannot control; this constant challenge has become my muse.

OPPOSITE ABOVE LEFT *Large Oak – Throop*
OPPOSITE ABOVE RIGHT *Corfe Castle seen from Sandy Hill Lane*
OPPOSITE BELOW *Five Fields to Winchester – Summer 2023*

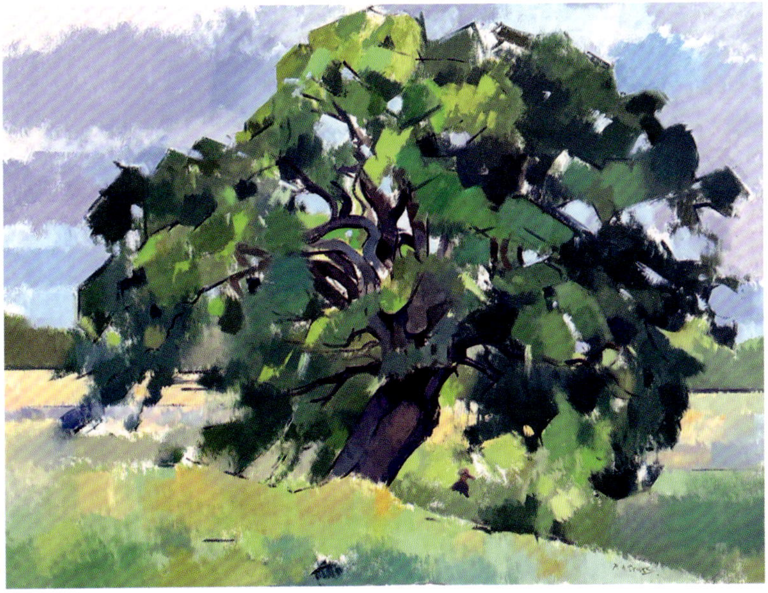

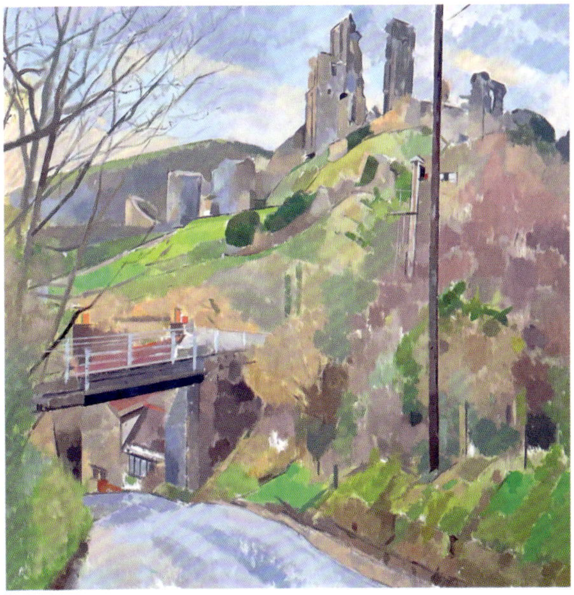

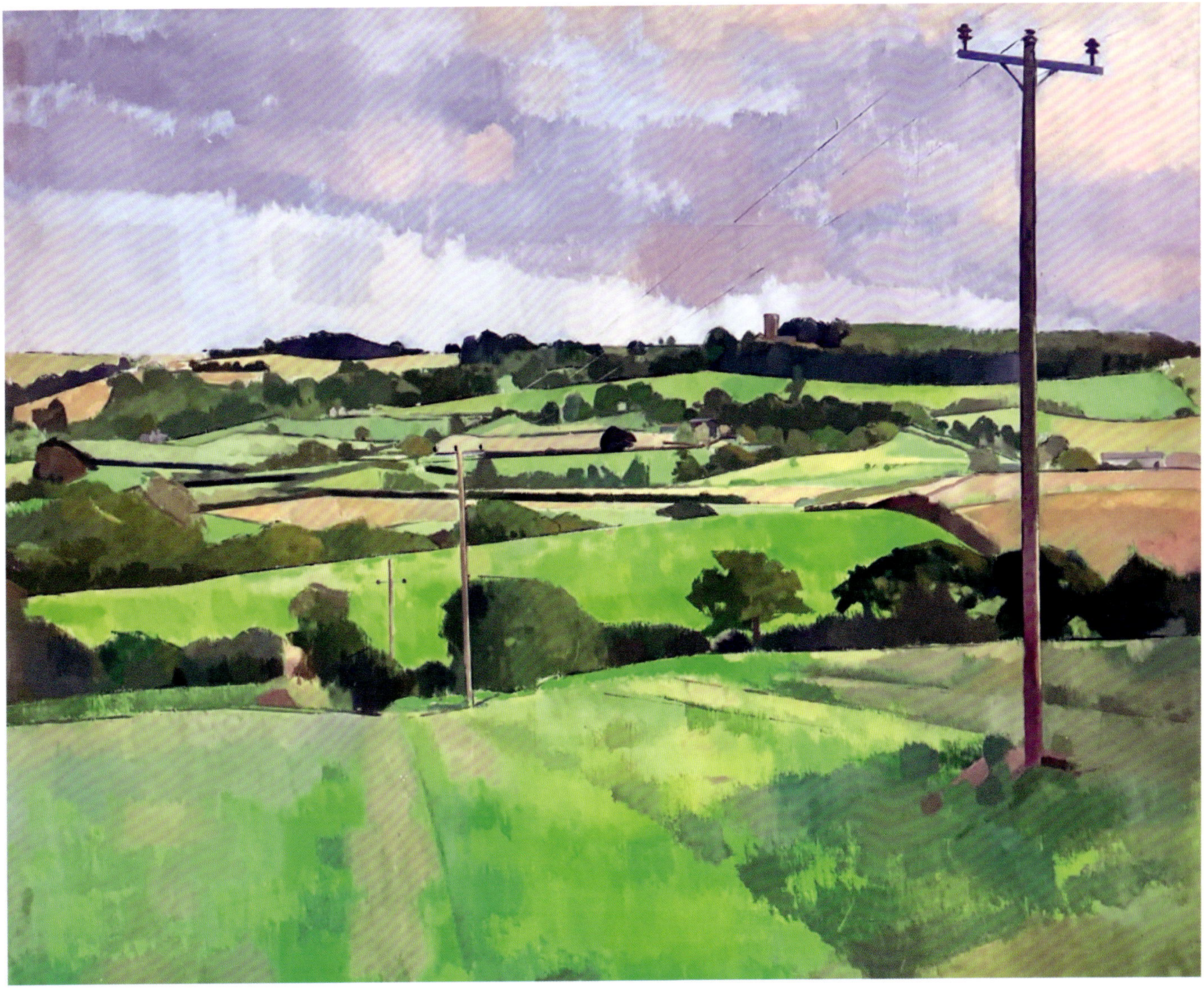

BELOW LEFT *Woodland Path, Kingston – Summer 2023*
BELOW RIGHT *The Great Oak, Kingston – Spring 2022*

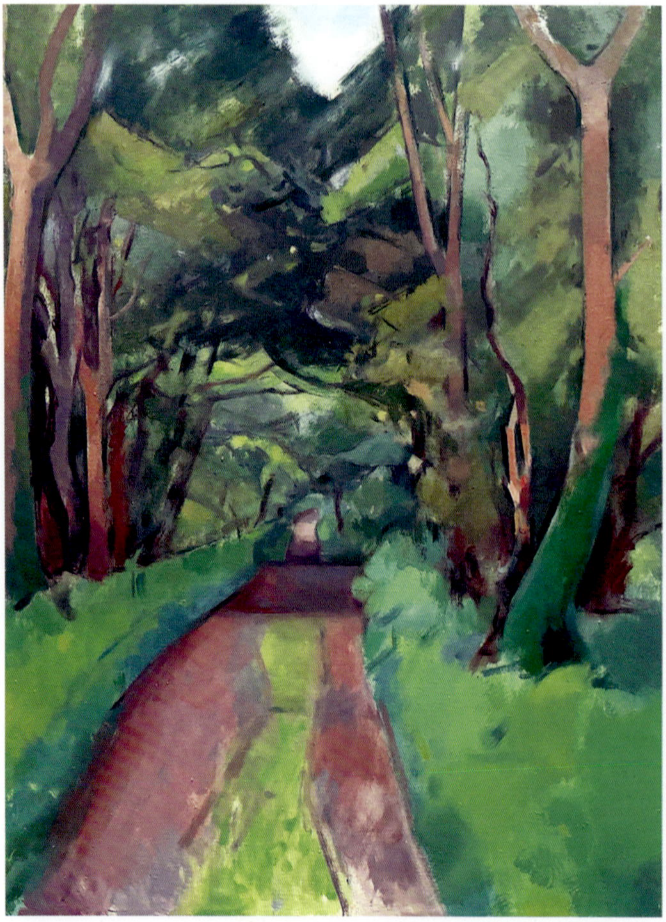

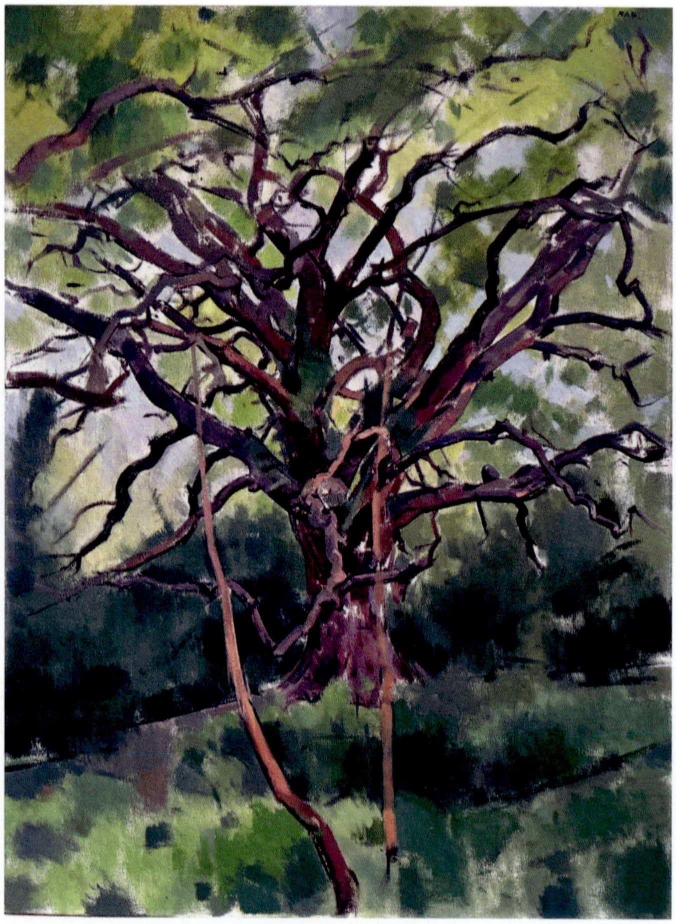

Jemma Appleby

My drawings are investigations into the complex relationship between architecture and landscape. The forest landscape is a haven for solitude and calmness, where the slightest change can result in phenomenological moments that twist the already sublime environment into moments of questioning. As with the forest, architecture has been a focus in my work, referencing utopias and enriched futures. Architectural forms have been used to explore the themes of shelter and protection, by generating structures of physical impossibility. I use charcoal to create chiaroscuro, which heightens the elements of space, volume and structure. This generates a synergy between the subject matter and the impenetrable velvet surfaces of the charcoal. This enables my landscapes that combine forests and architecture to merge harmony with variance. My images disconcert the viewer's perception, confusing reality and illusion, creating an encounter of the natural world and invention.

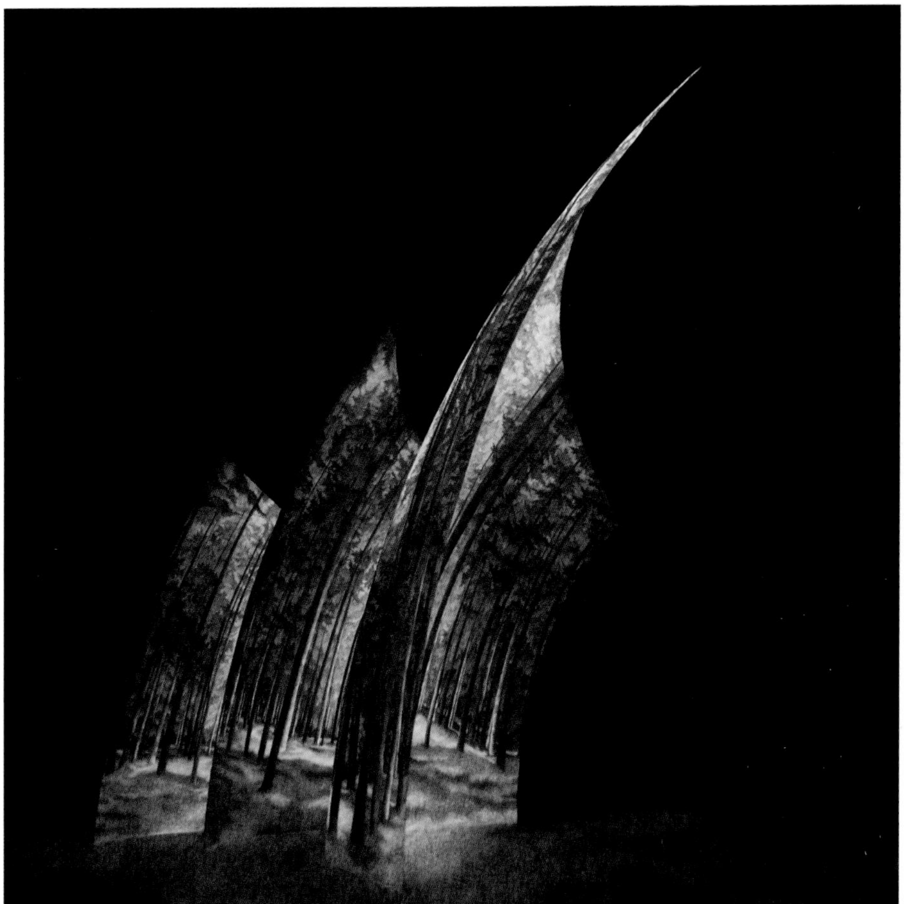

LEFT *Jubilee #1*

RIGHT *Affleck #2*
BELOW *Goetsch-Winckler #3*

OPPOSITE ABOVE *#3150918*
OPPOSITE BELOW *#1310823*

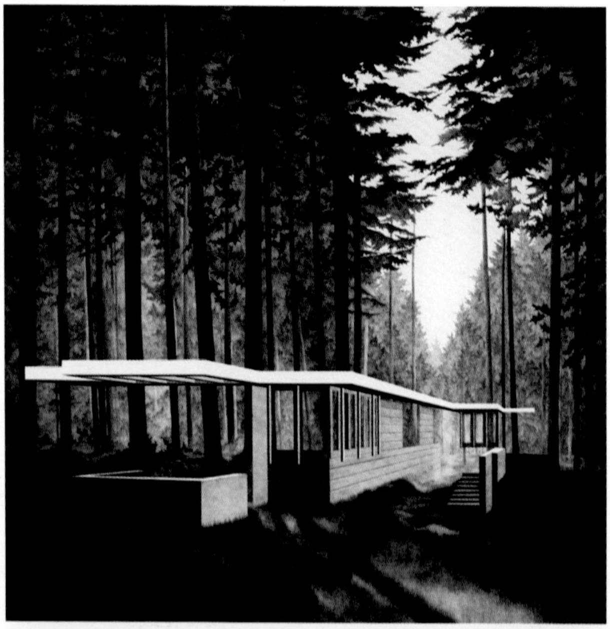

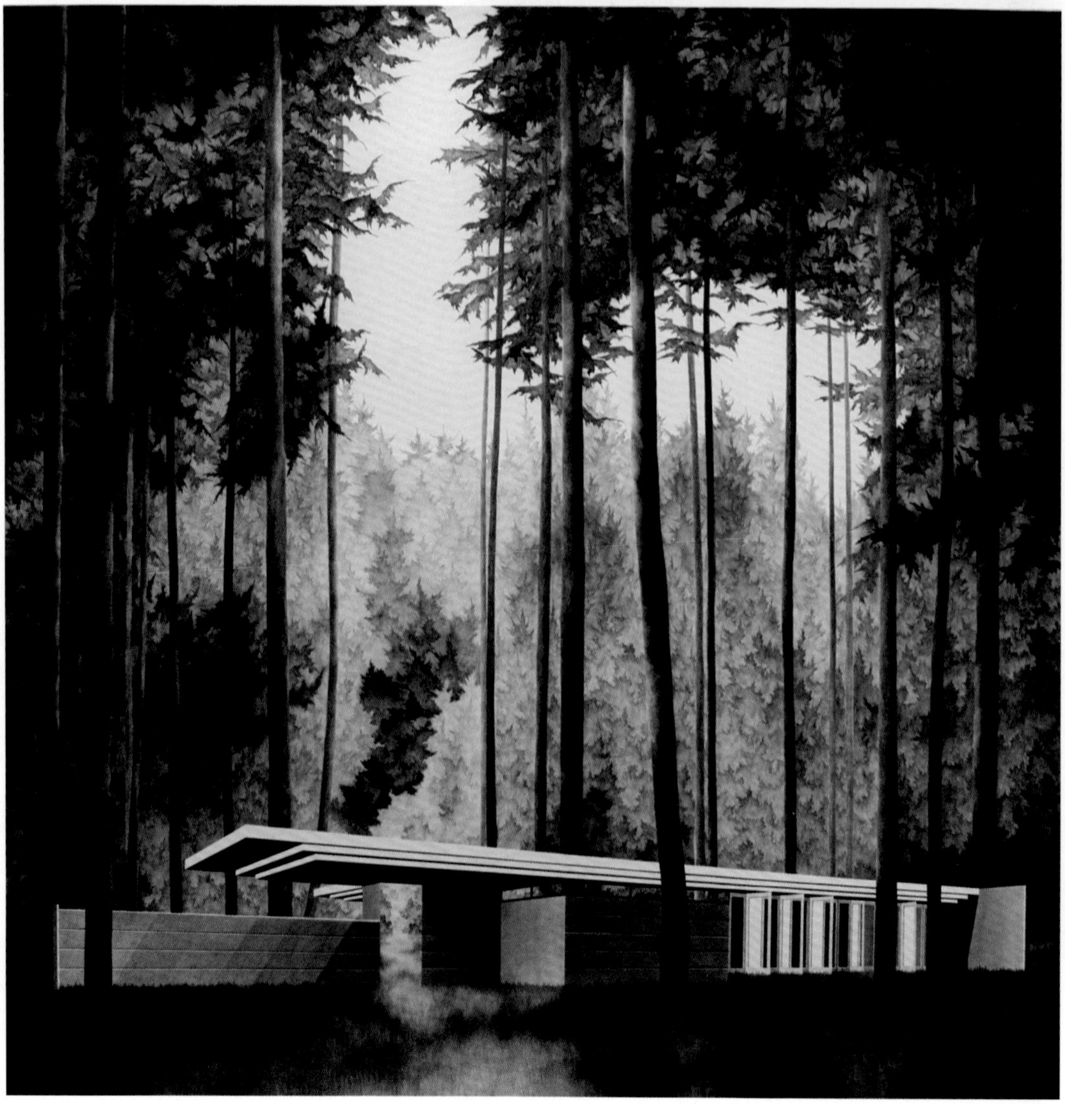

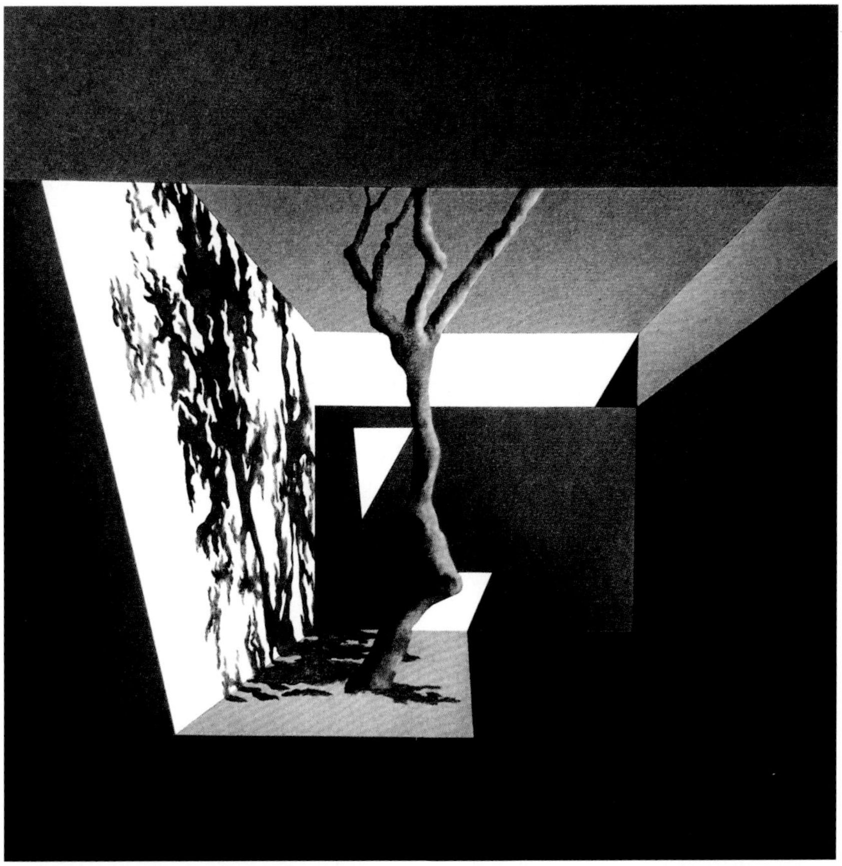

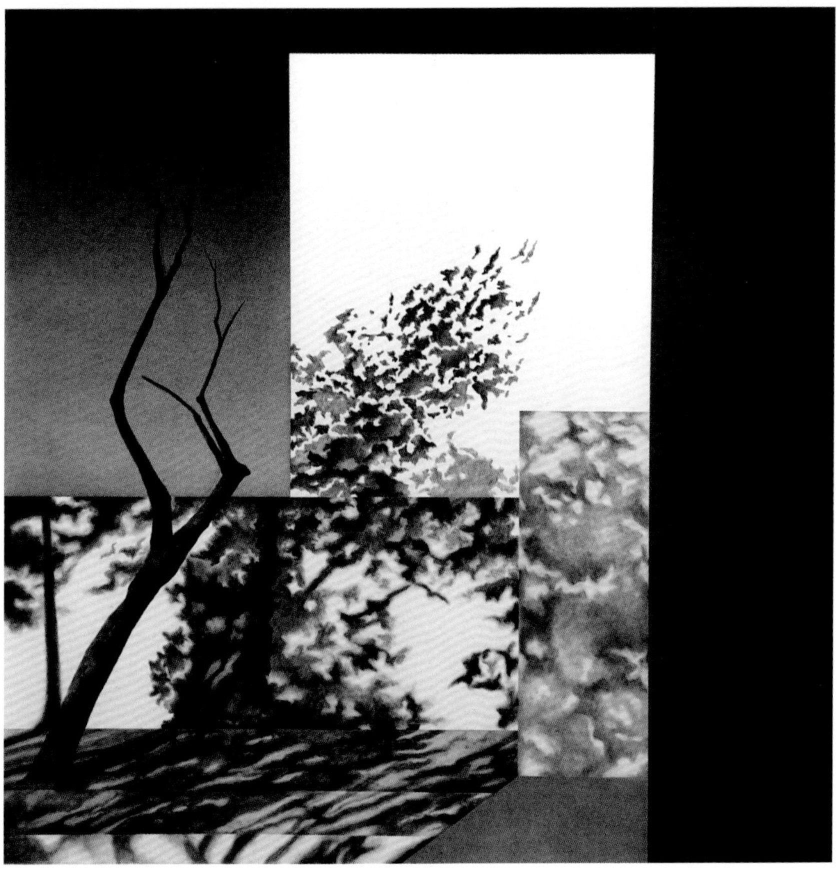

Richard Bavin

My work is motivated by a deep and abiding love for trees and woodland, which my mother, Jackie, kindled in my early childhood. I focus on long-term projects related to specific woodland and nature reserves, often partnering with Herefordshire Wildlife Trust. Spending time sketching in silence, surrounded by trees, is my place of peace and contentment. After a while the wildlife sees me as part of the habitat and comes surprisingly near. After drawing and painting trees for over twenty years, I know less than when I started, but I'm just as enthusiastic about communicating what I experience of their majesty and presence. Site work with the Arborealists and experts, including George Peterken, has brought fresh insights and ideas that have changed my perspective. Trees transform the world around us and give so much to human beings. It has always felt important to try and understand them for what they are: separate beings with behaviours, needs and characters in their own right.

My love for trees has turned increasingly into positive action, including surveys and conservation. My latest art project is about our native black poplar, which is close to extinction but has many champions striving to save it.

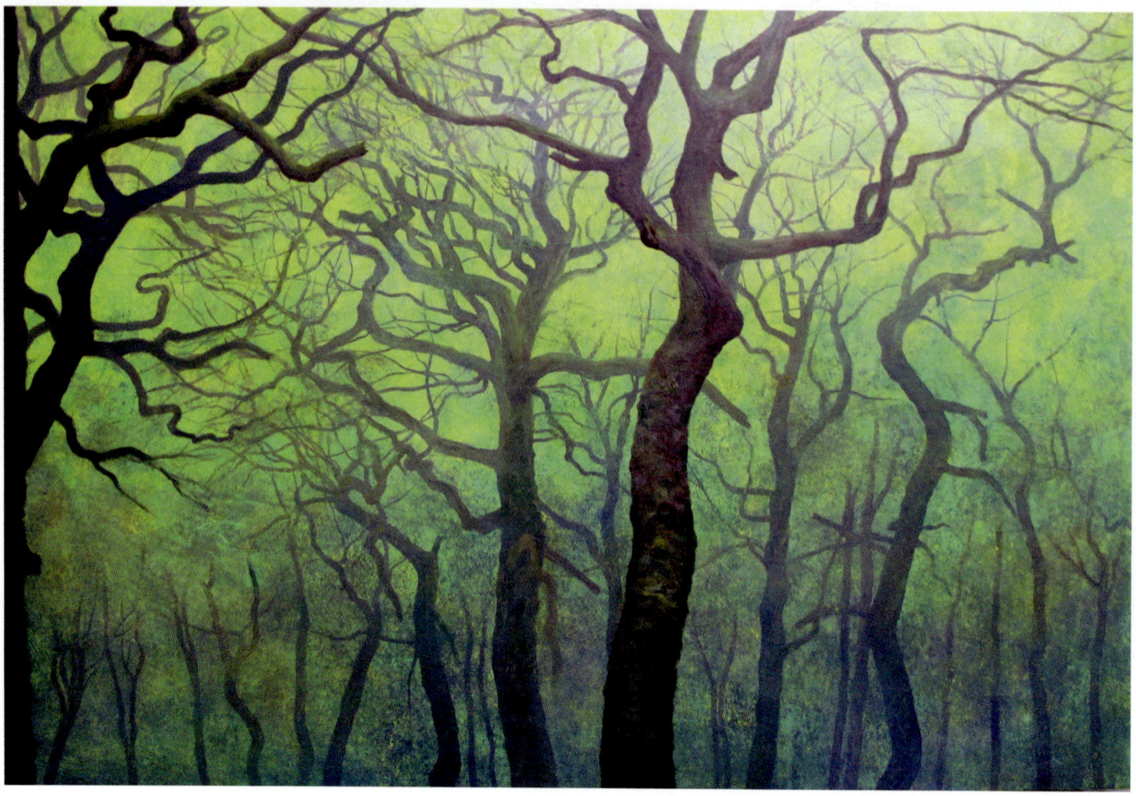

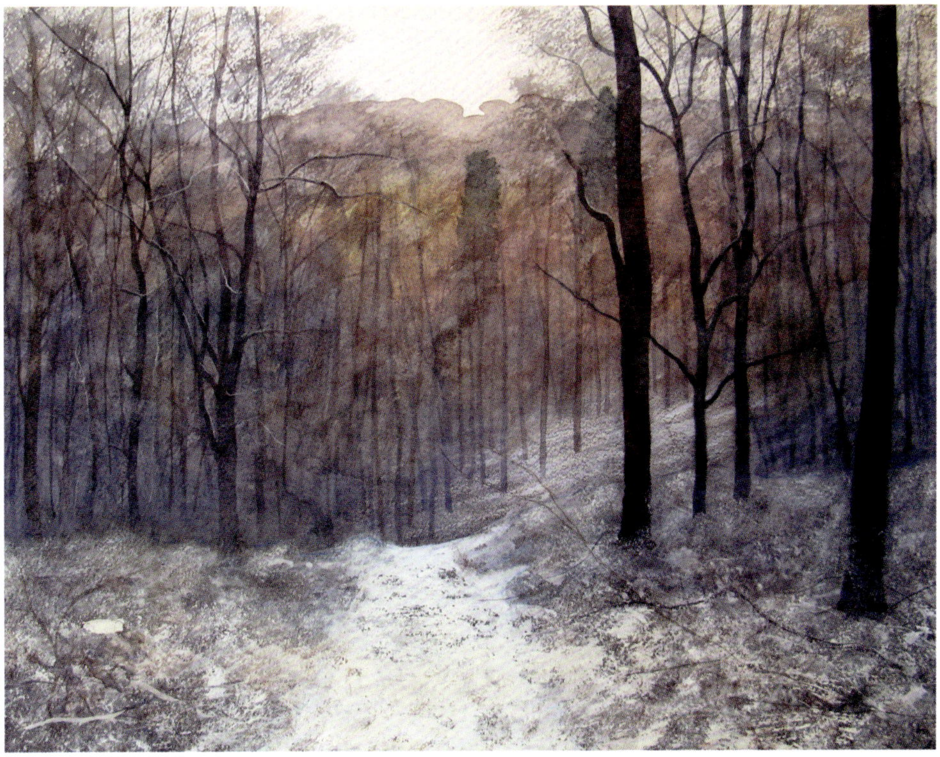

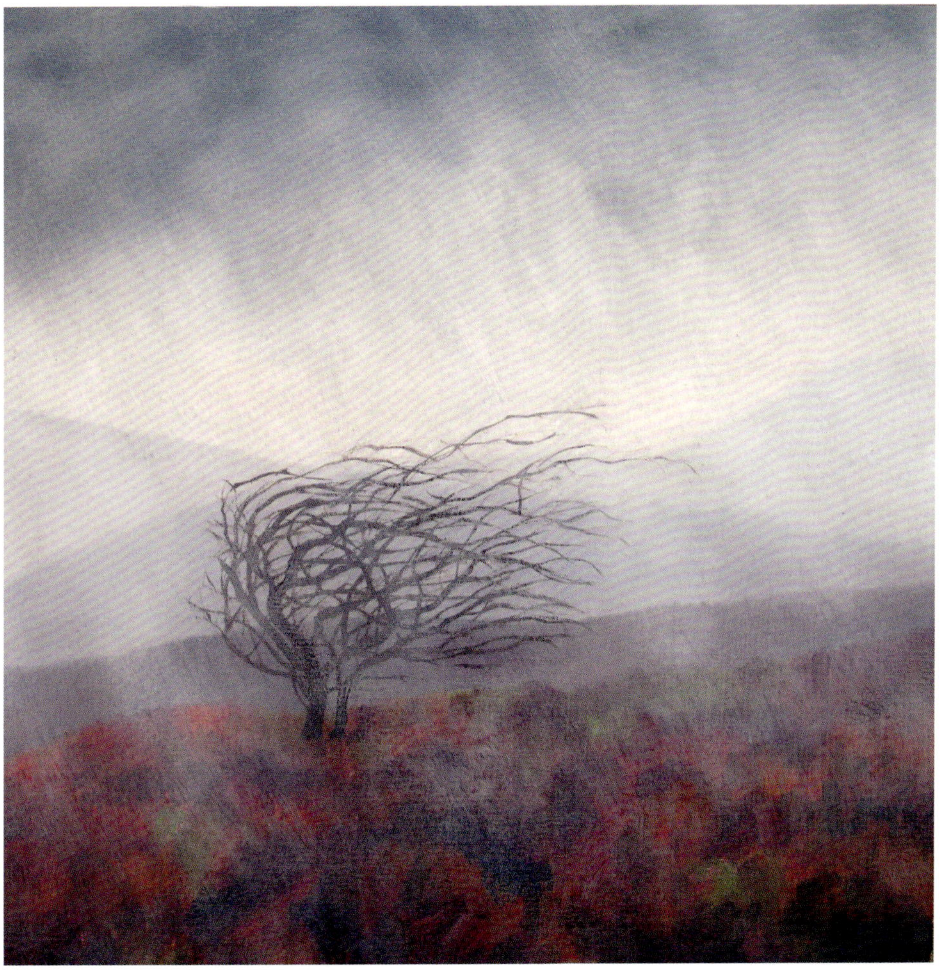

OPPOSITE *White Wood Spring Light*, 2019

LEFT *Winter Crisp and Cold*, 2020
BELOW *Hawthorn in October Squall*, 2019

RIGHT *Native Black Poplar, Herefordshire*, 2024
BELOW *Late Afternoon Light*, 2024

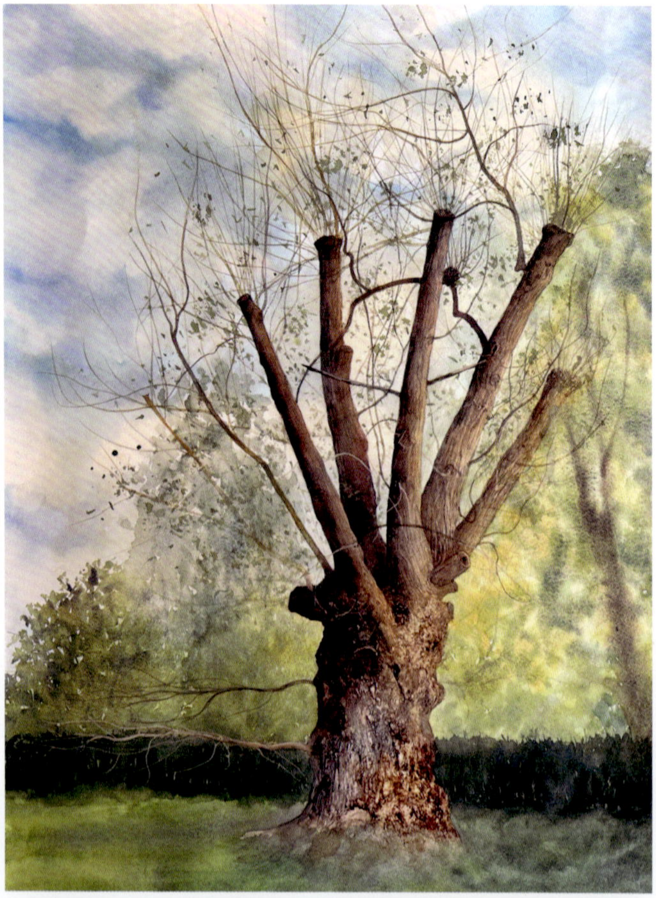

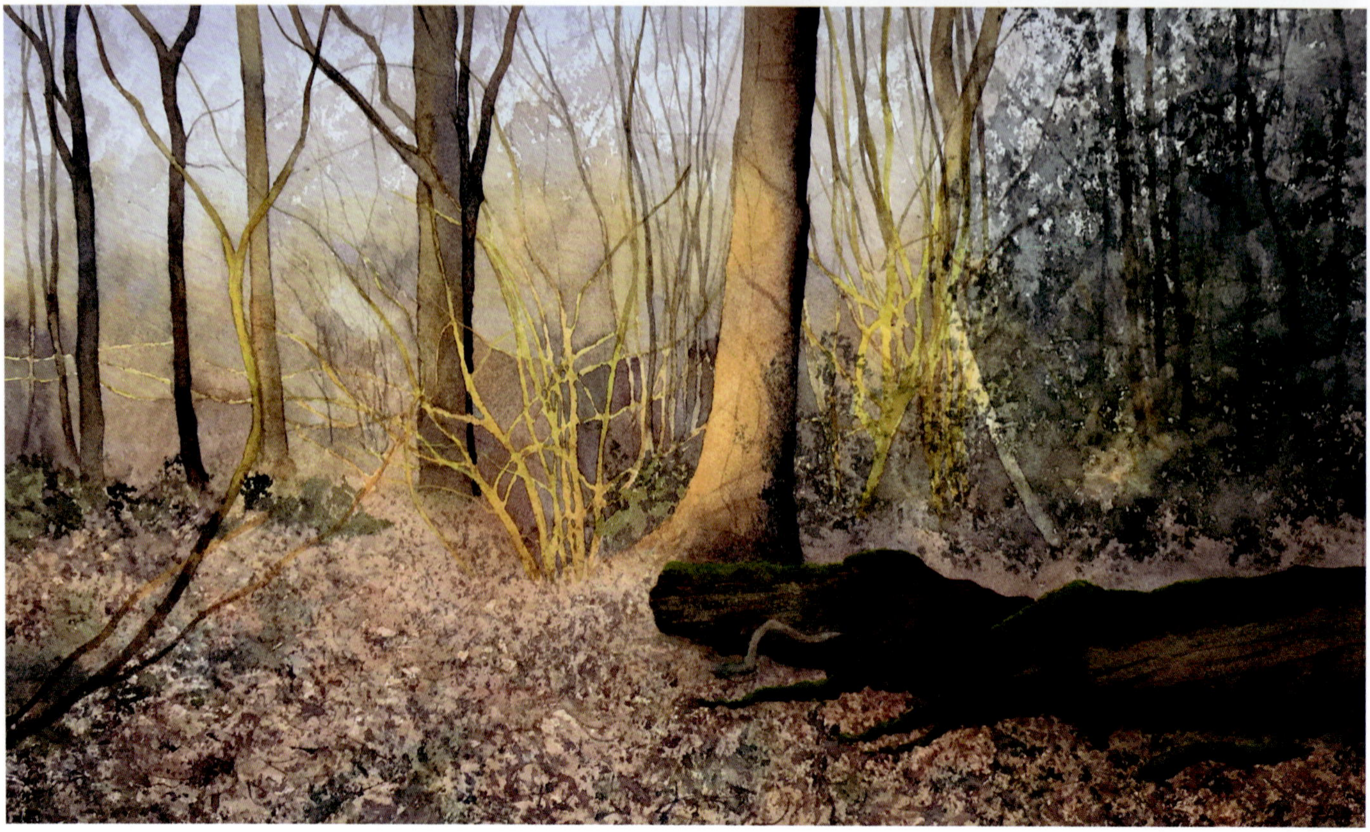

Philippa Beale

While most people share concerns about the conservation of sites of natural beauty, they feel unconnected to nature due to daily constraints on modern living. There is a consensus that fostering some personal connection with nature is vital to enabling a largely urban population, particularly in times of war, conflict and crisis, to benefit from images of the landscape. I feel my role as an artist, drawing directly from specific tree and woodland sites like Exmoor, Dartmoor and Staverton Park in different seasons and making new works for special exhibitions, enables me to bear witness to the greater environmental campaign. While there is no simple solution to our environmental problems, I am able, through my discreet activities, to provide some of the public with visual experiences that enable the viewer to feel connected to nature and their love of trees.

BELOW *Tree Bathing*, 2014–24

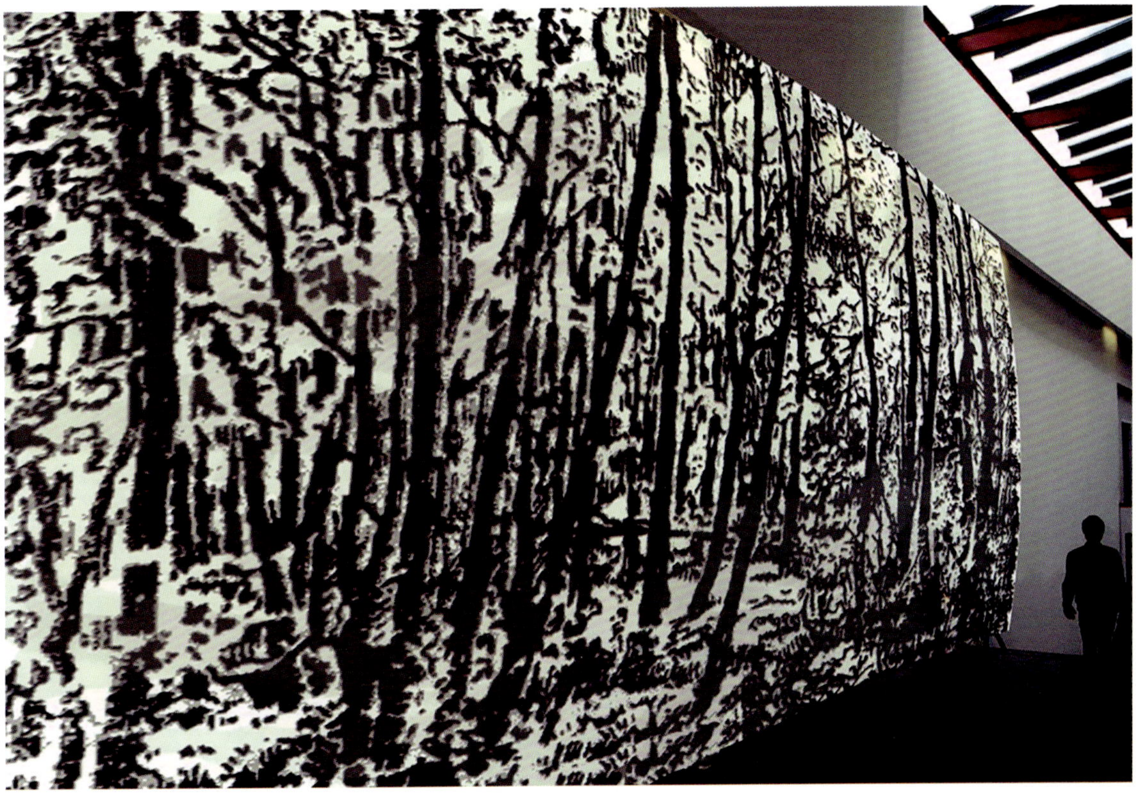

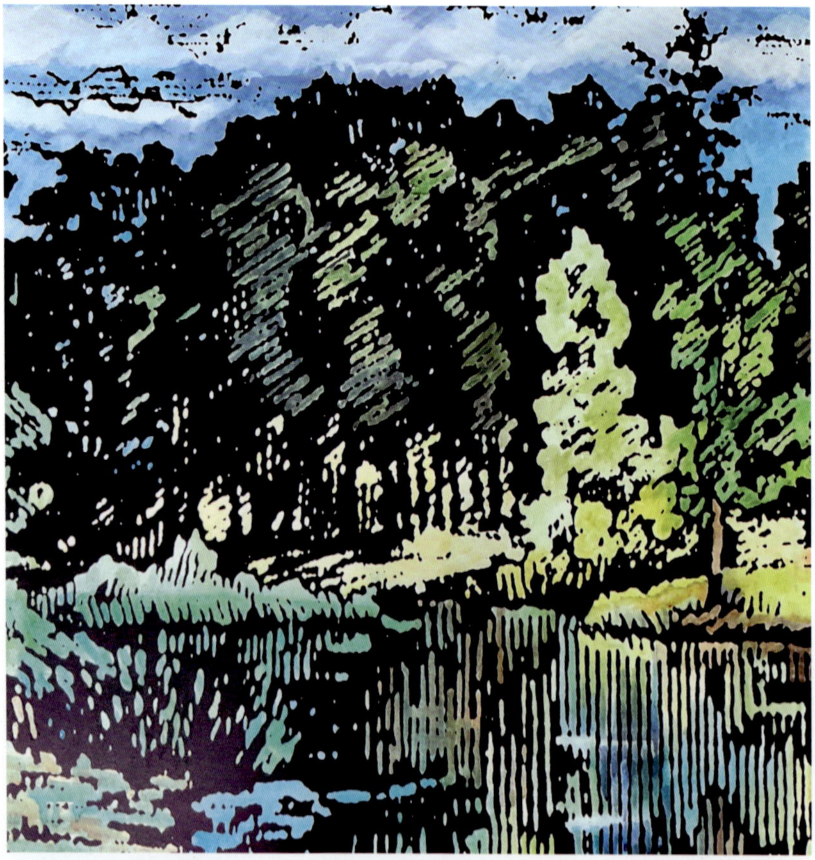

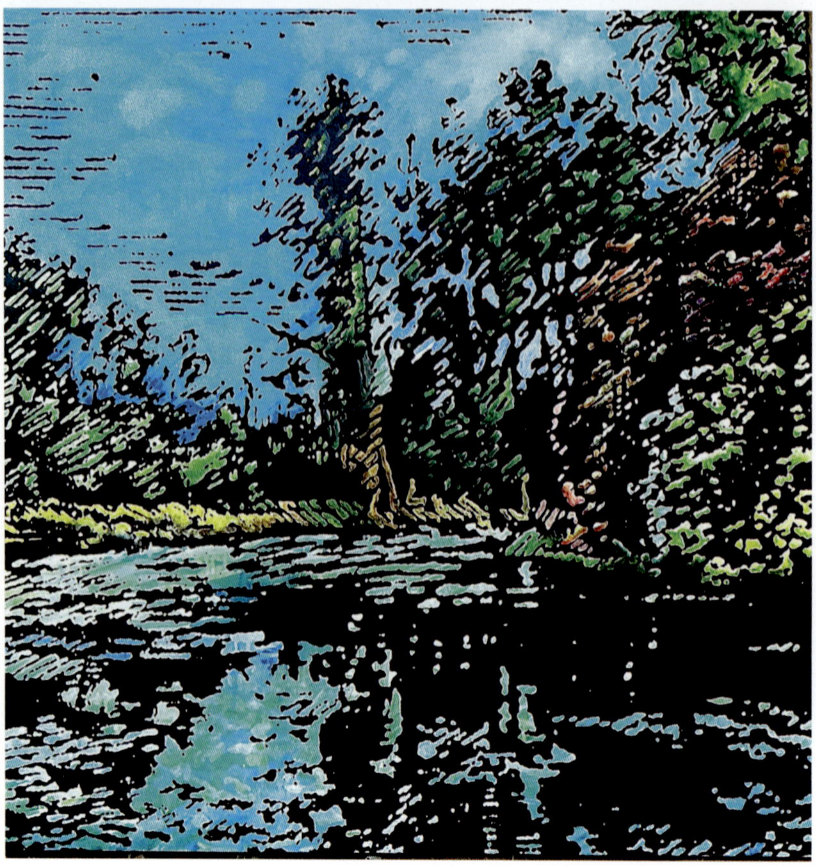

OPPOSITE ABOVE *The Edge of the Burrator*, 2023
OPPOSITE BELOW *The Water's Edge*, 2023

BELOW LEFT *Contrasts*, 2019
BELOW RIGHT *Oak Trees in the Hunting Wood*, 2023

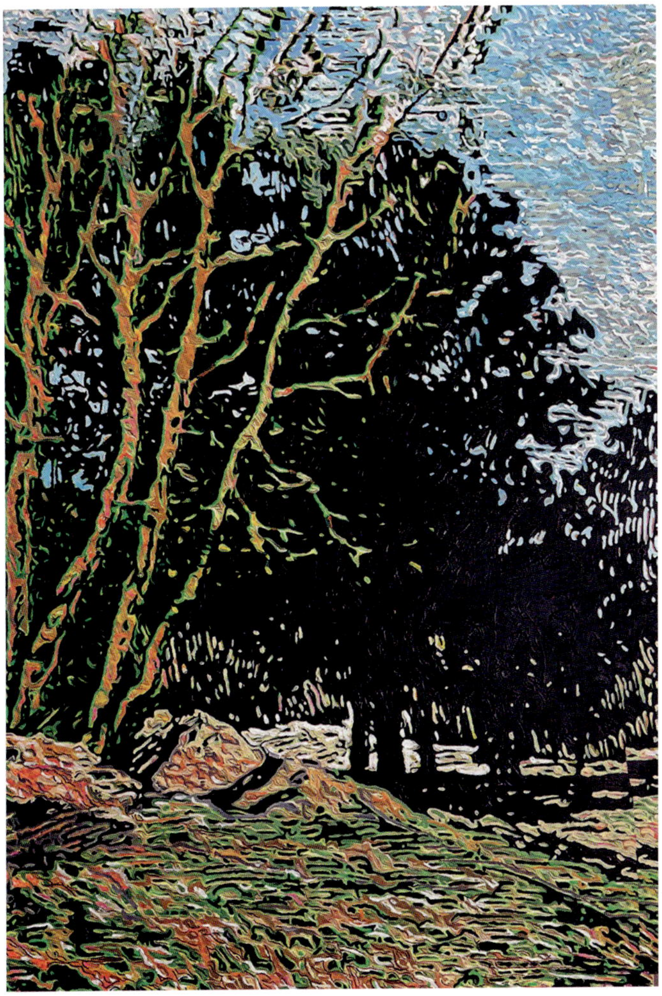

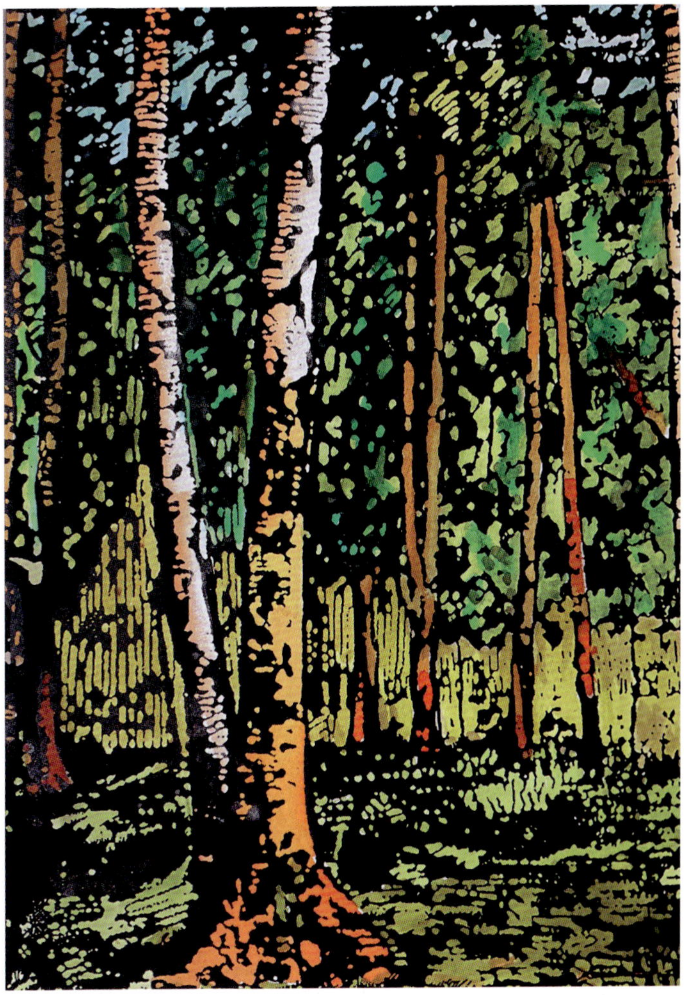

John Blandy RCA

John Blandy, a landscape artist, follows an individual tree through the seasons to build up a longitudinal portrait. John works in pastel on paper *en plein air*, completing each work on location. Timed and dated, they stand alone, or can be viewed as part of a sequence. Each overall portrait has its own sequence or time intervals. *Following a Lime Tree*, painted in London's Queen's Park, is selected from a series Blandy worked on from 1997 to 2020. Stood at his easel near the cafe, he became a familiar sight. The series consists of more than three thousand images, which are used as a visual bank to compare the subtle ebb and flow of long-term change year-on-year. The tree was subsequently blown over.

Since 2015, Blandy has been an Artist in Residence in Wytham Woods, a scientific research facility for Oxford University. The work produced is about recording change, over a longer timespan. The series Blandy is currently working on is following an apple tree. This project aims to complete a pastel of the tree each day, posting on Instagram @john2art. What began in lockdown has continued for four years, producing daily images of the tree. As the work is in a restricted space, and the easel in a particular position, plants often obstruct, becoming part of the portrait.

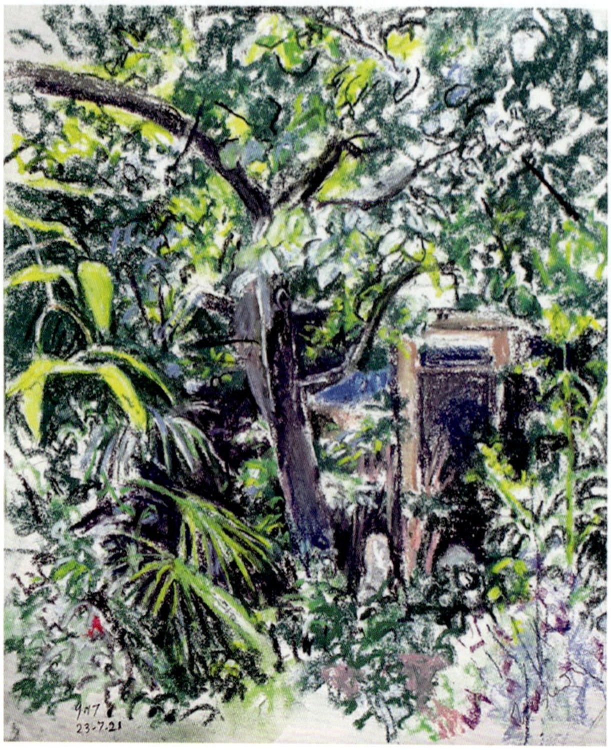

LEFT *Apple Tree 9:17*, 23rd July 2021

OPPOSITE *Following a Lime Tree*, 27th September 2018 – 8th January 2019

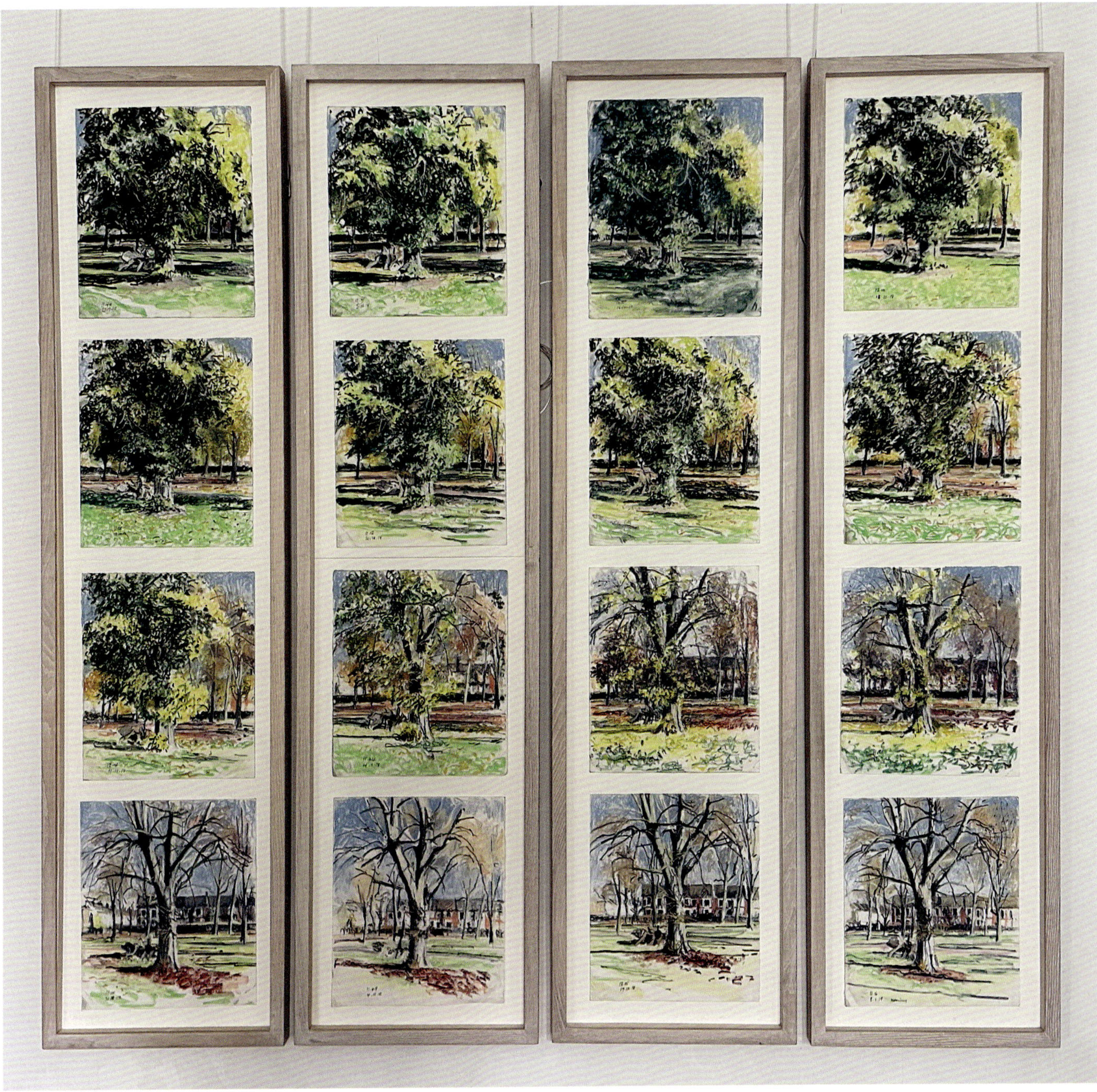

Ann Blockley

As a child, I lived at Beechwood Lane near ancient woods where we climbed, gathered conkers, built dens and memories. Two large ash trees stood like sentinels, guarding the bottom of the garden. I obsessively painted and drew their patterns and shapes through their seasons. They represented safety, familiarity and beauty. Today, I watch over two old ash trees in my own woodland garden. I see them wither; their diseased branches and twigs are snapping and crashing to the ground. They may have to be felled next year, and I feel sad to see these icons fading as the world around us rushes relentlessly towards change. The woodlands I once took for granted are now vulnerable. I paint them to cherish and relish in their abstract tangles and textures, trying to capture some of the old-fashioned magic I still feel. I dream I can cast a spell within my painted pieces, a nature-prayer that all the ashes will not return to dust. I experiment with paint and different mediums, adding recycled collage. Sometimes, I incorporate photographic elements as a reminder of the underlying realities behind my imagined, whimsical interpretations.

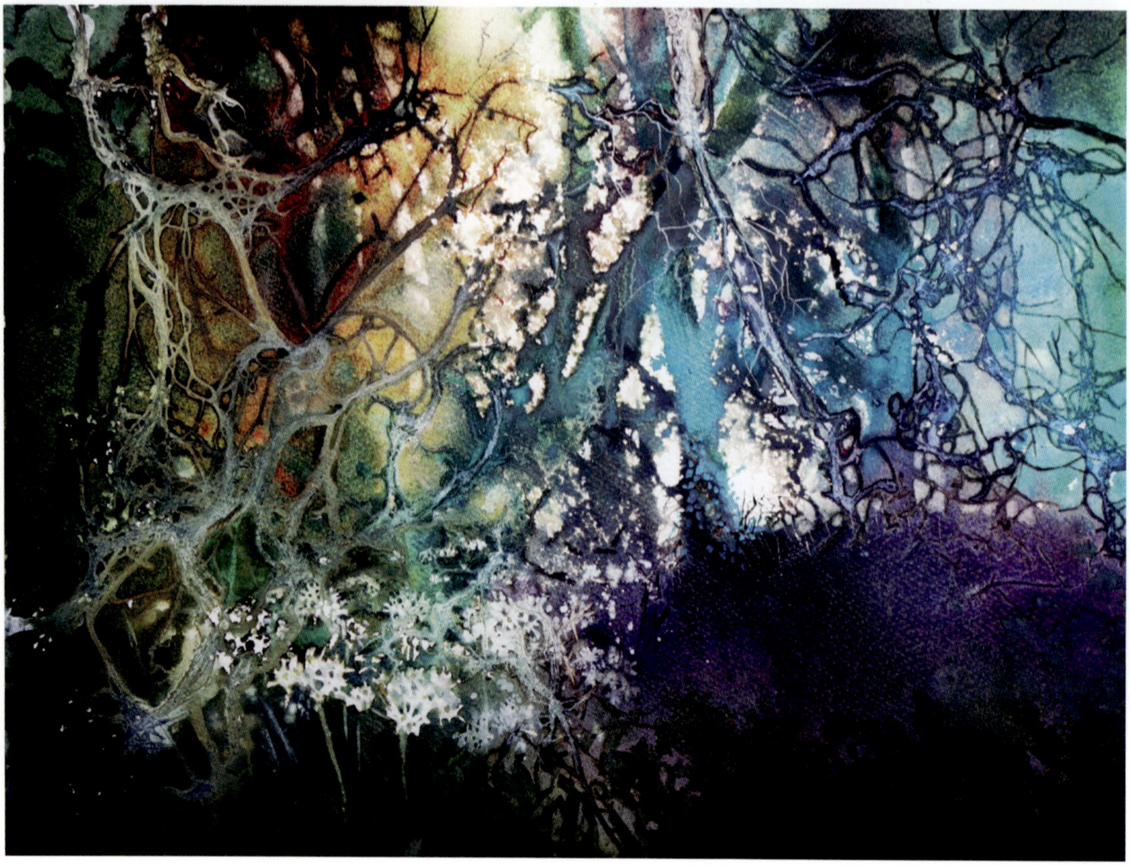

OPPOSITE *Wild garlic in the wood*, 2024

RIGHT *Faerie foxglove wood*, 2022
BELOW *The tangled grove*, 2022

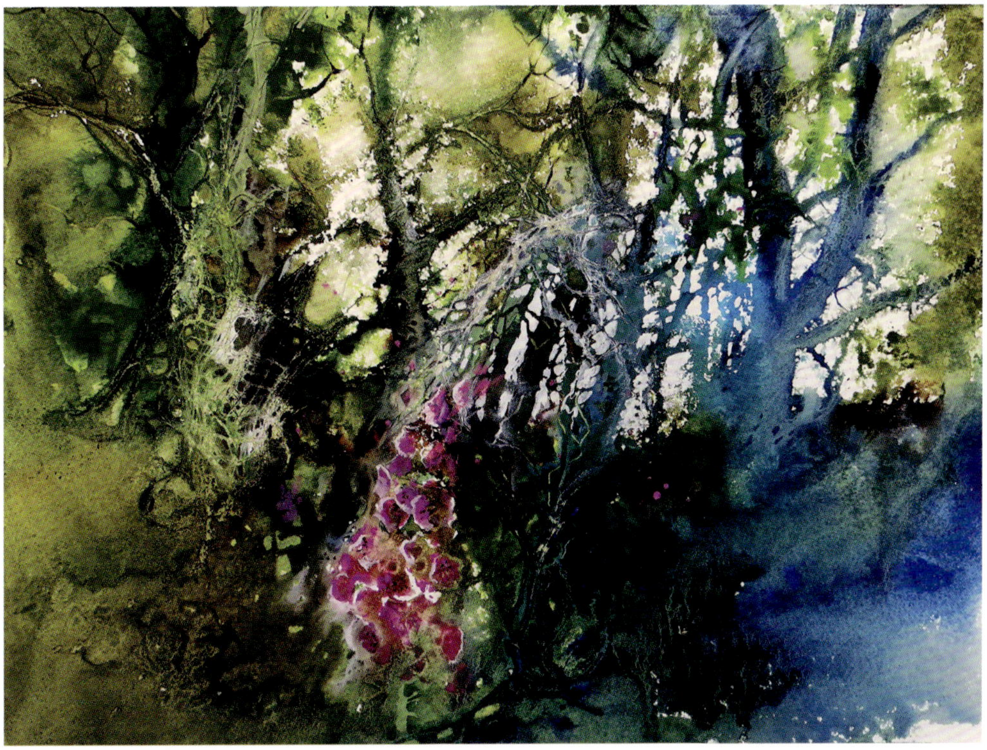

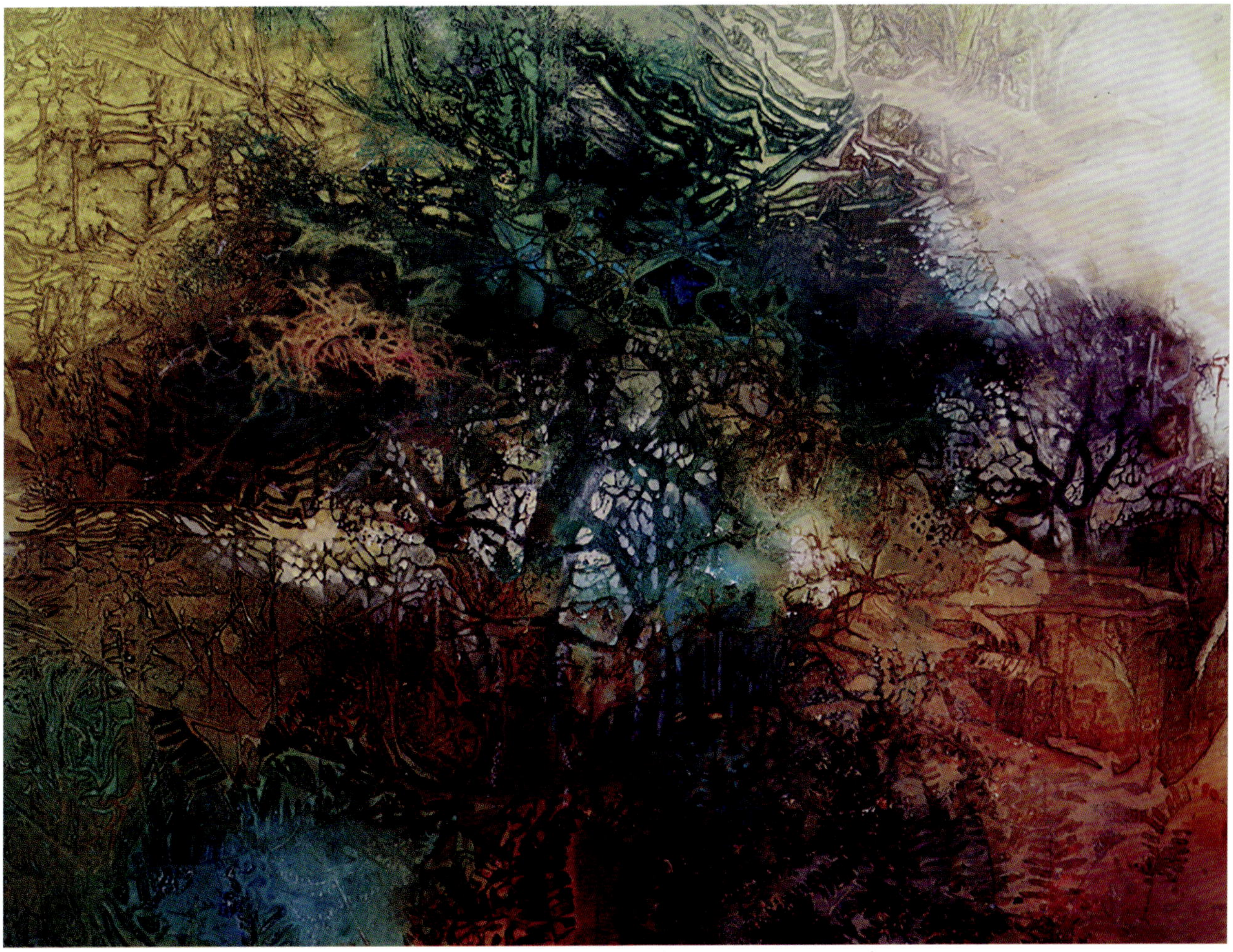

BELOW LEFT *Frosty moonlit tree*, 2023
BELOW RIGHT *Scarlet moorland thorn*, 2023

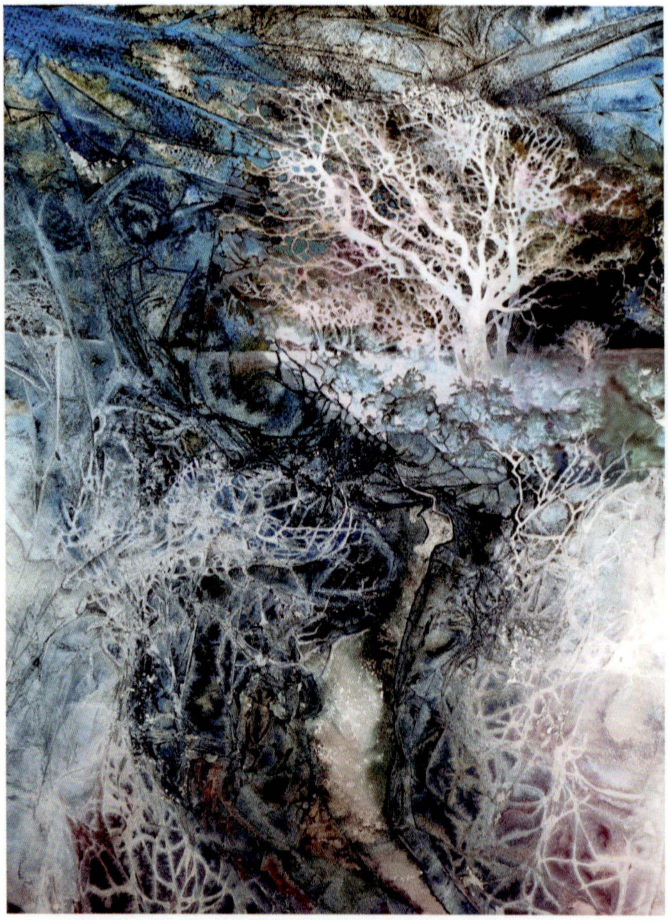

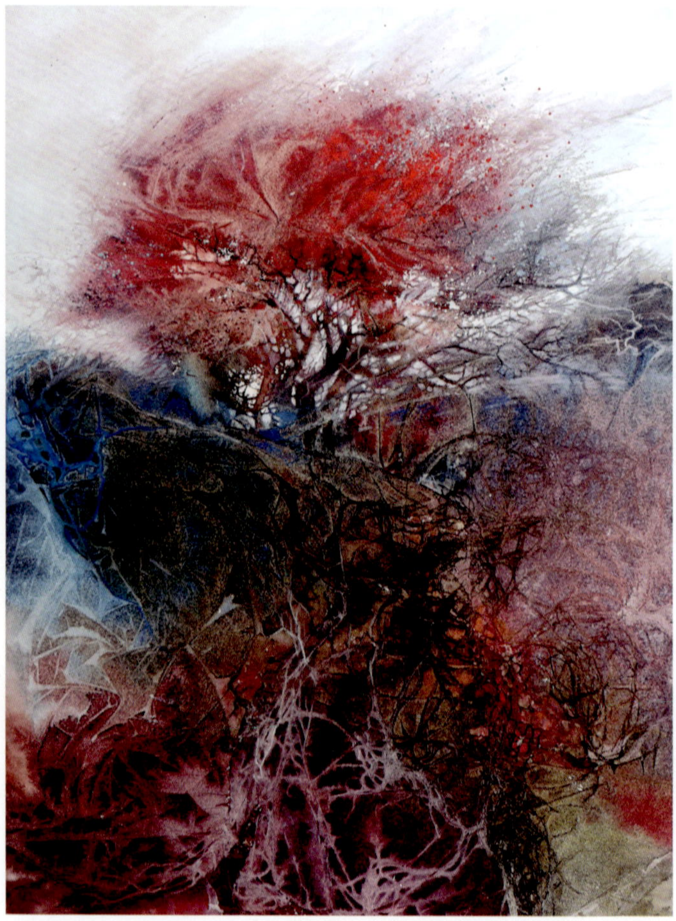

Claire Cansick

I realised the power of trees to transform a landscape when the elms which had always lined the road I grew up on succumbed to Dutch Elm Disease in the late 1970s. Since moving to a house that is nestled against a small wood, my love and appreciation of trees and their biodiversity has deepened.

When I look at a tree, I sense it as a marker of time, an observer of history as much as a living organism. They give off an aura I try to tune in to when painting, concentrating on their energy, silhouette and colour against our grey English skies. Winter light appeals to me more than sharp summer shadows; it suits my muted palette, and the greens of a tree work perfectly with a soft violet-grey blanketed sky. It is these colours which bring me back time and time again to painting trees. My work has also turned towards the plight of trees against climate change and their fight to survive against fire and flood.

BELOW *Thank You for the Days*, 2022

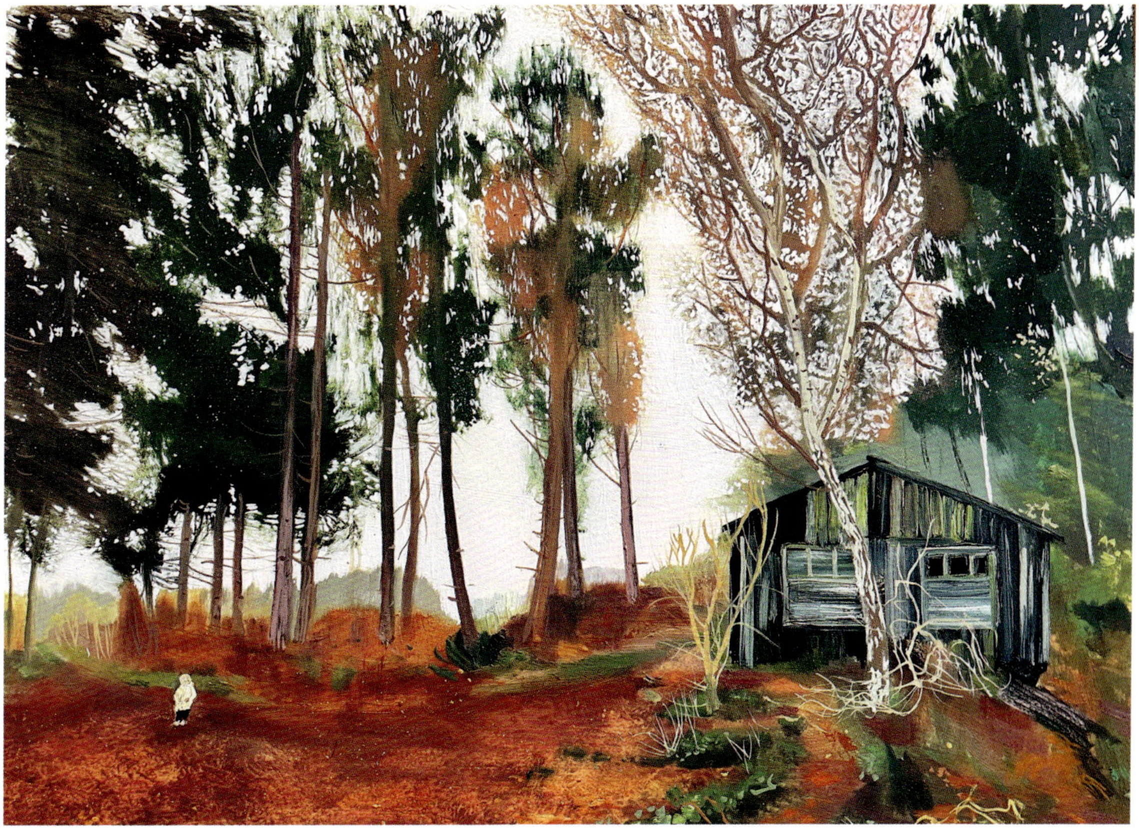

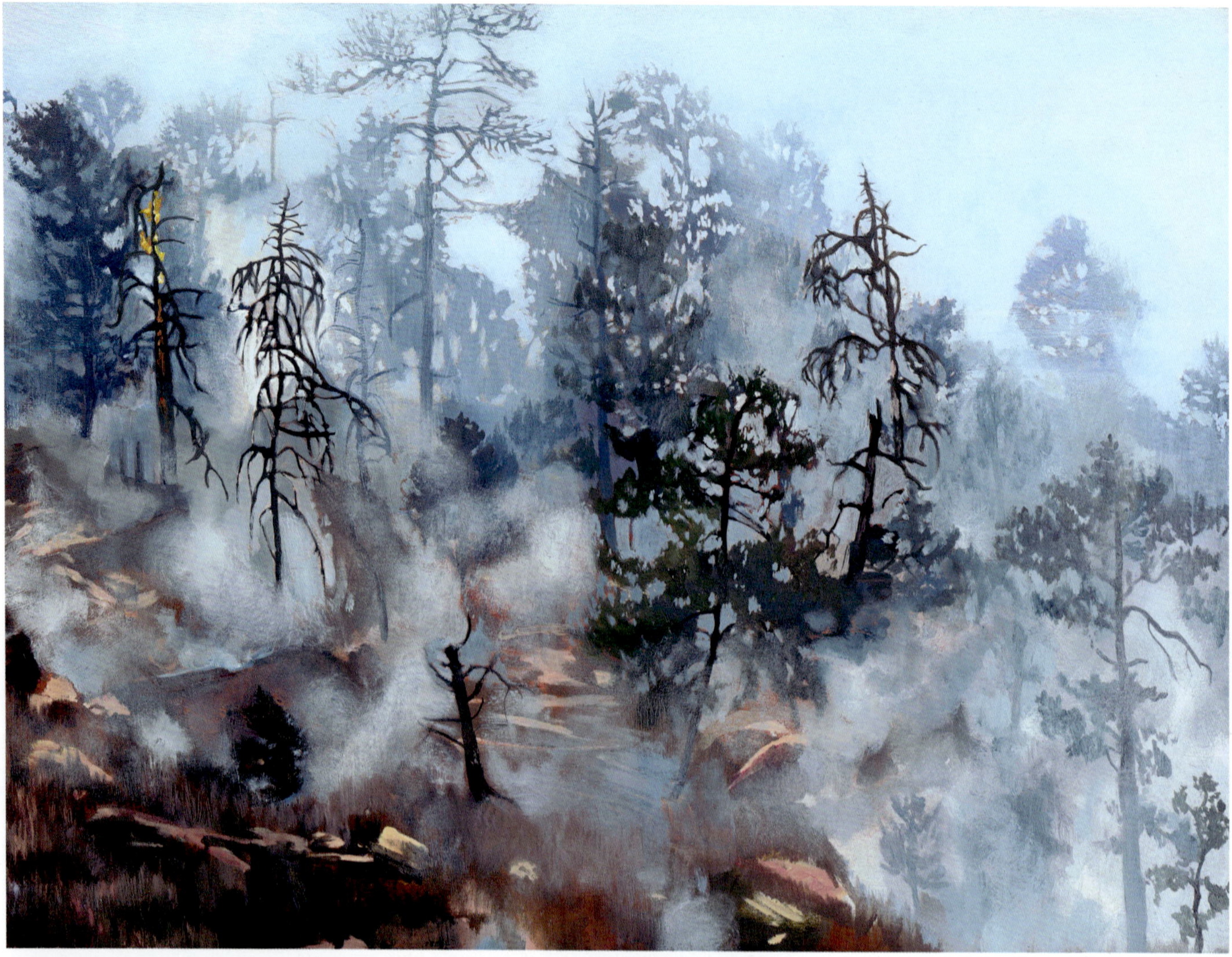

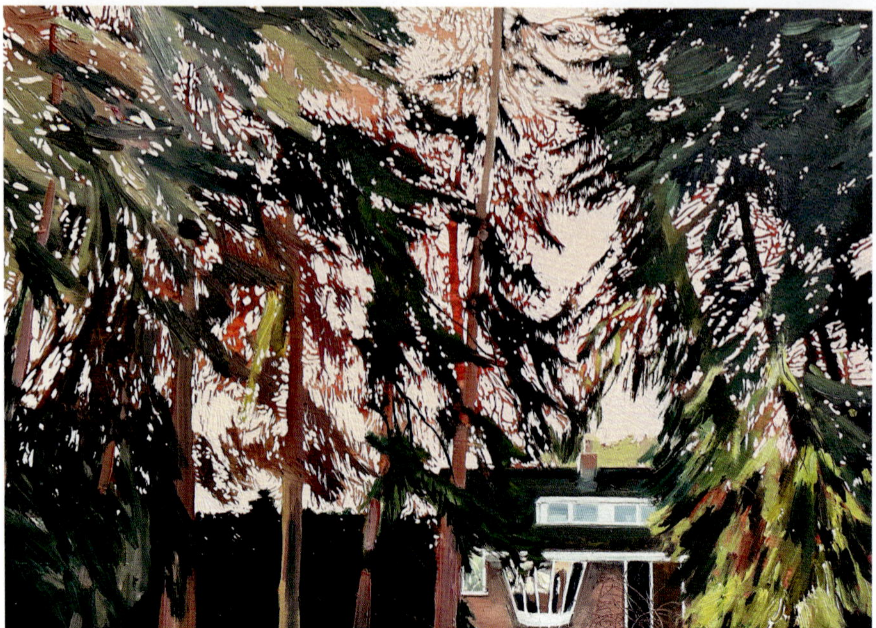

ABOVE *Albuquerque*, 2022
LEFT *Covet Thy Neighbour's House*, 2022

OPPOSITE ABOVE *It'll Always Belong to Them*, 2022
OPPOSITE BELOW *Not a Drop to Drink*, 2021

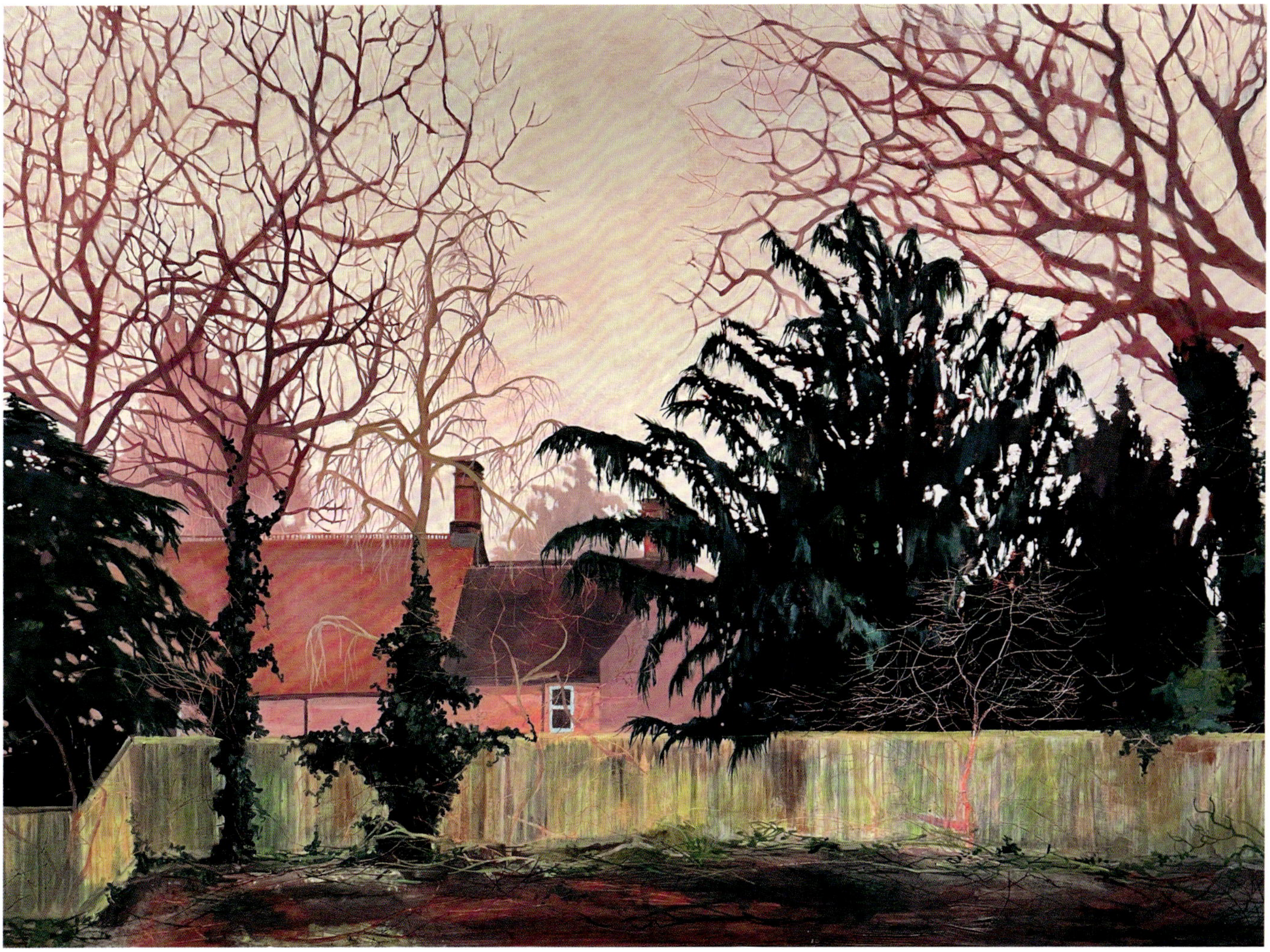

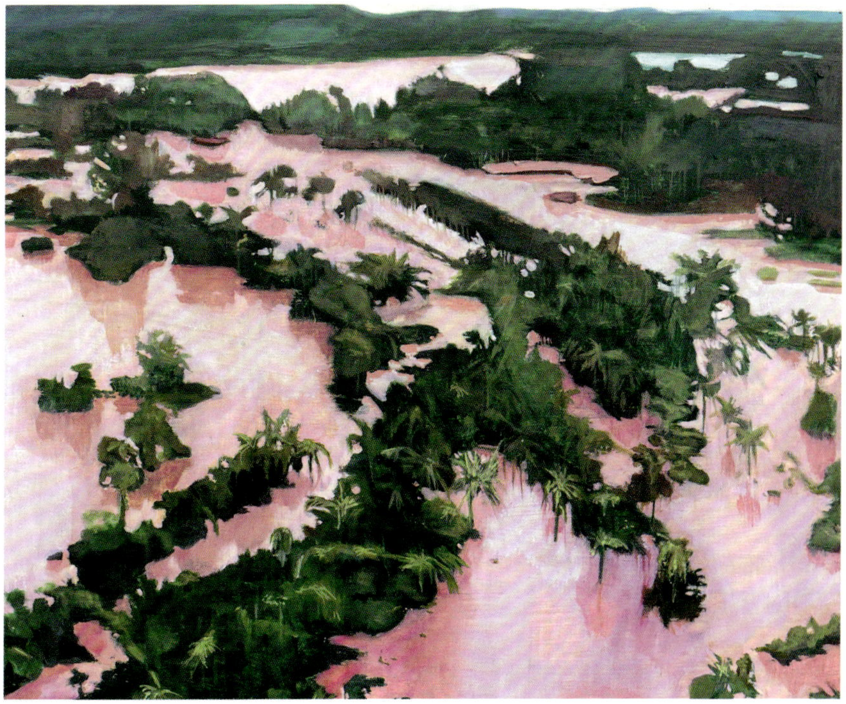

Andrew Carnie

My main concerns focus on the interface of art and science, often working in collaboration with scientists, though not exclusively. My approach to media is agnostic, using methodologies and media as informed by the context, concepts and concerns. Drawing, painting and sculpting have an enduring place in my practice, but video, projection and installation are my primary interests. I create environments around subjects like heart transplants, metabolism and neurological conditions, and the web of life is what intrigues me. I am particularly interested in the tree-like forms in our bodies and the dendritic networks outside our bodies. The Italian biologist and pathologist Camillo Golgi discovered that neurons are the principal building blocks of the brain when he mistakenly left brain samples overnight in a sink with silver nitrate photographic solution. Fortunately, only one in a hundred of these 'tree-like' cells stained black, allowing them to be seen for the first time – for him to see the wood for the trees. The Spanish neuroscientist Santiago Ramón y Cajal perfected the technique and went on to develop 'neuron theory', exploring the structure of the brain in significant ways, describing the form of our brains as a forest of independent but linked neurons and using the term 'arbour' to describe this forest.

At our core, and in fact, entering and leaving our physical heart and every organ of our bodies, are tree-like structures, 'dendritic' forms, nerves, arteries and veins that fundamentally make our bodies work. As in wider nature these systems supply, transmit and remove, all that make us work. We are intimately linked to these forms. I am fascinated by how this all operates. My work, in all its forms, including painting, sculpture and projected pieces, tries to explore these ideas: the complex trees in and around us.

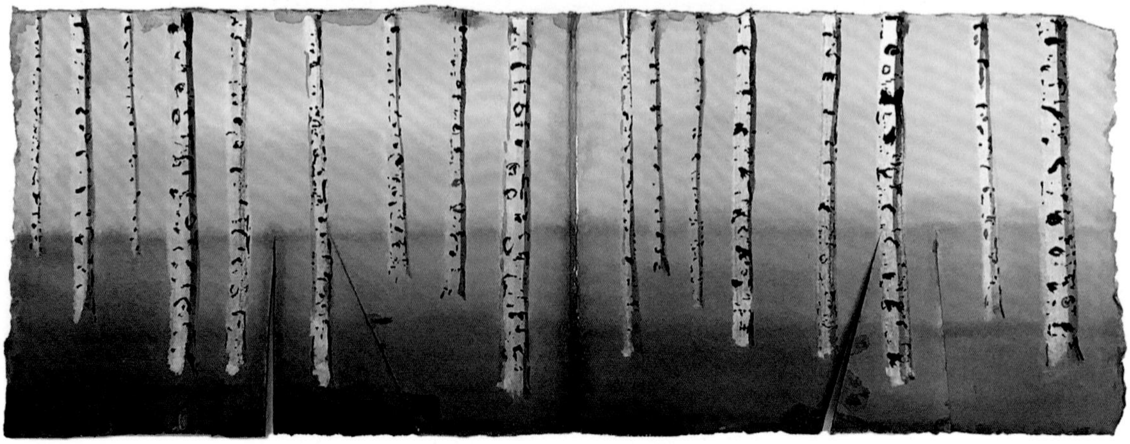

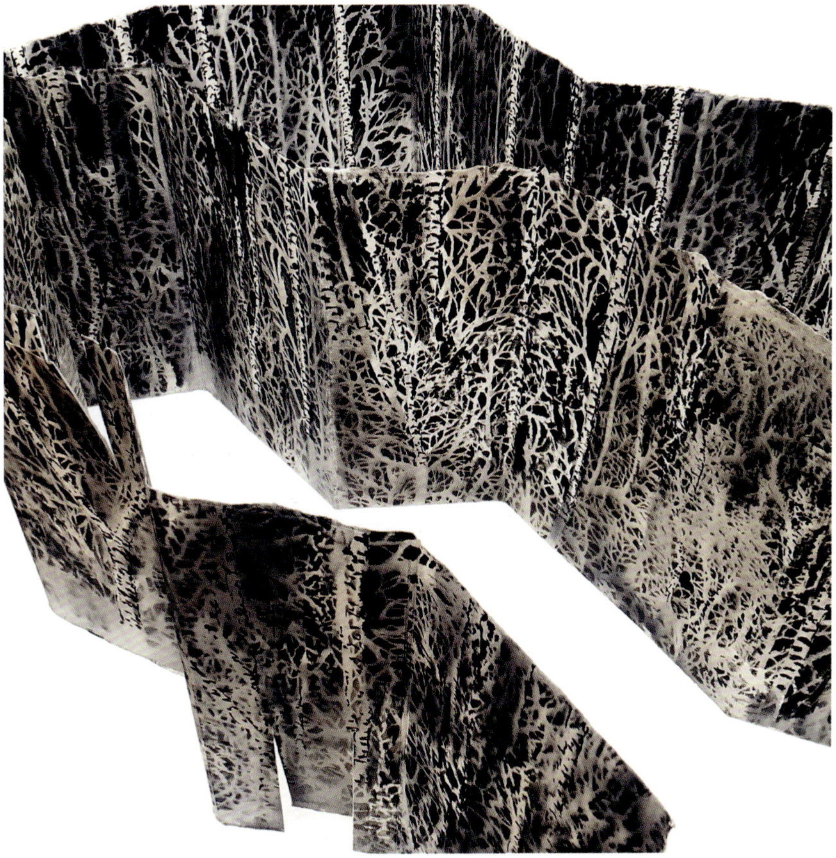

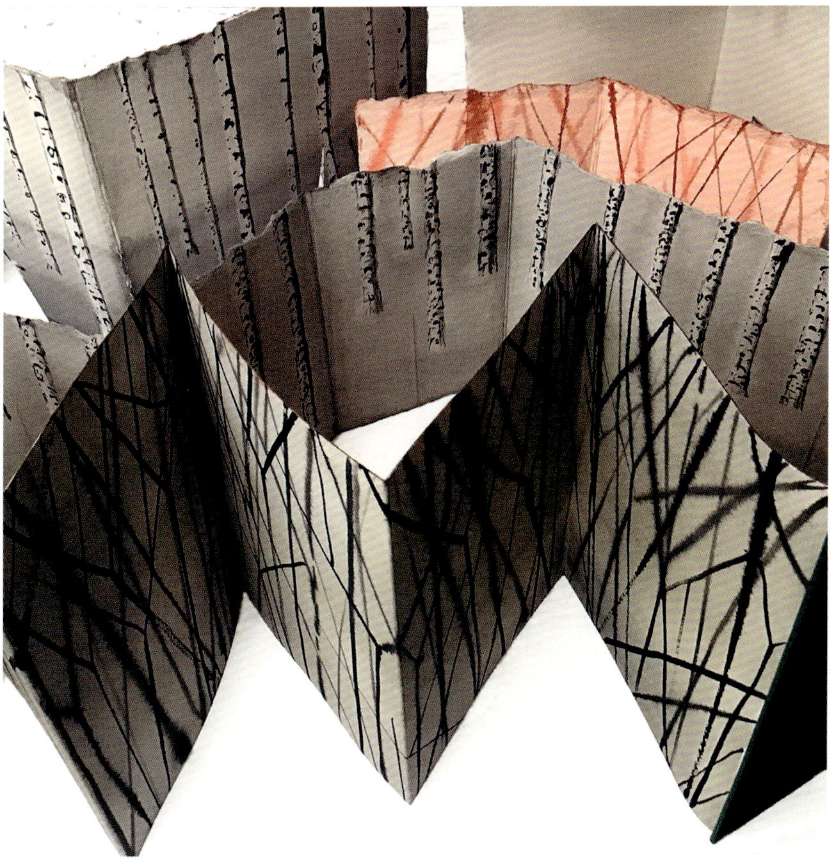

OPPOSITE *Grove: Future*, 2024

ABOVE *Mixed Forest*, 2024
RIGHT *Black Birch Network*, 2024

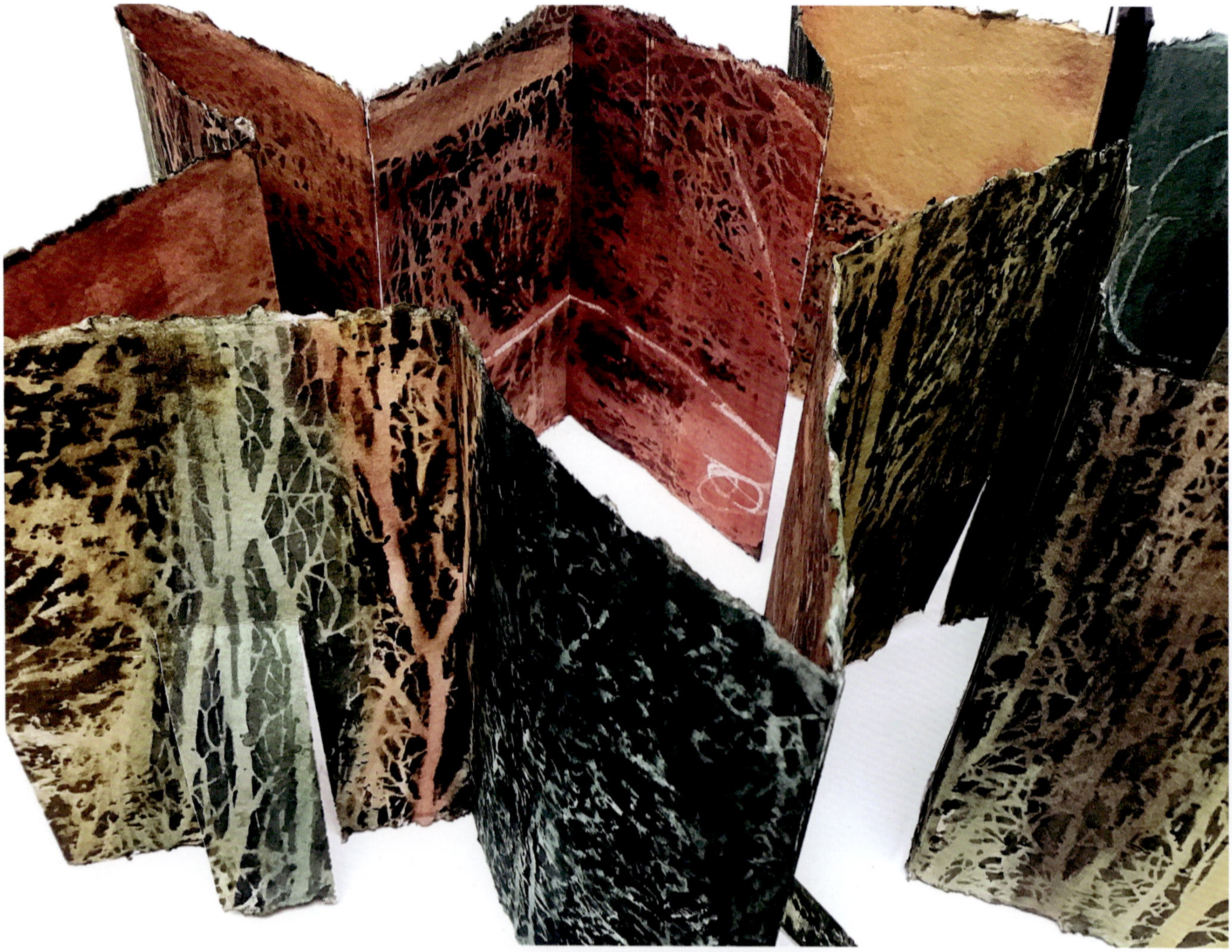

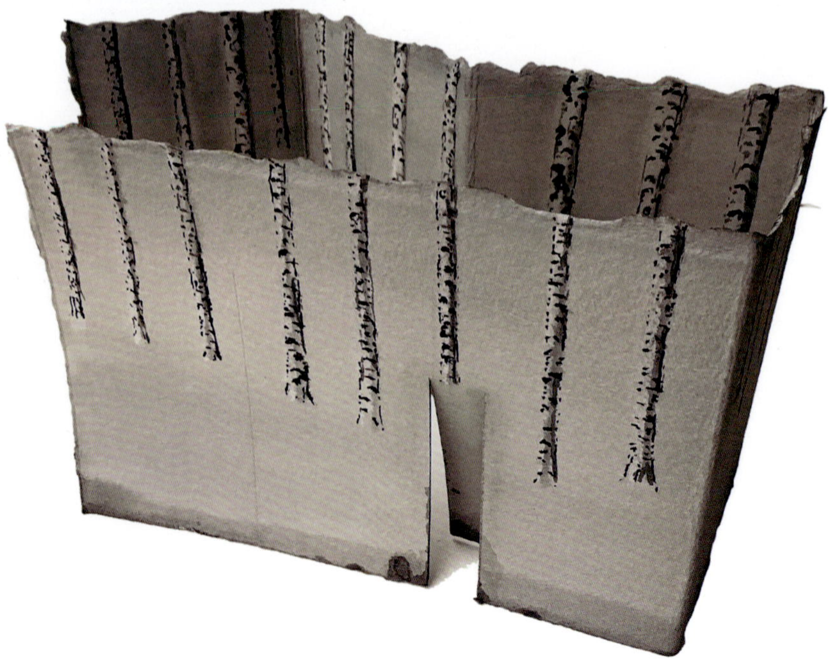

ABOVE *Bile 1*, 2022
RIGHT *Grove 2: Hut*, 2024

Stella Carr

Stella Carr is a painter, examining the symbiotic relationship between the seen and felt in the natural world. Her paintings focus on trees as a locus of pattern and energy, honouring deep ecology and exploring the tensions between manmade landscapes and wildness. Carr's work dramatises the mutual vulnerability of artist and environment, both in her process, which often involves a somatic response to her subject, and in the finished work the viewer encounters. Her paintings document an inextricable connection between the evolution of her work in response to nature and the inner ecology of the self. Carr's eco-centric approach to creating is complemented by her work as a gardener over five decades. In this work, she uses the same intuitive response as in her paintings, working with texture, shape and pattern. Her work in both disciplines highlights the essential value of every cell, atom and microorganism as part of a boundaryless, interconnected whole whose imperilment threatens the loss of what it means to be human.

BELOW *Infinity*, 2019

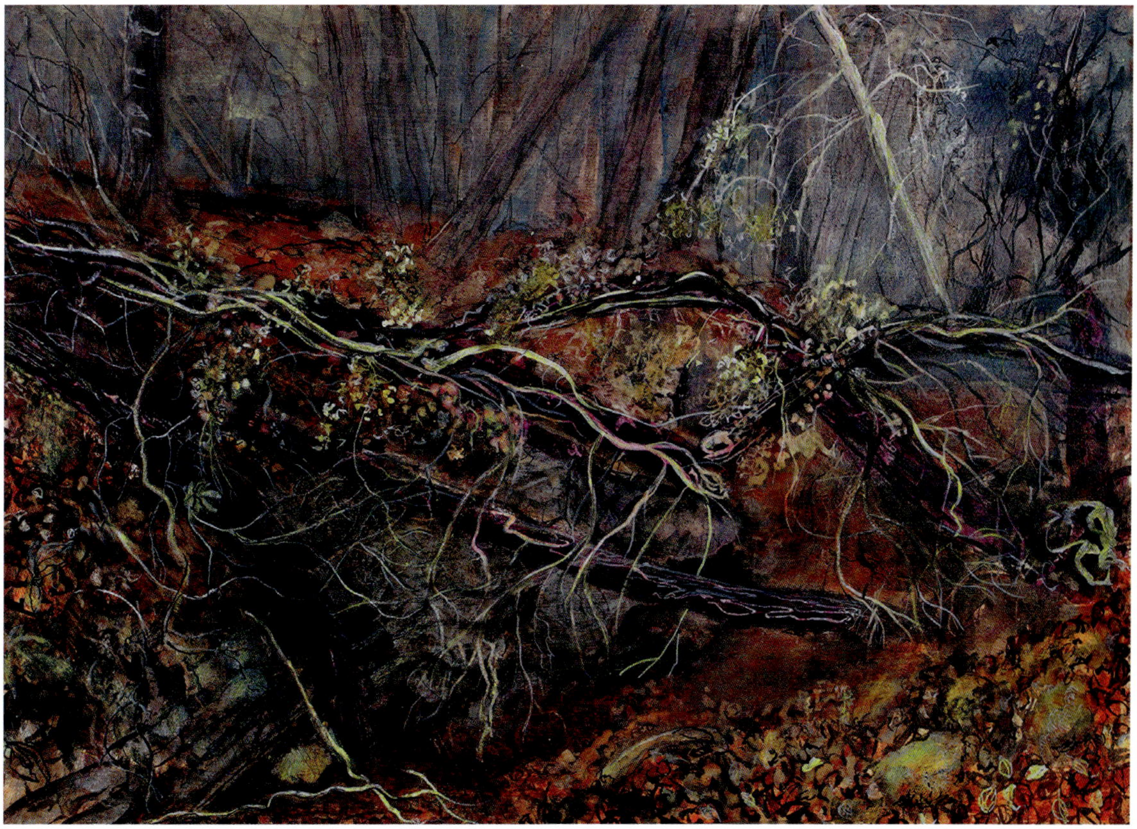

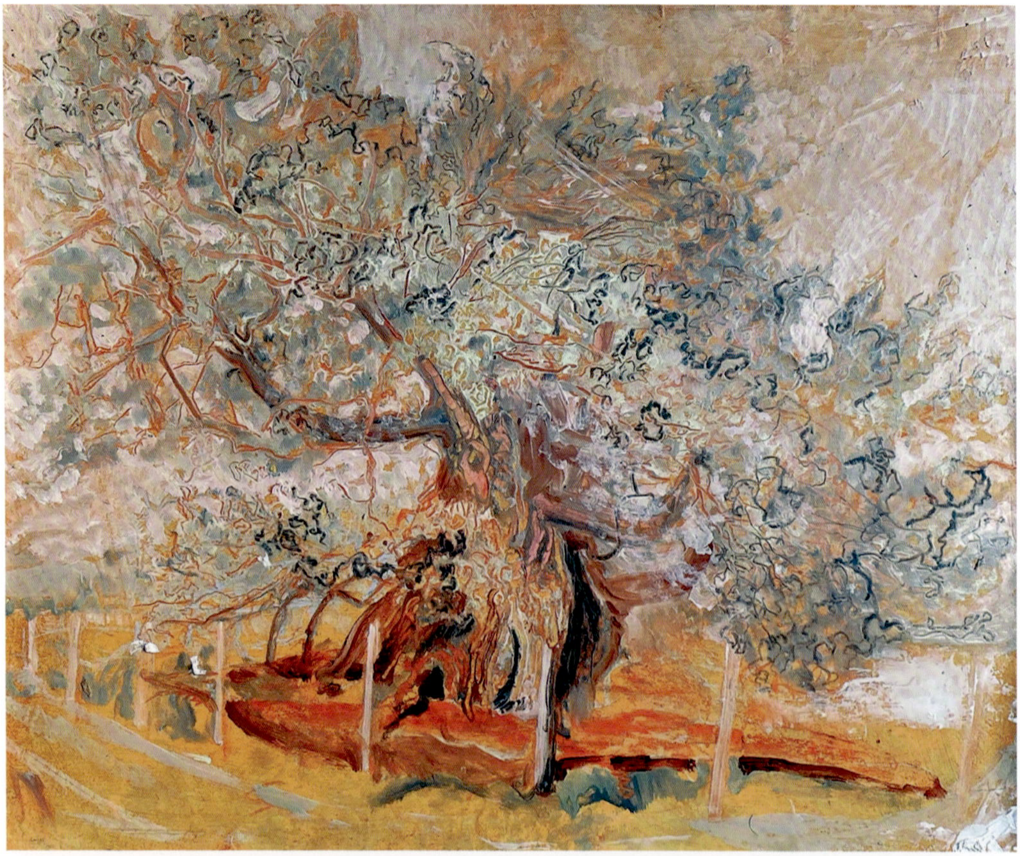

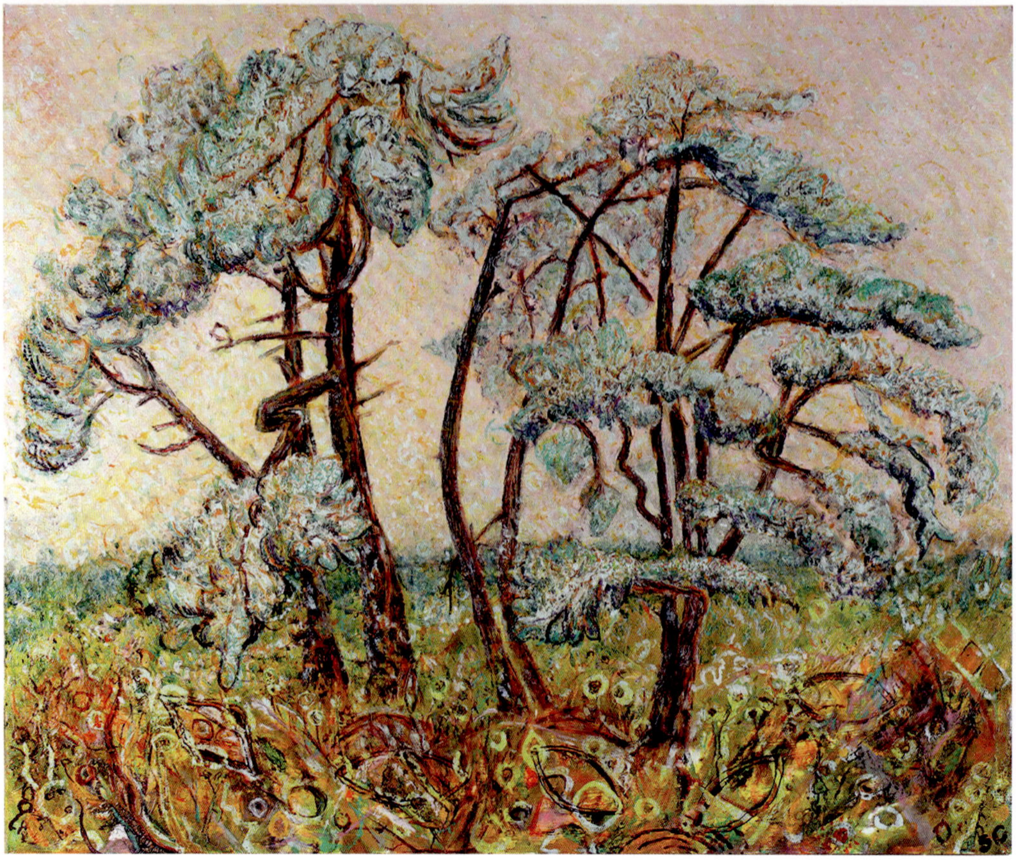

OPPOSITE ABOVE *Bowthorpe Oak*, 2023
OPPOSITE BELOW *The Infinite Field*, 2022

RIGHT *Charlotte's Walnut*, 2023
BELOW *You Said Meet Me There*, 2024

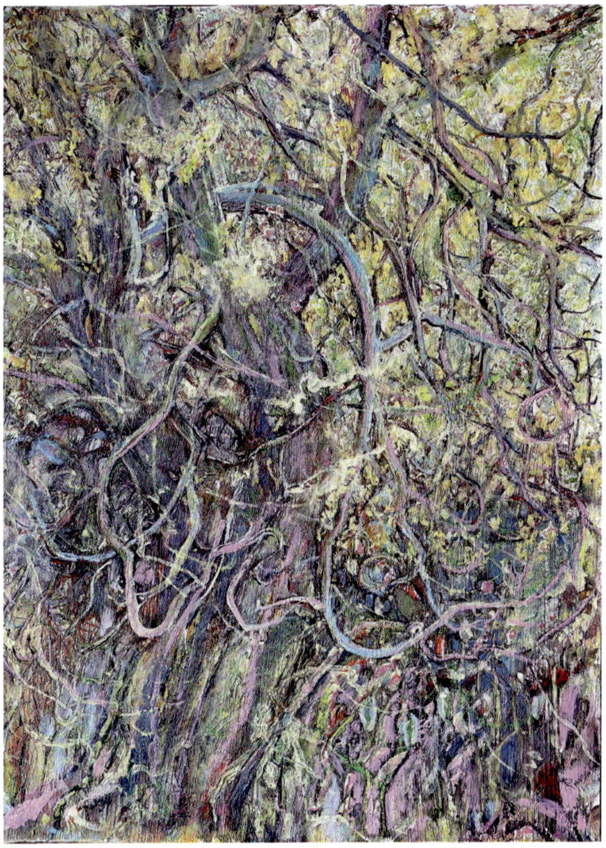

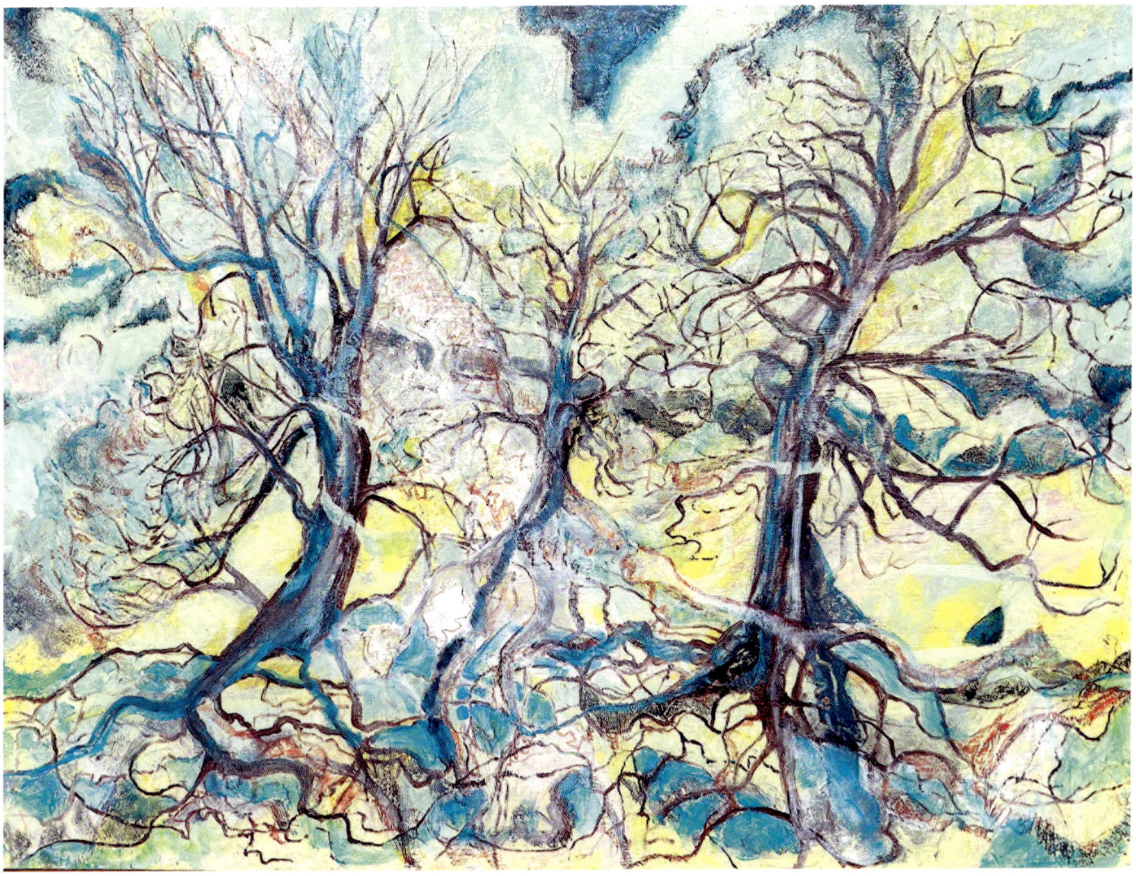

Lara Cobden

I feel most at home among trees. Wherever I am, the woods offer a place to retreat, reflect and inspire. Trees are eternally generous and serve as a benevolent source of healing and wisdom, rooted in a central theme of recollection and sense of place; my paintings are informed by observation, memory and dream. They are a subjective and individual response to my surroundings, calling on an imagined, coveted past that is unreal, a magical realism. Pulling between the chimerical and the familiar – I hope there is both a stillness and fluidity in my work and a sense of reverence in the ordinary. I like to inhabit and explore this in-between place, and try to collect and recreate that residue of experience, like recording details and grasping at the gossamer fabric of waking from a dream. Trees and forests offer a unique space for this journey to begin, between the interior and exterior. They offer both refuge and unease, a starting point for untold stories and portals into another world.

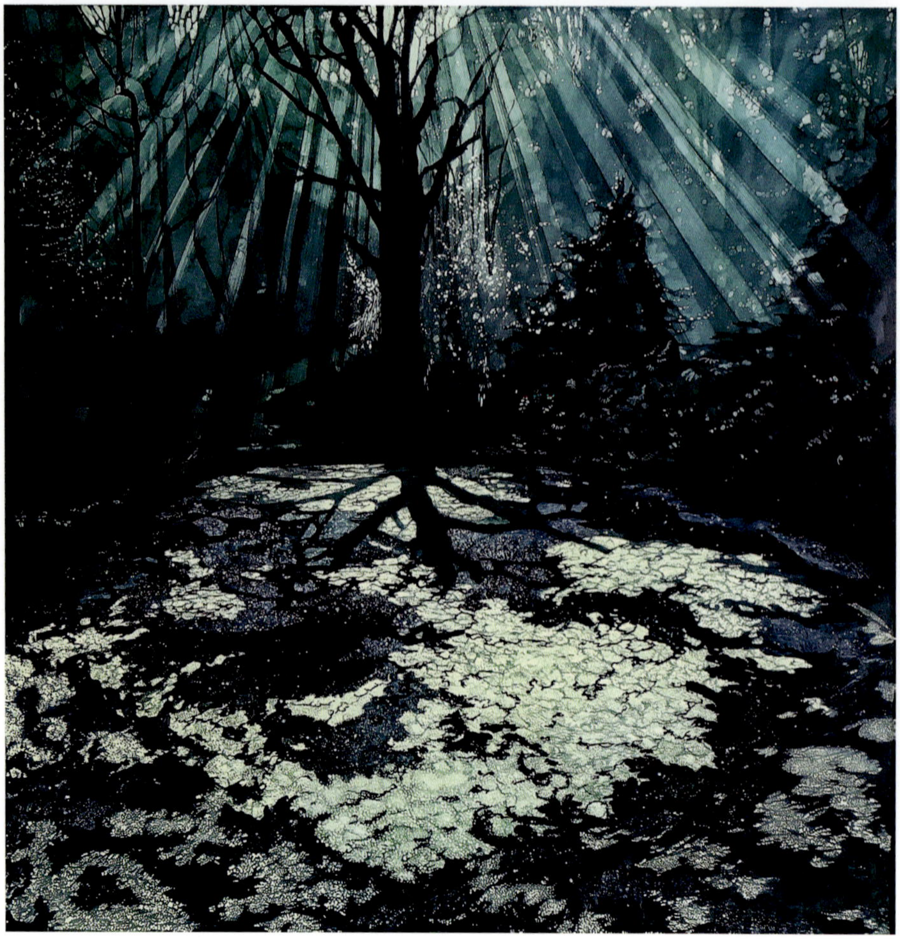

OPPOSITE *Shadowtackle*, 2022

BELOW LEFT *Still Here*, 2024
BELOW RIGHT *Winged Man and White Moths*

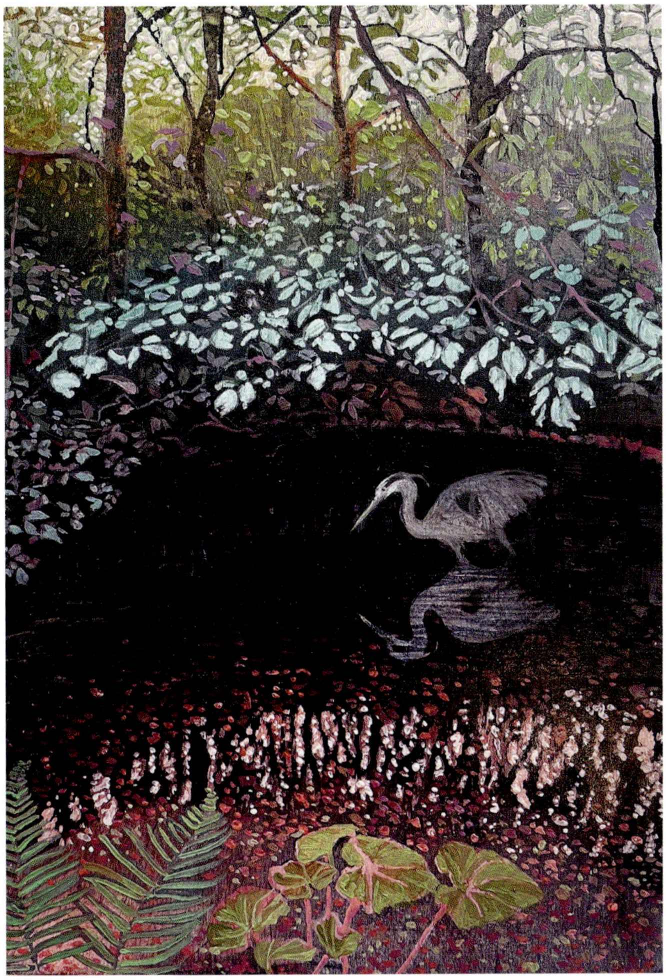

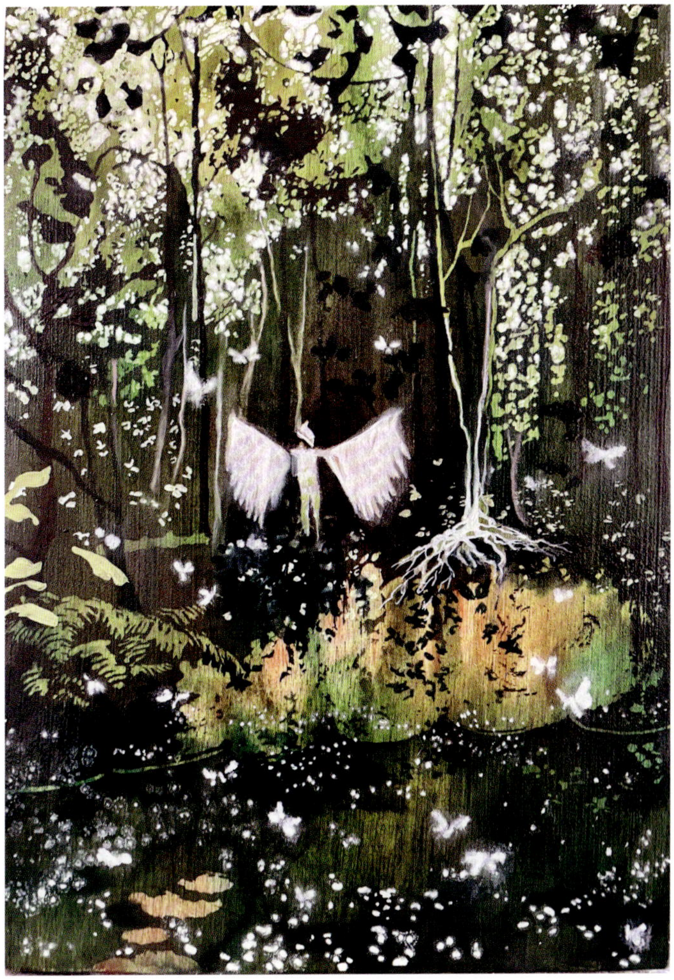

BELOW LEFT *The Pollen Path*, 2024
BELOW RIGHT *A Year of Ghost Wishes*, 2020

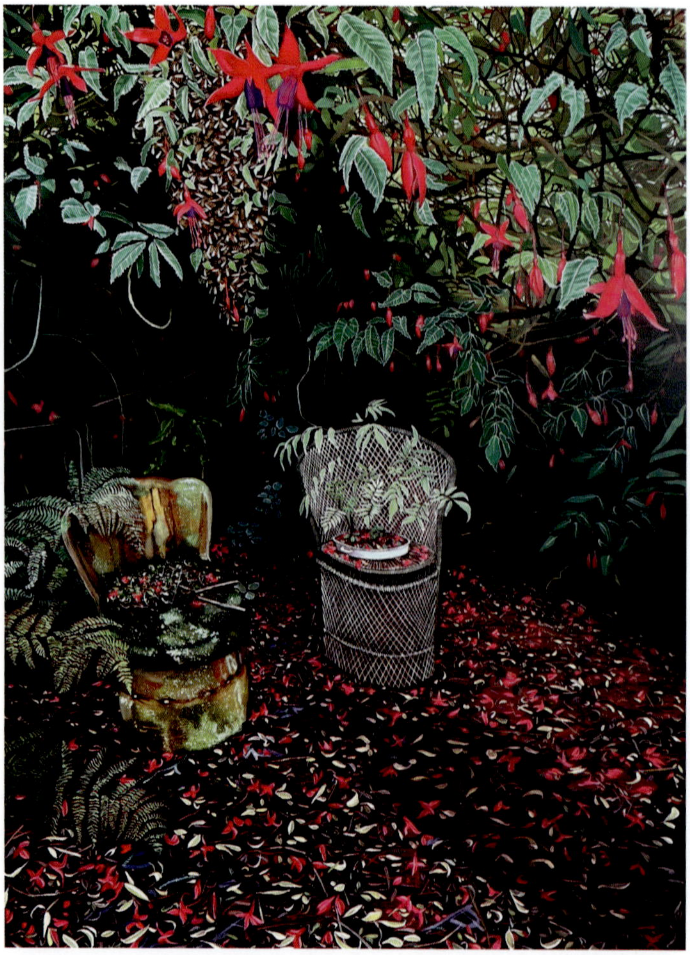

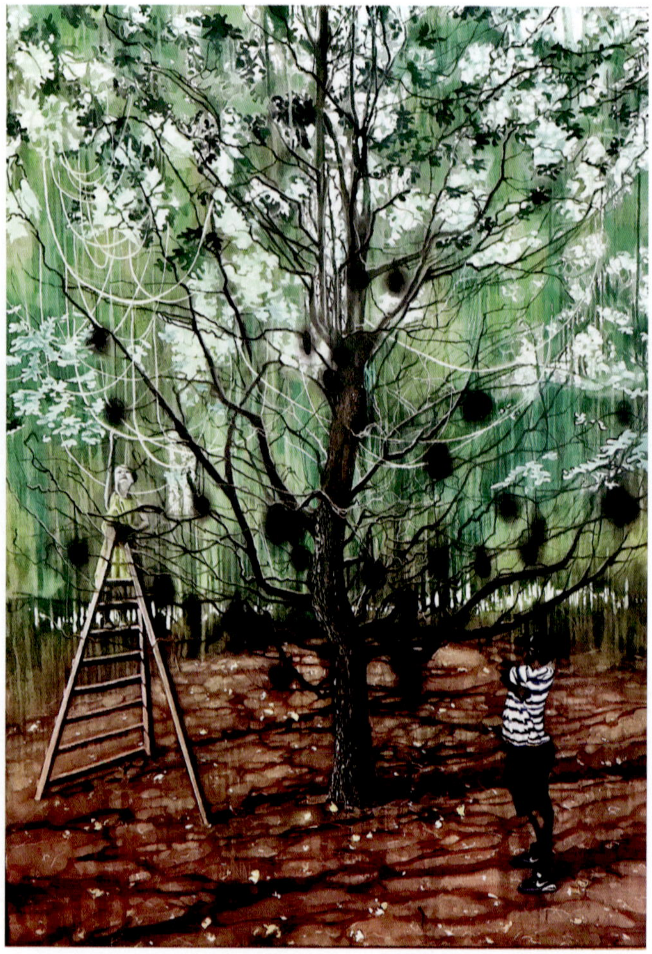

Tim Craven

My work explores the dichotomy and long relationship between painting and photography. I am drawn to complex and rhythmic imagery when flattened and abstracted by photography. My paintings are often monochrome or muted in colour, evoking memory and nostalgia. I contrast deadpan and anonymous Photorealism with English romantic subjects such as trees. I am drawn to the strong, dynamic verticals (as opposed to the supine horizontals of topography), spatial drama and abstract qualities of tree forms.

After training in Fine Art and the conservation of paintings, I joined the staff of Southampton City Art Gallery in 1980. I remained there, working closely with one of the finest regional public art collections spanning eight centuries, for more than thirty-five years. This has proved a privilege and stimulus for my own art practice, which I have always rigorously pursued. My work is, therefore, inevitably informed by a diverse range of styles and ideas, and the legacy of British art history. I admire the English pastoral landscape tradition, notably the Pre-Raphaelite landscape painters, such as J W Inchbold, and its links with Surrealism through Paul Nash and others, along with various abstract and contemporary movements, including Land Art, Op Art and the Systems Group.

BELOW *October Frieze (Lady Park Wood)*, 2018

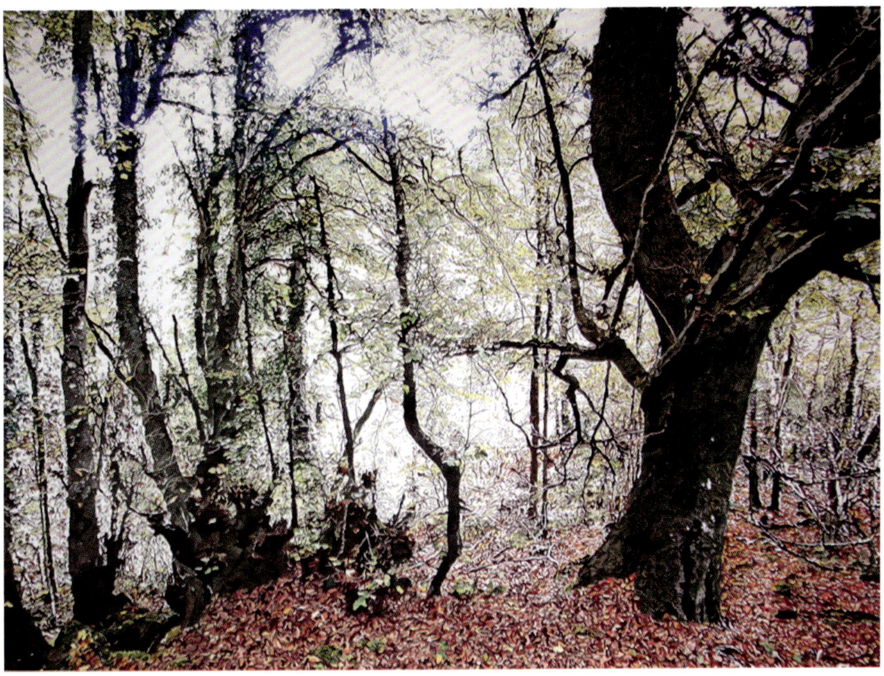

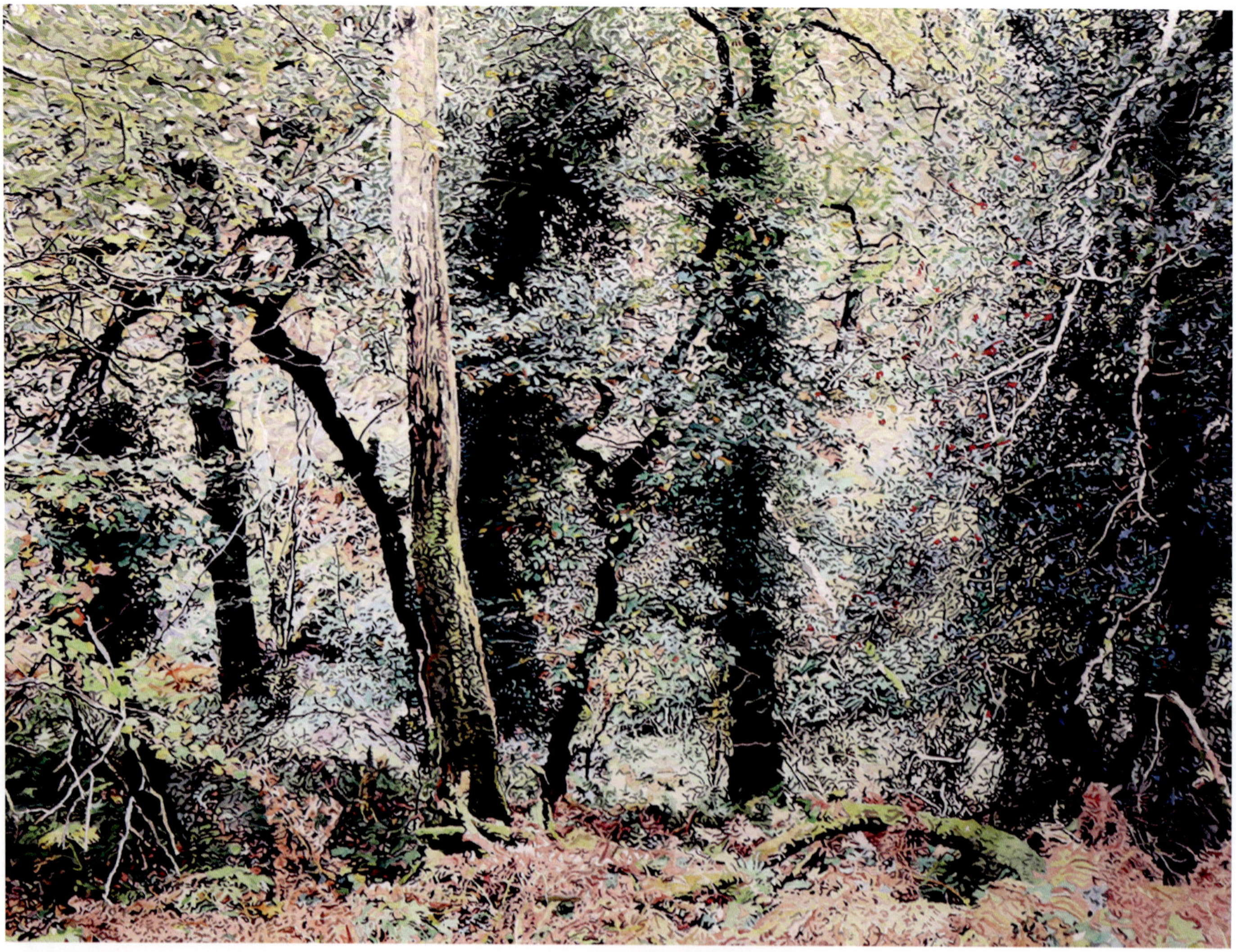

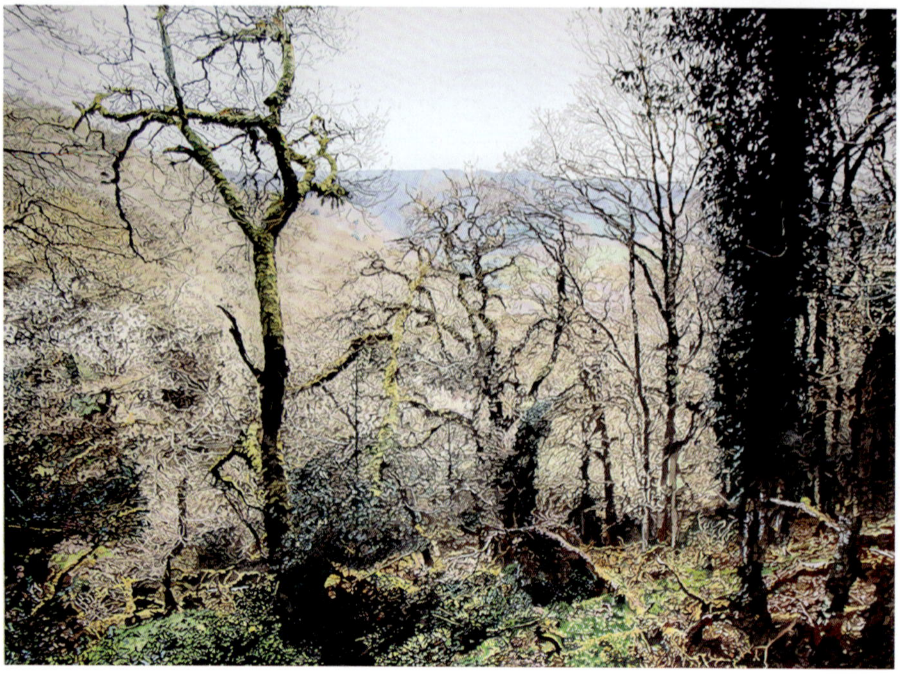

ABOVE *East Water Valley (Exmoor)*, 2021
LEFT *Rey Combe (Exmoor)*, 2018

OPPOSITE ABOVE *Tortworth Chestnut*, 2021
OPPOSITE BELOW *Twin Pillars (Lady Park Wood)*, 2018

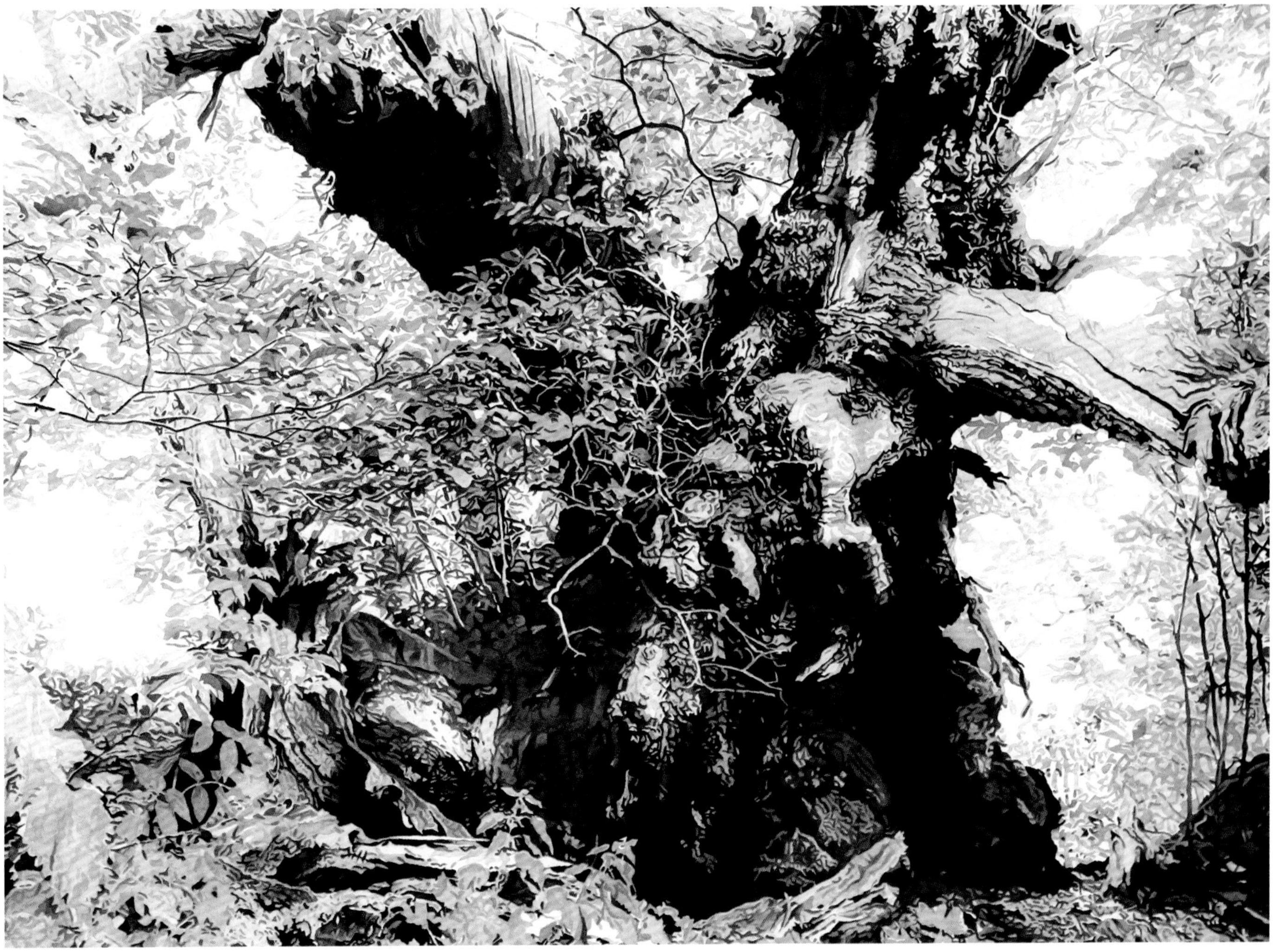

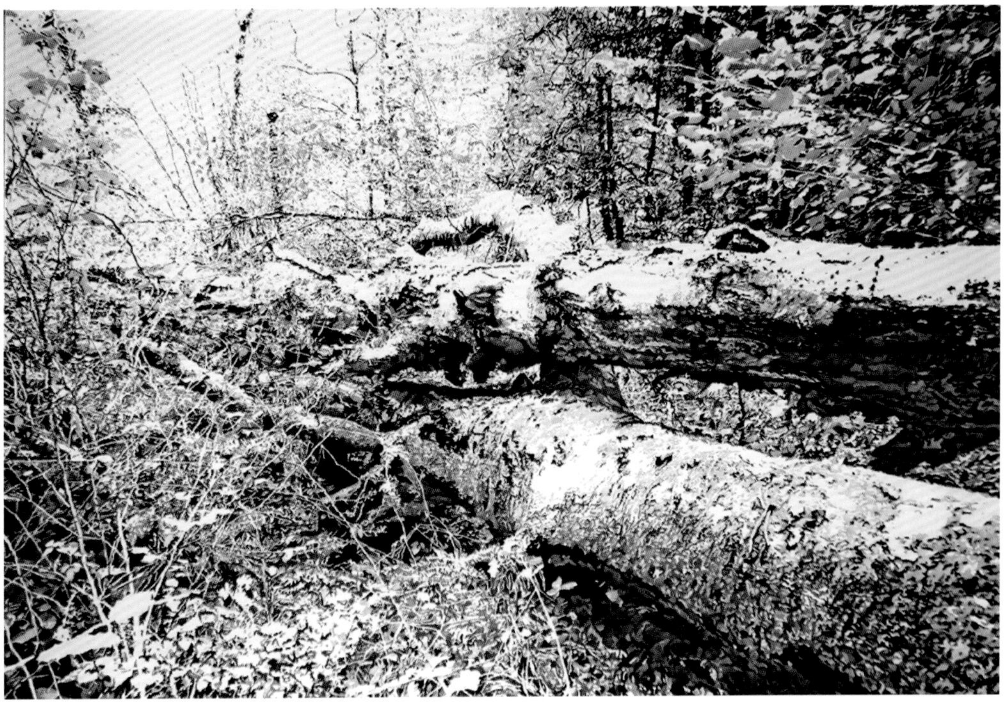

Annabel Cullen

As a painter of the human figure, my interest in and feeling of connection with trees arise in part from their anthropomorphic and emotive qualities. I enjoy the correlation between their sinuous, jointed limbs and human anatomy; movement and feeling are often suggested in their static forms. The physical presence of great ancient trees can be quite overwhelming. For me, they are powerful and poignant protagonists of the human condition. The medium of drawing is my preference; its speed and immediacy allow me to respond directly to the subject. Most of the work is made on-site using various drawing materials, predominantly charcoal and ink.

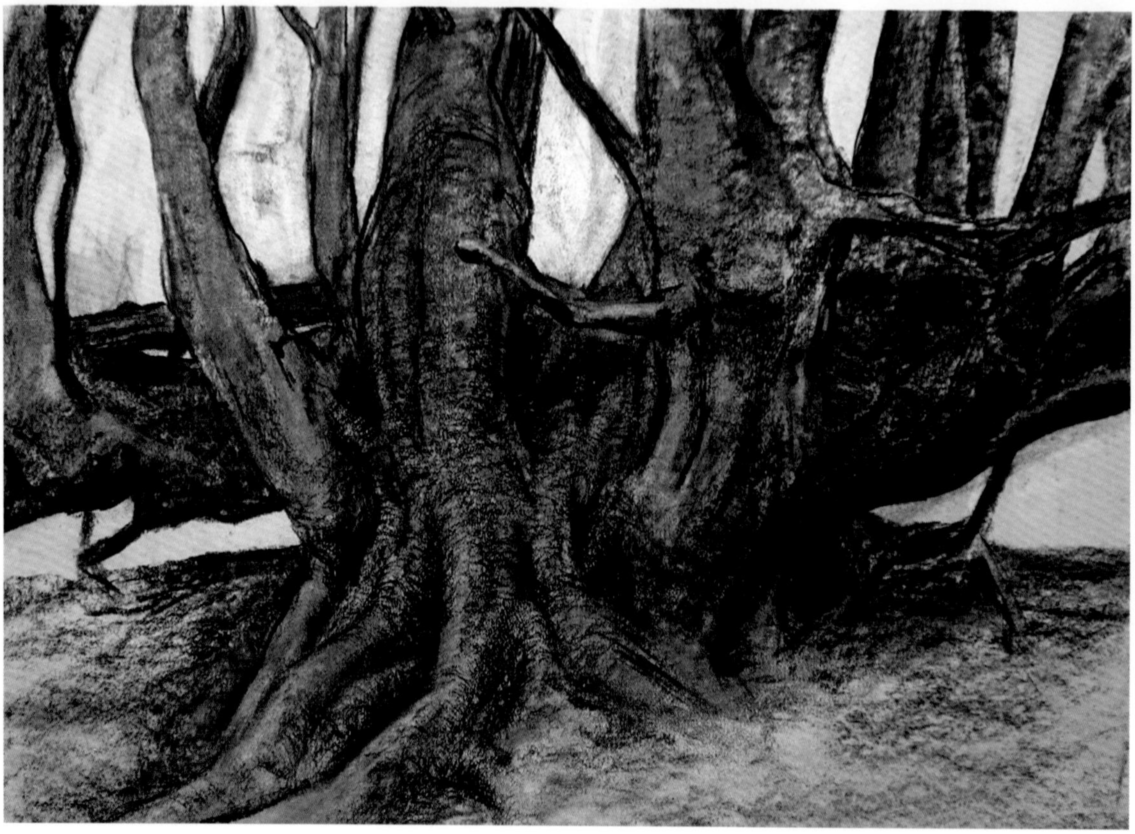

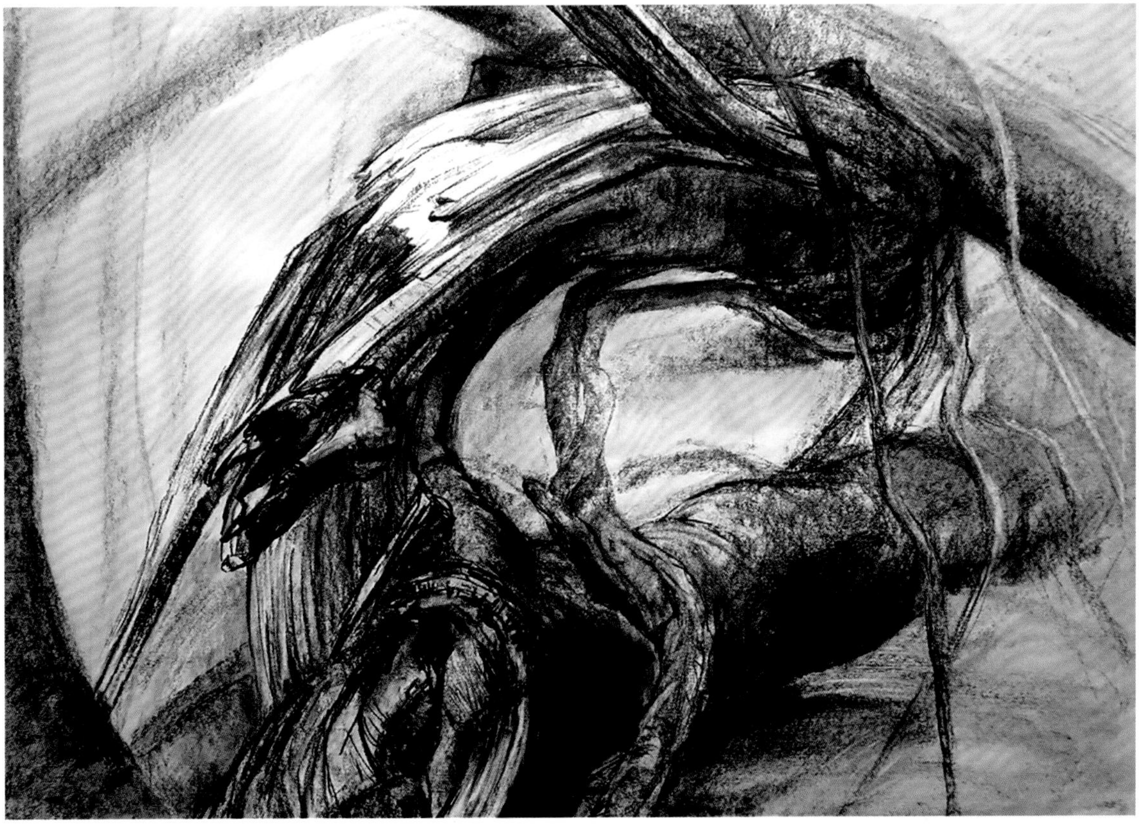

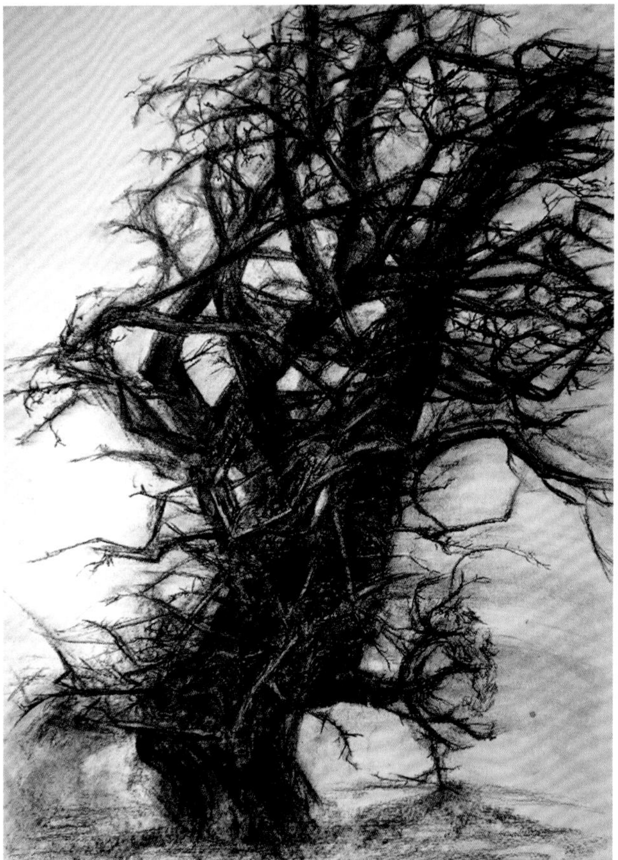

OPPOSITE *Laid Beech Hedge, Exmoor*, 2018

ABOVE *Forces of Nature, Lady Park Wood, Wye Valley*, 2017
RIGHT *On Winsford Hill, Exmoor*, 2018

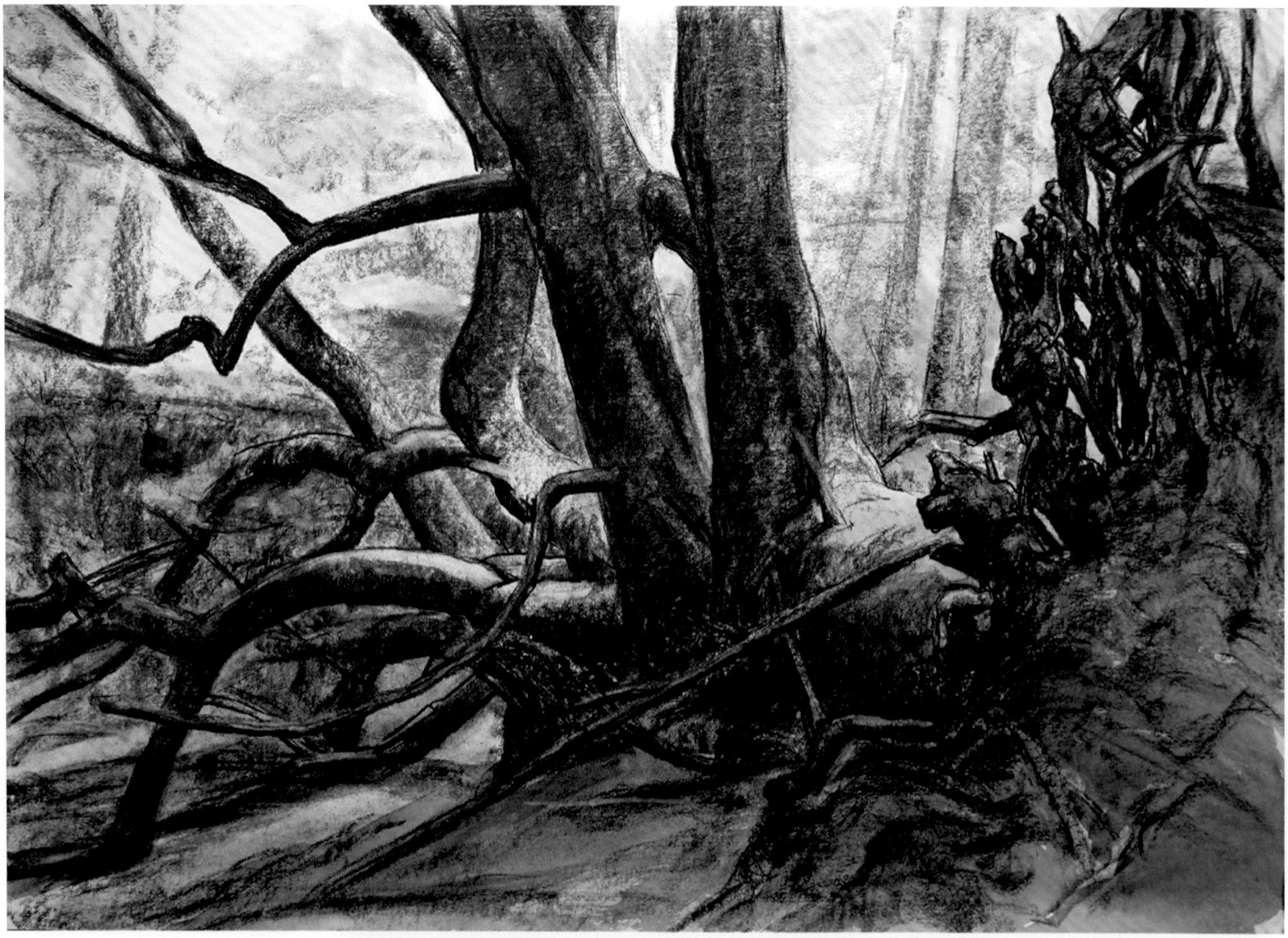

ABOVE *Regenerating Beech, Lady Park Wood, Wye Valley,* 2017
RIGHT *Holly and Oak, Staverton Thicks, Suffolk,* 2024

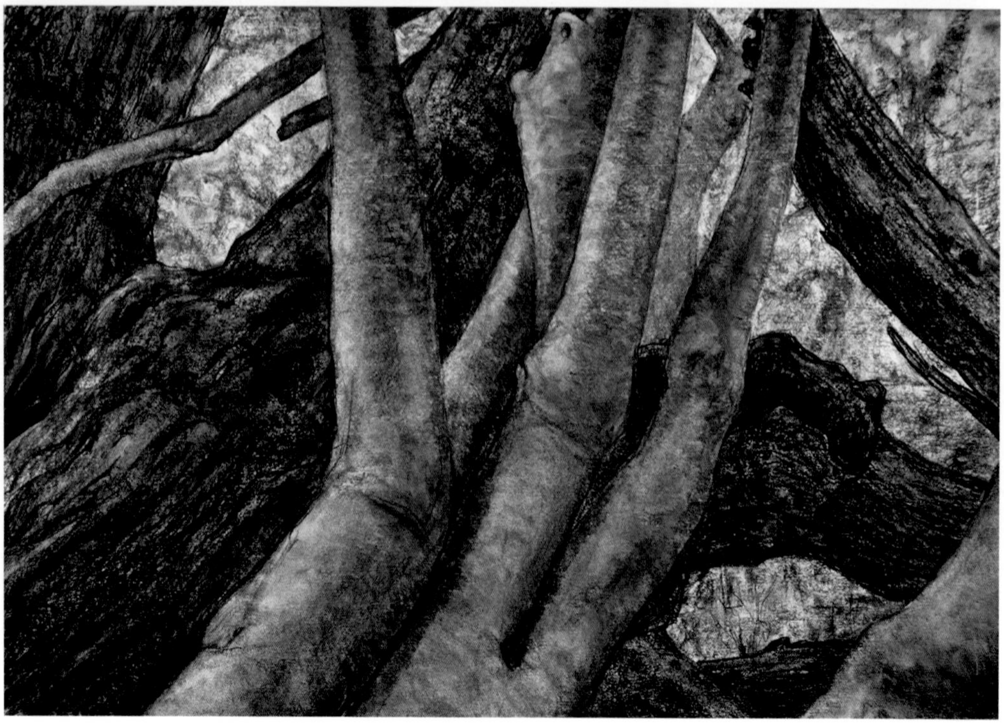

Blaze Cyan RE, SWE

Ecology and the plight of trees are very close to my heart; that said, it's not the sole reason trees are my subject matter, but just one of the reasons I seek to draw attention to them. Their elementary and complex beauty and structure, their simple dignity and yet mighty sense of presence, and the peace they bring to the landscape and the human mind are just as important to me. Trees are fundamentally an essential component to life, ecological diversity and the planet's well-being; without them, we would not survive.

I first began working with trees over 15 years ago and knew from the outset that they were a subject I could never exhaust, and would never tire of. Trees travel with us through time, through life, and my personal interpretation of them is as unique and changeable as the weather. They take the position of unconditional love, a soulmate.

BELOW *Wardour*, 2023

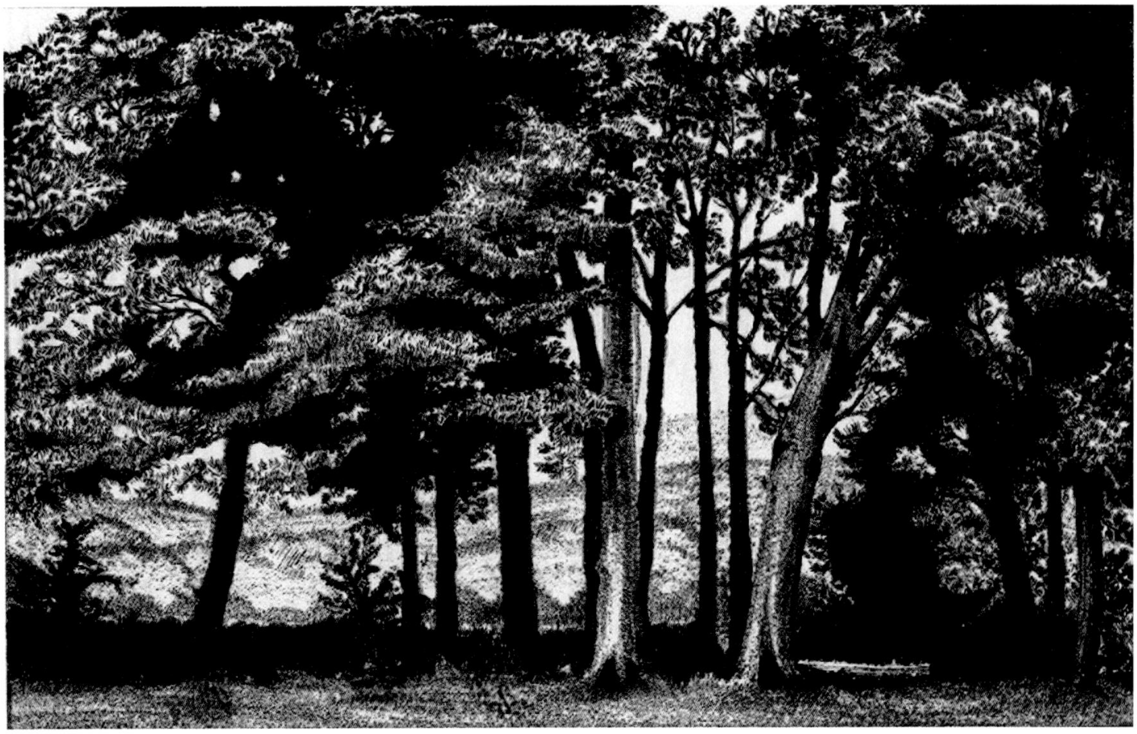

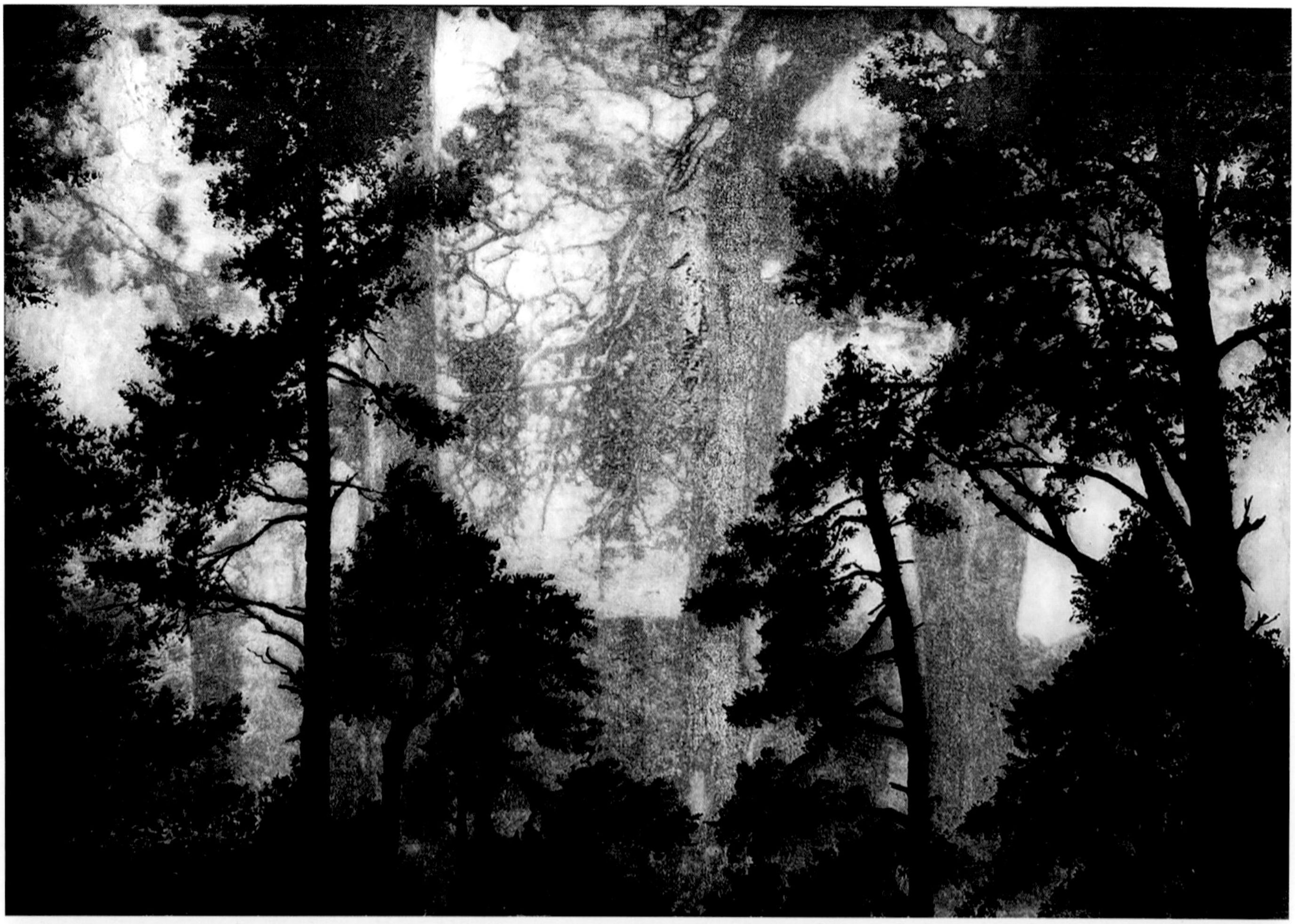

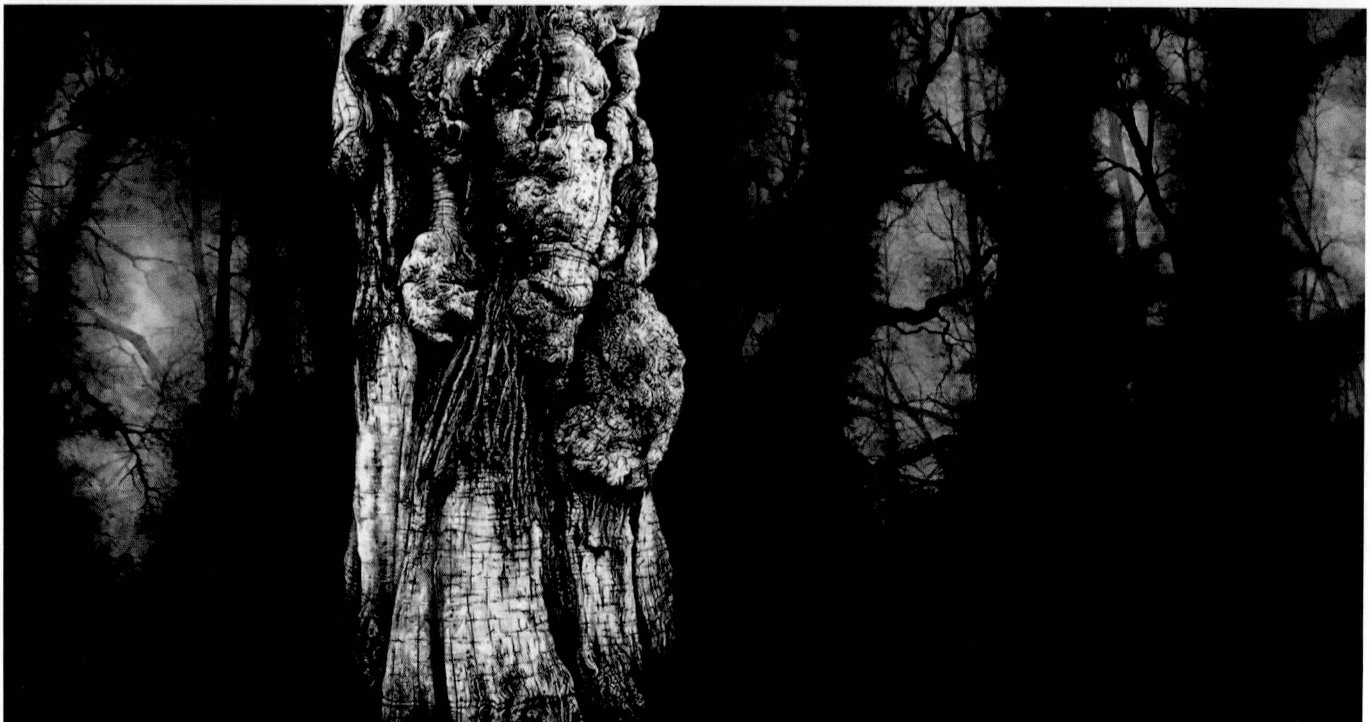

OPPOSITE ABOVE *Forest of Ghosts V*, 2023
OPPOSITE BELOW *Windsor Forest*, 2016

BELOW LEFT *Dappled Oak at Petworth*, 2023
BELOW RIGHT *Croft Castle V*, 2017

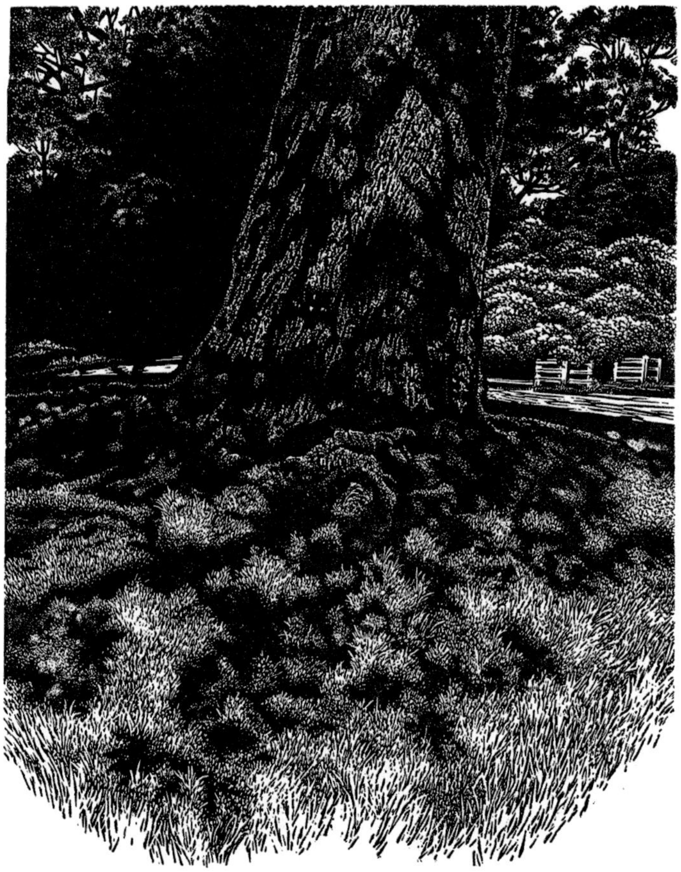

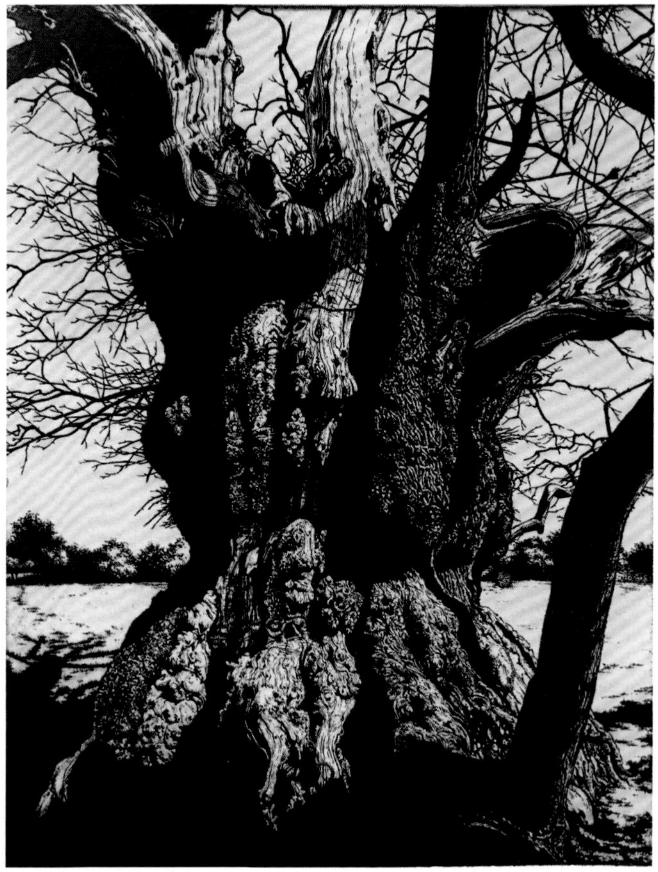

Mike Dodd

The main focus of my two-dimensional work has settled on trees as a subject, through my admiration of a grand old grey poplar that dominated the vineyards close to my home in Southern France. I regard trees as sentinels and witnesses to the comparatively brief span of a singular human life, and human history in general. I am especially drawn to trees like Kett's Oak and the Glastonbury Thorn, which have a specific link to a particular historical time or event, whether factual or mythological. My source material is photography because I want to engage my audience as directly as possible, with the intricately realistic detail of the branch formation, bark, tree roots, fungi, etc. associated with trees; these aspects offer incredible complexity when represented in works of art. I am searching for a subjective response from my audience regarding an objective representation of the trees' detailed reality, while simultaneously embodying my feelings of awe and wonder at the trees' beauty and majesty.

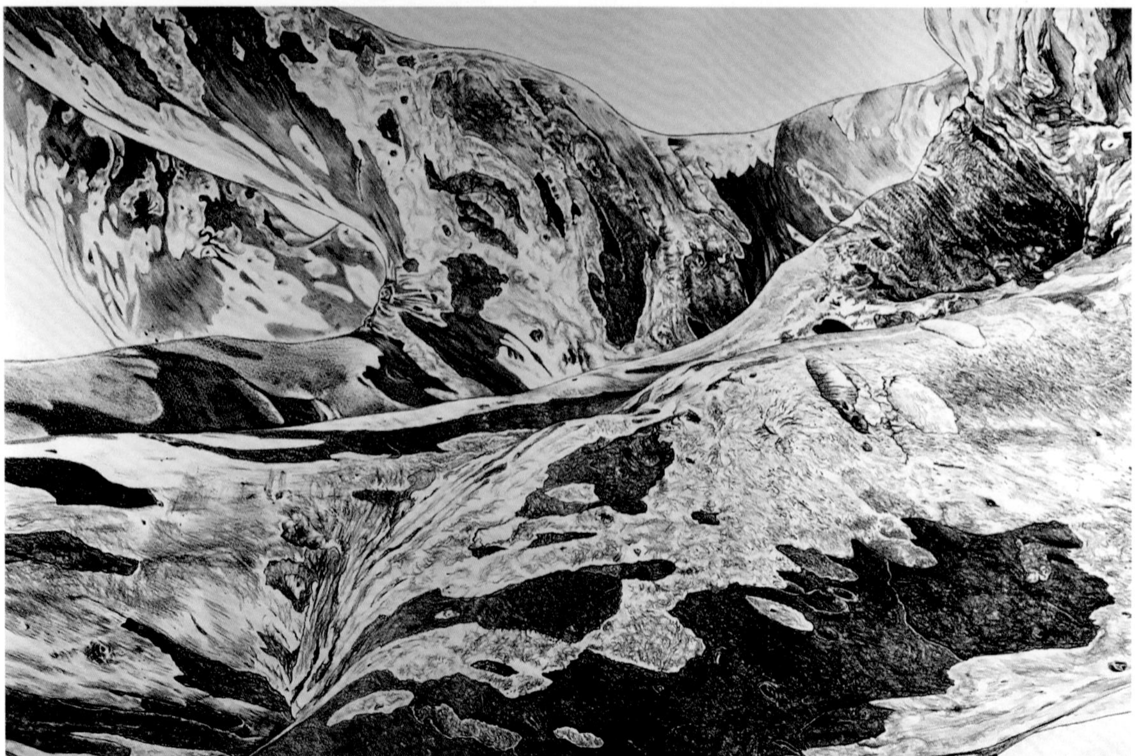

OPPOSITE *Eucalyptus*, 2018

BELOW LEFT *The Defynnog Yew*, 2023
BELOW RIGHT *Old Knobbley*, 2024

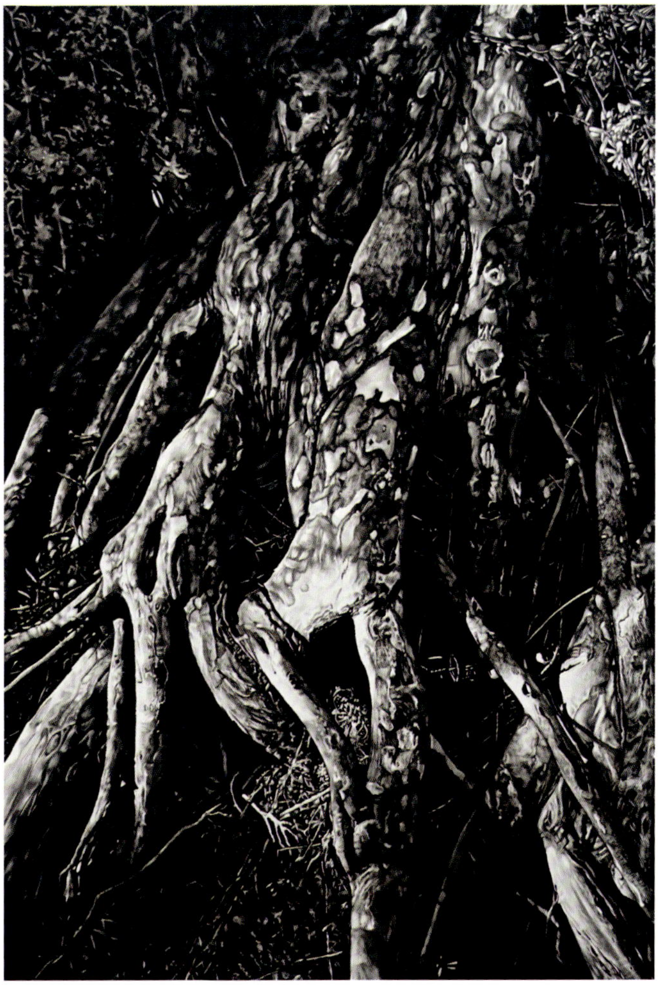

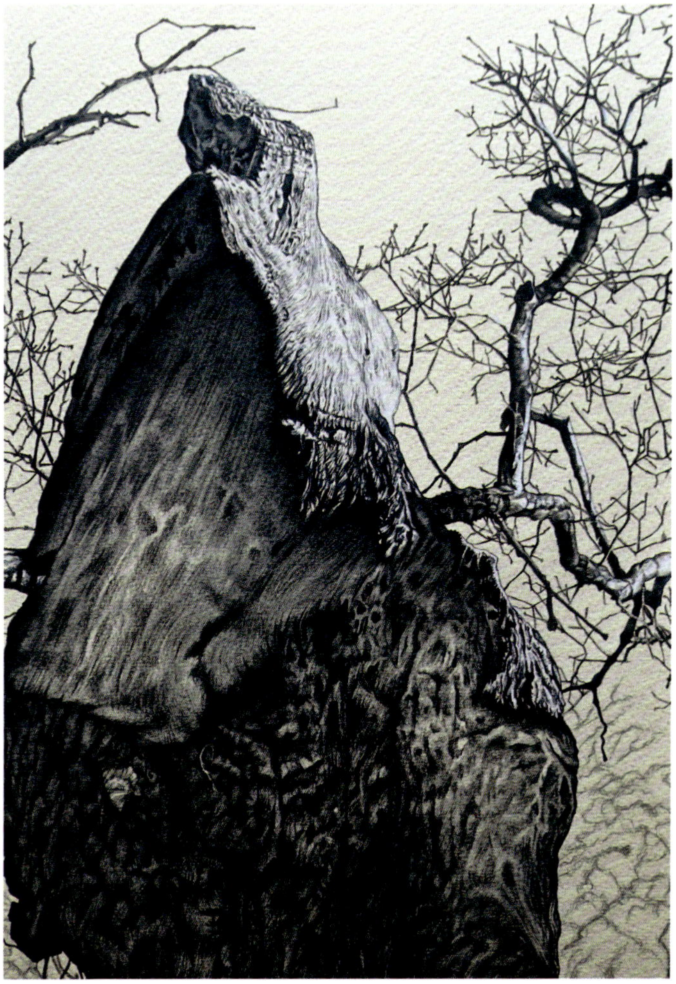

RIGHT *Turkey Tail Fungus*, 2021
BELOW *The Glastonbury Thorn*, 2022

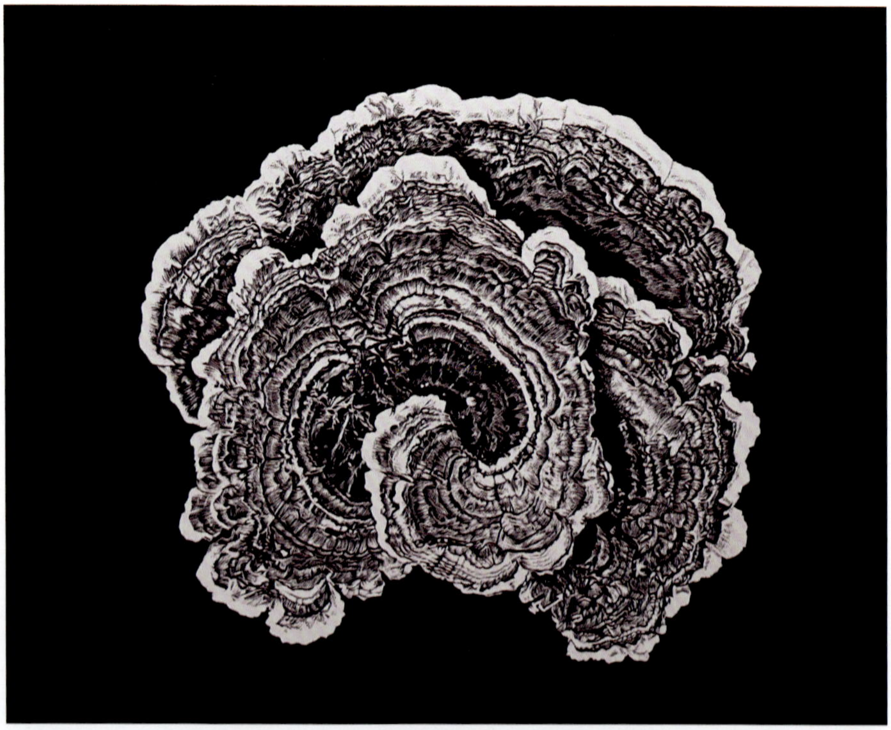

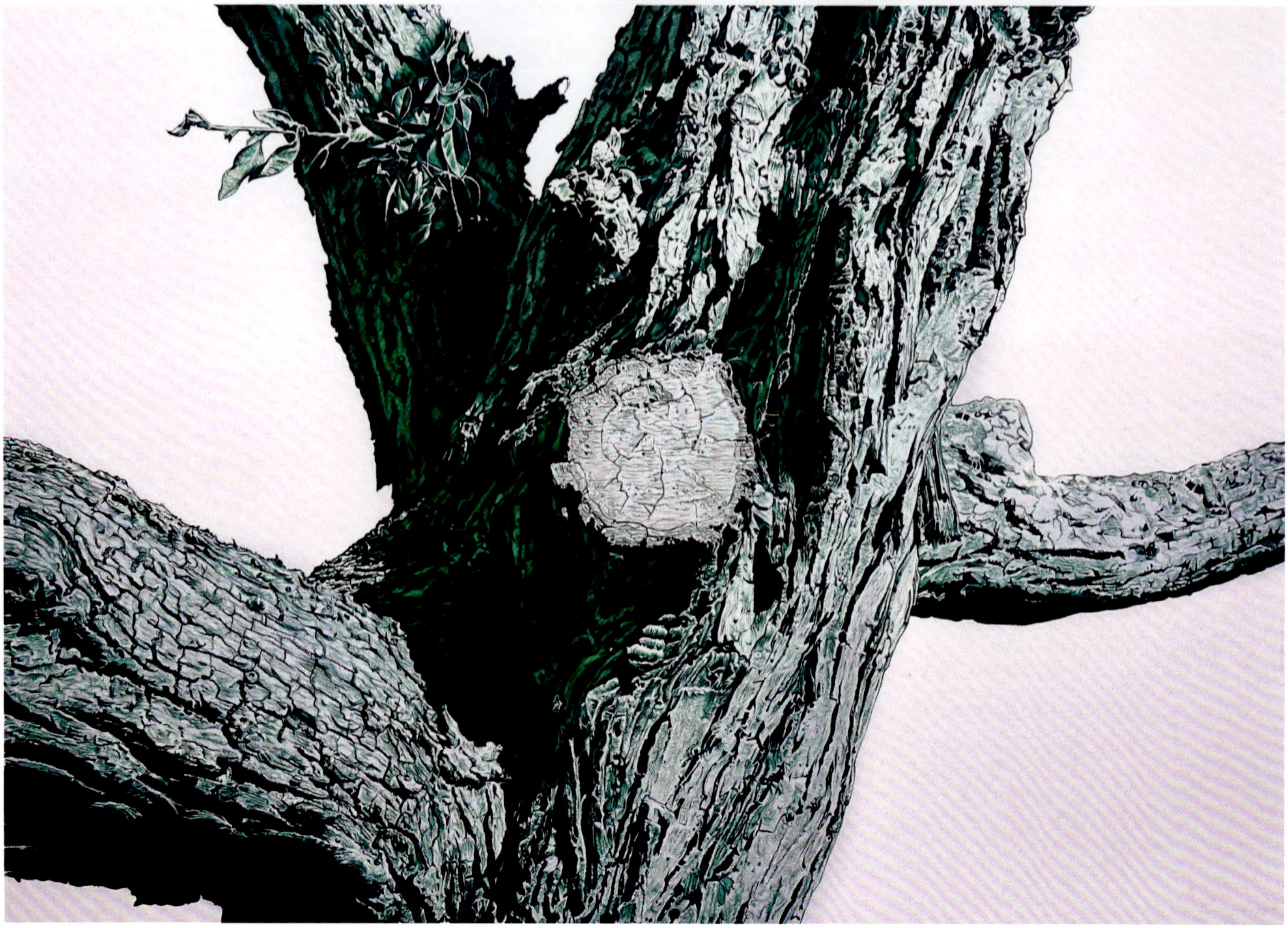

Alex Egan

Why trees?

I look back through sketchbooks and search through scattered memories, and there they are, constantly in my vision, but was I really seeing them? I was using them as still life, part of a landscape or a means to further my practice. A few years ago, this sense of purpose began to embed itself, a longing to spend time portraying these serene life forms. Perhaps the trees have been messaging me, and for years, I was unaware. It has taken me an awakening of sorts to realise and hear them. I am, without shame, a tree hugger; their energy is powerful in their stillness. I seek to discover a way of depicting this through my art.

BELOW *Lady Park Wood sketch*, 2019

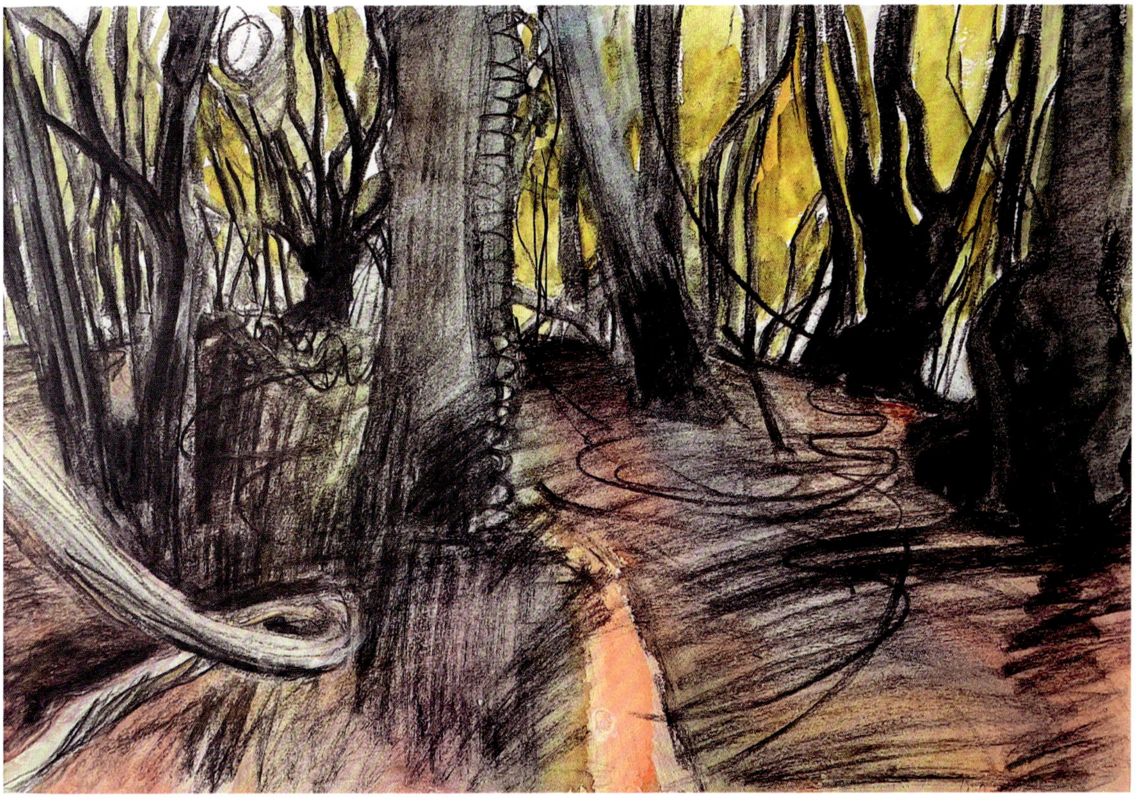

BELOW LEFT *Floating points field, woods, forests, groves*, 2023
BELOW RIGHT *Horner Wood, Exmoor*, 2020

OPPOSITE ABOVE *Tree of Wonder, Beech Grove Marchmont*, 2021
OPPOSITE BELOW *Treelife 2*, 2023/24

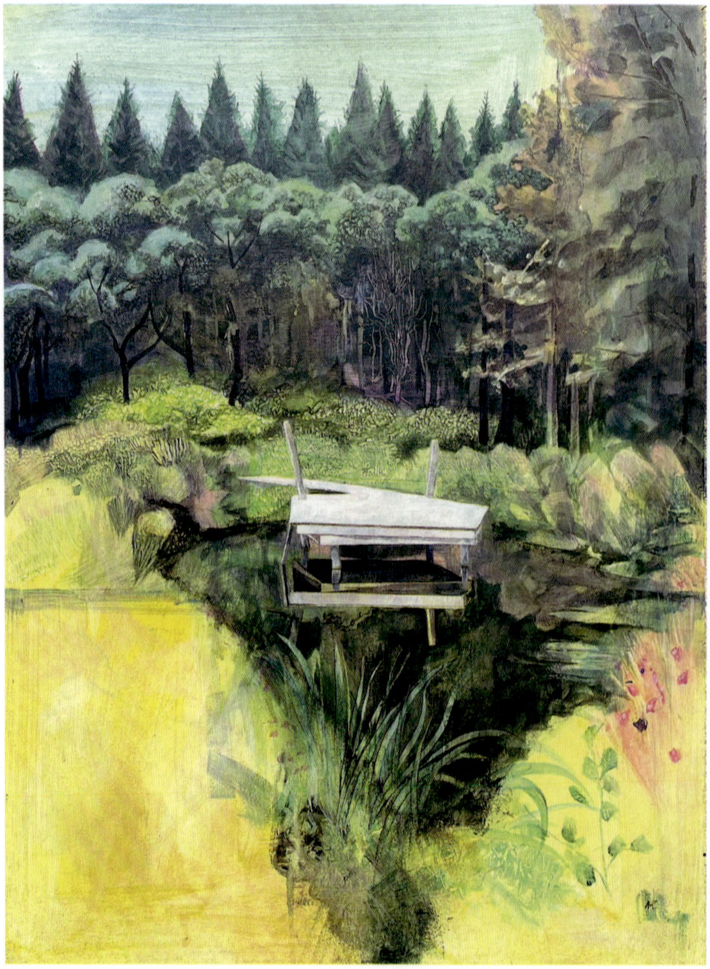

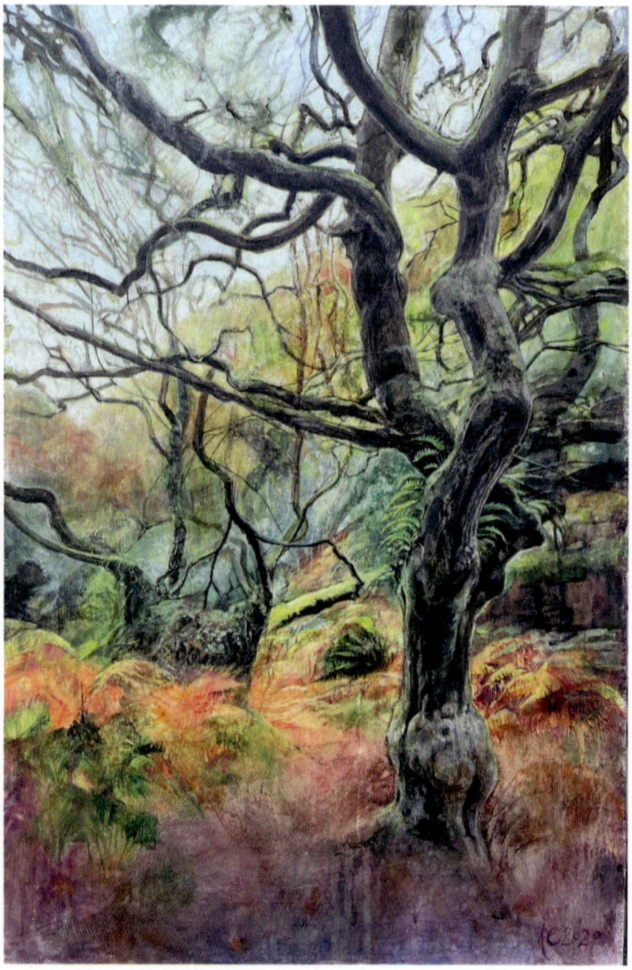

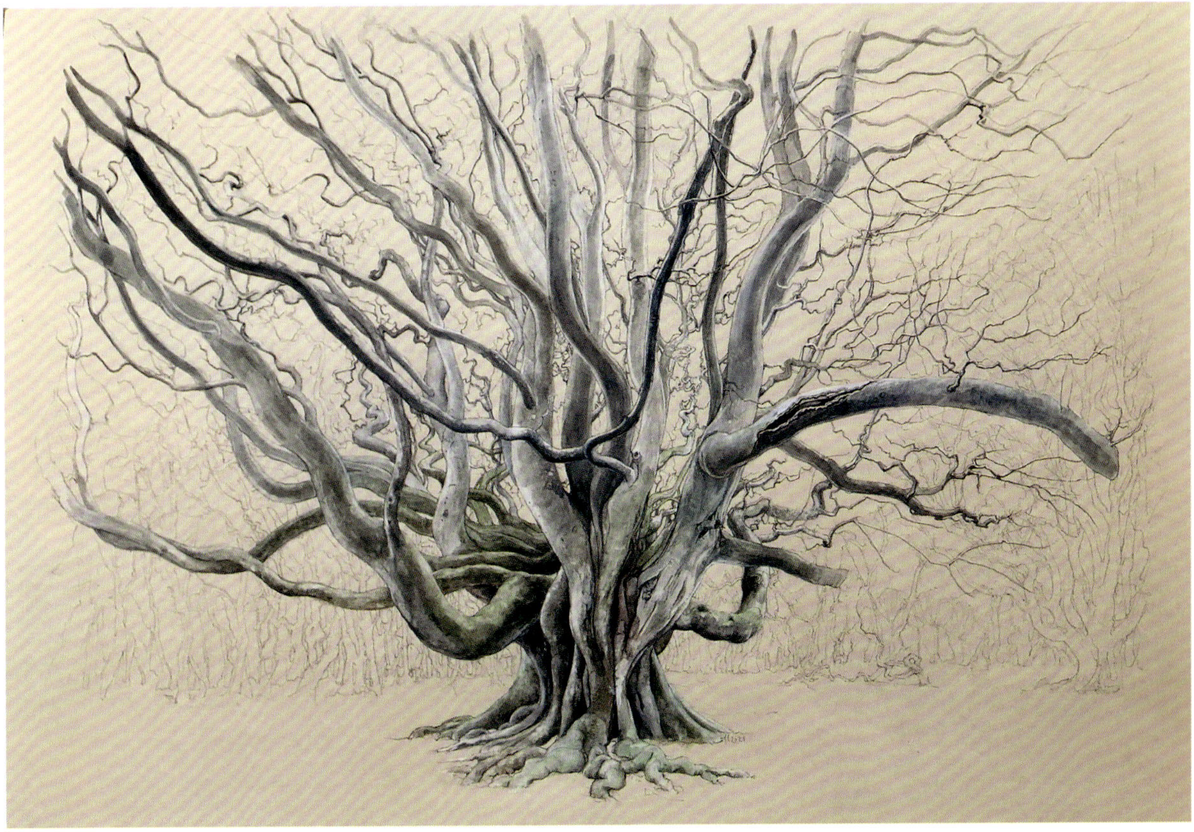

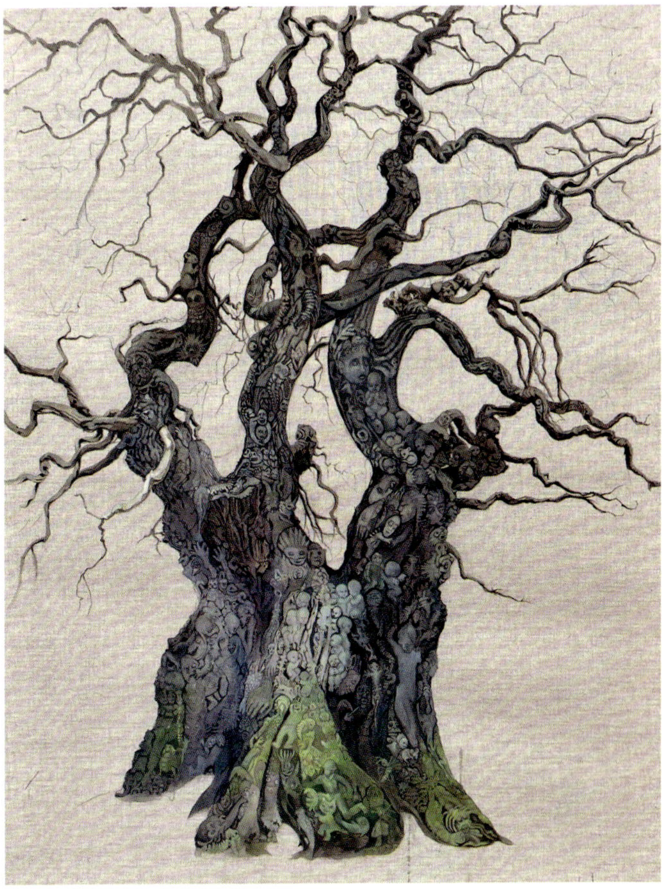

Alex Faulkner

I am drawn to the pastoral, as it is as much an image of loss and longing as an image of paradise. My painted and printed work is about storytelling. In the end, myths are rooted in the groves of the past… the mind finds a home in the garden, woods and valleys. These are the places of paradise lost and the places of paradise now. Trees and woods are the places of memory and of longing. My recent work is in books, written texts and printed images… the two things that inform each other. They are poems of myth and the unseen; most recently in prints made from marble fragments found in the hardcore of the paths through the woods where I live in Somerset. I engraved these found shards with arboreal scenes, and the shapes and dimensions of the fragments reveal a mythical land contained within their own form…

And behind us, a place of fauns,
where once we sprang from trunks of oaks,
lingering beneath the pines,
loafing at dusk on the cold iron of the Wicksteed horses.
(*Like Odysseus* by Alex Faulkner, Ball-Press Editions, 2023)

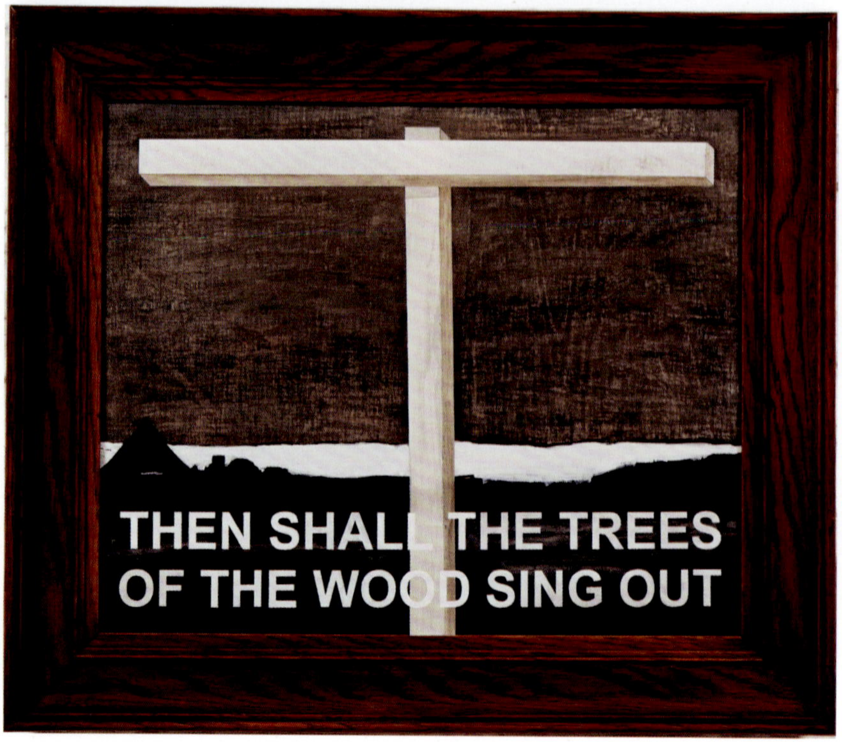

OPPOSITE *Then Shall the Trees*, 2022

BELOW LEFT *A New Kind of Tree*, 2018
BELOW RIGHT *The Fruit from the Wood*, 2021

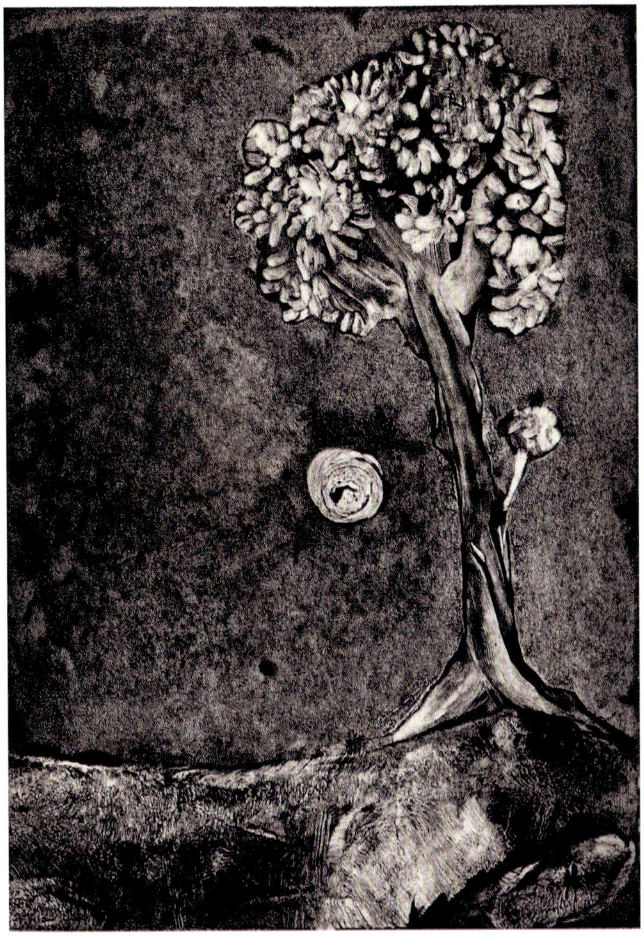

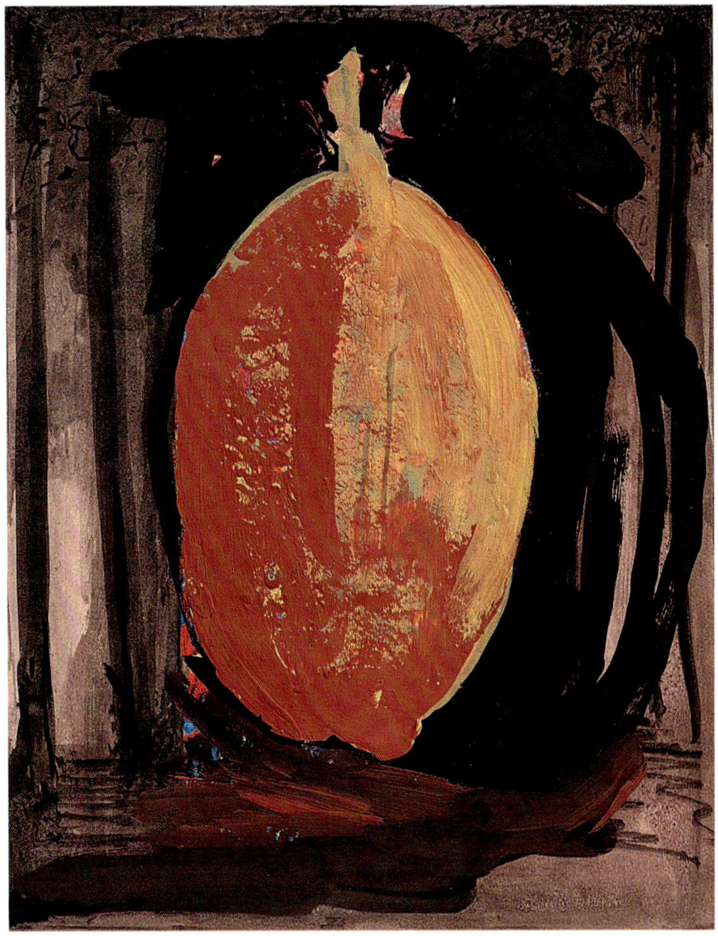

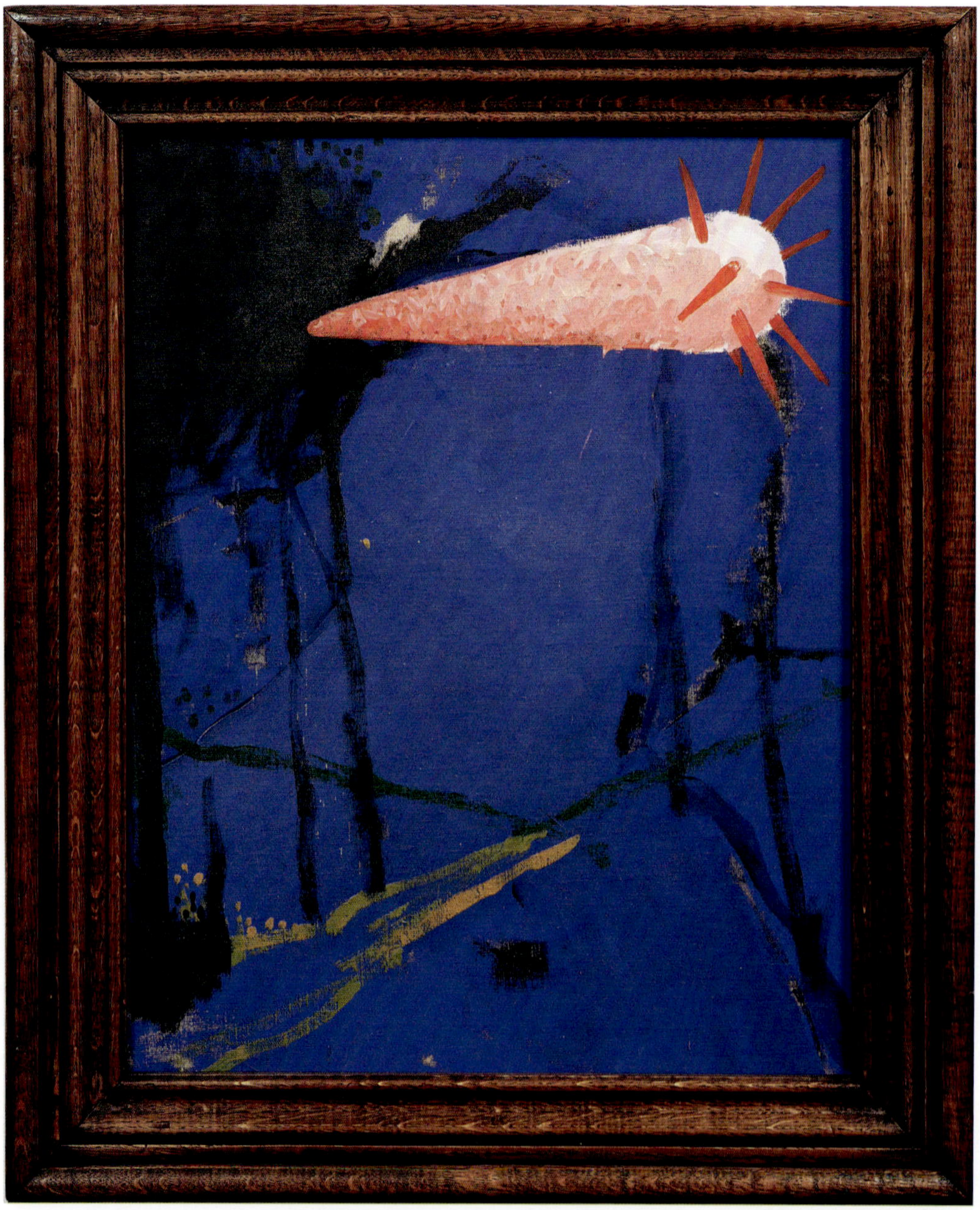

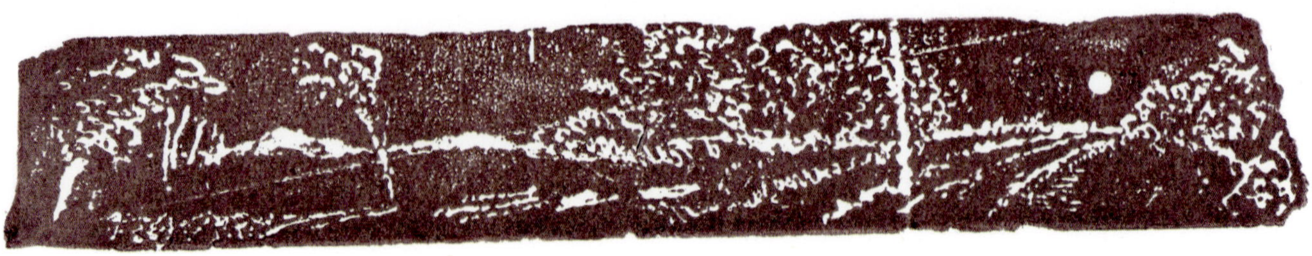

LEFT *The Shining Glory of the Woods*, 2019
BELOW *As I went Out One Morning*, 2024

Stephanie Fawbert

I am a painter, living and working in Hastings, East Sussex. I studied Fine Art at Newcastle and pursued a career in Community Development in Africa and the UK. My paintings deal with our connection to nature, built up in thin layers and washes of translucent, intense colour, making the most everyday landscape become magical and unearthly. I allow the paint to drip and blur to create a sense of light coming through the branches and leaves. There is often water alongside the forest, depicted with thin washes of oil and glazes to evoke places of stillness and calm. Figures are included, to give a sense of scale and our experience of being within them. The figures are often small, enfolded by forests, dwarfed by landscape and immersed in the world around them. There is a strong sense of both their vulnerability and tenacity. The places I depict are anonymous and familiar, taking the viewer to a place of collective memory. I want the viewer to remember the forest glades they have been in, the paths walked, and their feelings. In this sense, I am looking at how our interior world is shaped and takes its cues from the exterior around us. The paintings are about the interaction between the two and a longing to connect. In this way, they act as psychological spaces where different narratives can be unearthed.

BELOW *Walk in the Woods*

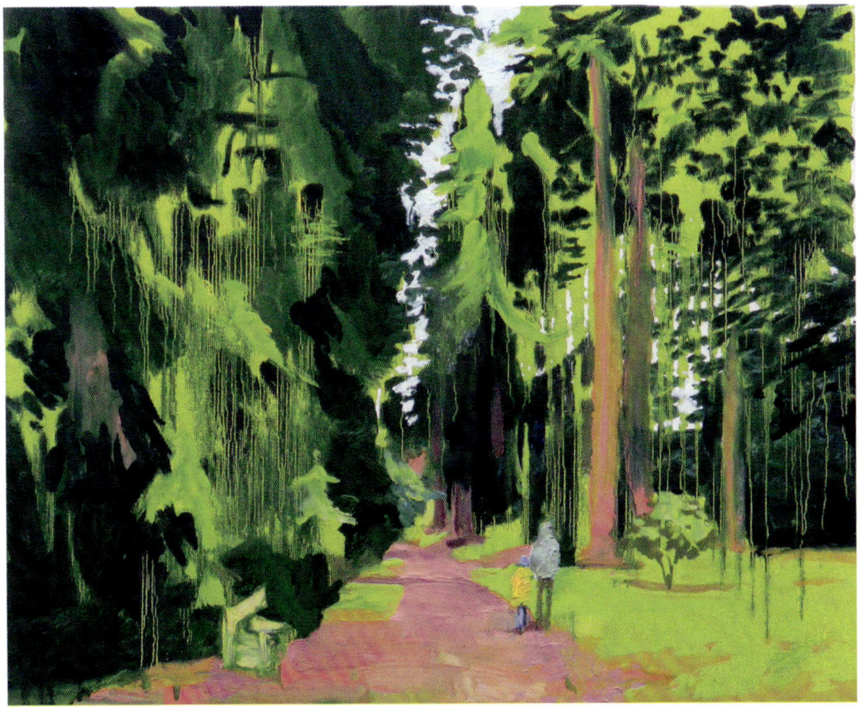

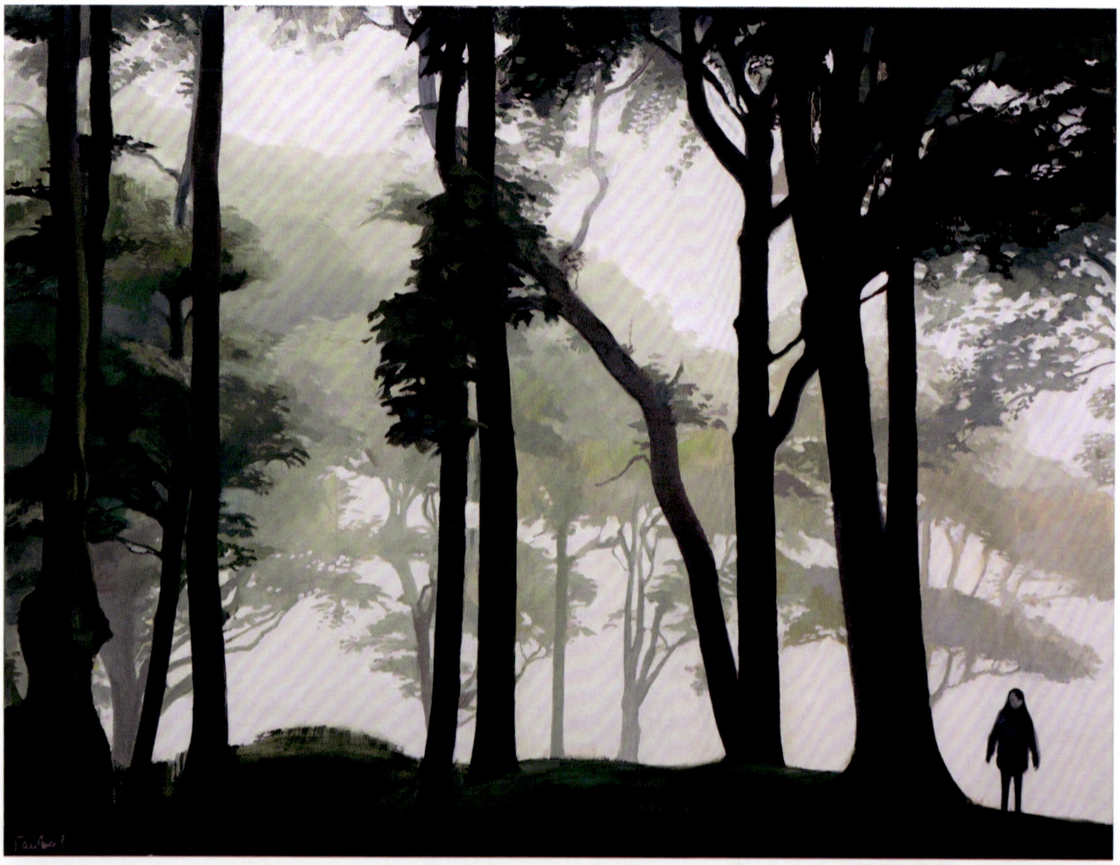

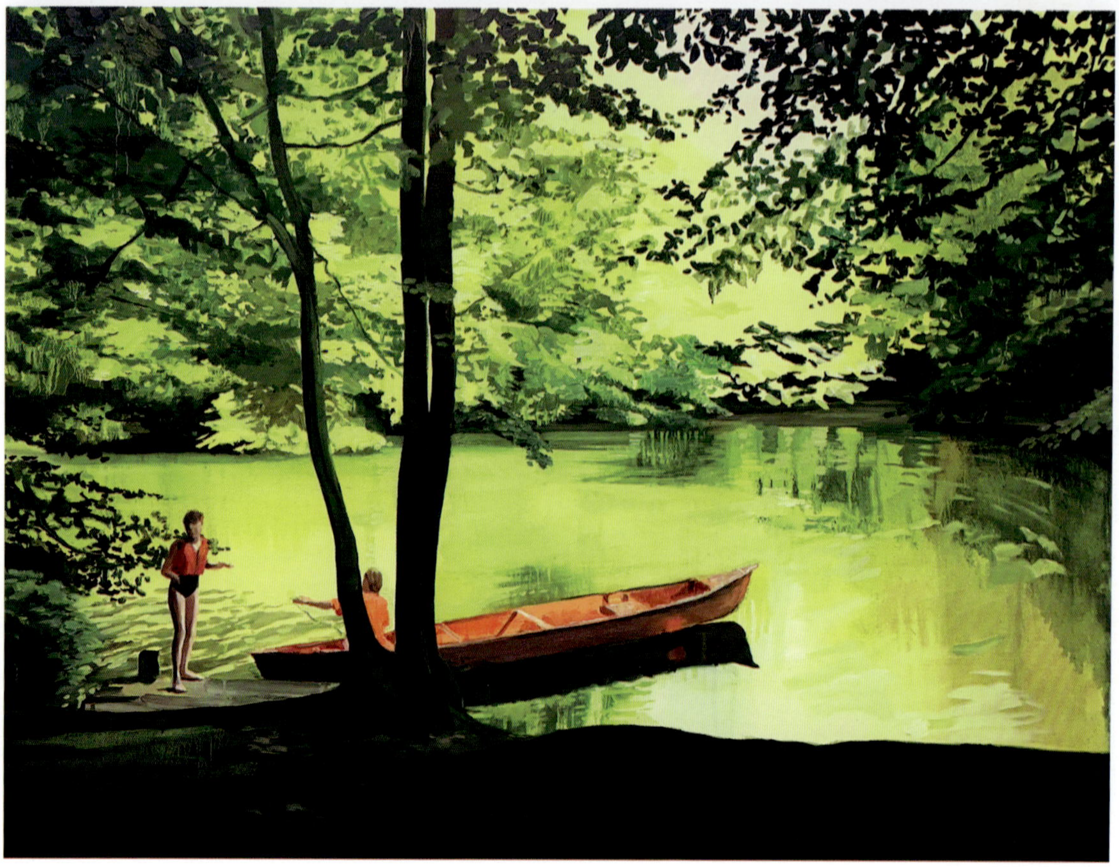

OPPOSITE ABOVE *Chanctonbury Ring*
OPPOSITE BELOW *Green Lake*

BELOW *Tree Climbing*

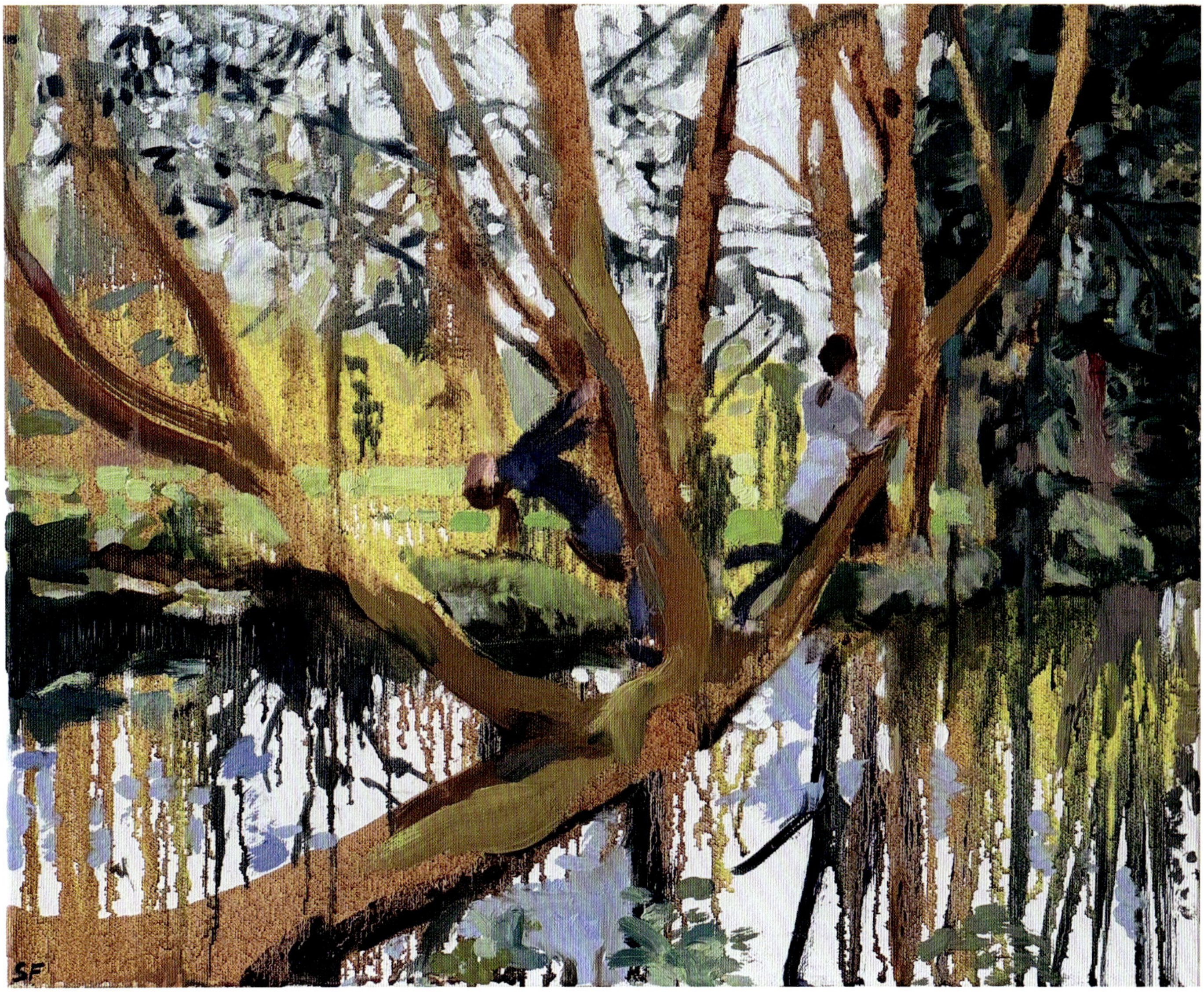

Paul Finn

I am primarily a landscape painter. Of course, trees are an important element in the places where I work, and depending on this, they can take on a range of meanings. I like to work in edgelands (secret places) where nature has taken over former industrial or military sites. Recently, I've been inspired to paint in new places: in the Blackdown Hills in Devon, I saw groups of trees acting as a barrier before a beautiful landscape, obscuring it and acting as strong vertical elements in a composition. Ancient woodlands, such as Staverton Thicks, offer complex interwoven branches of oak and holly, which somehow develop into abstract paintings. Working recently on the South Downs, I loved painting trees that are growing horizontally due to being buffeted by high winds, and closer to home in London, an ancient oak tree sits among suburban houses, a 350-year-old tree in complete contrast to 1930s architectural forms. I love the variety of trees, how they differ in different settings, how their forms and textures differ and, of course, how they change throughout the year. Having said this, the spaces around, in between and through trees are as important to me as the trees themselves.

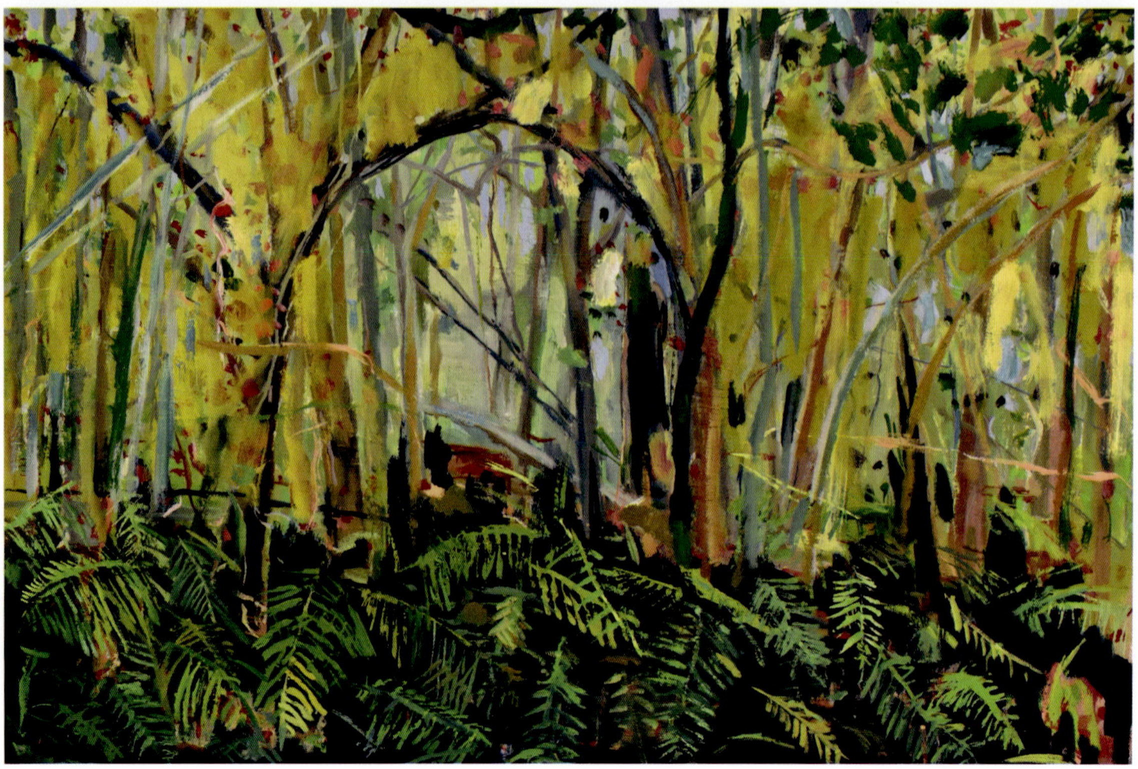

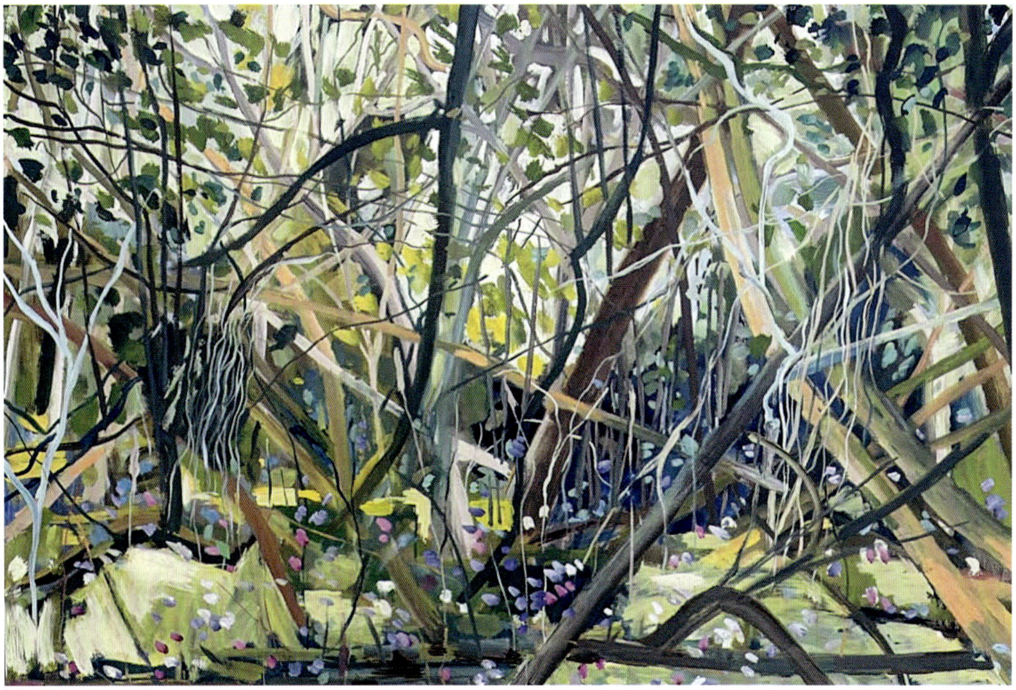

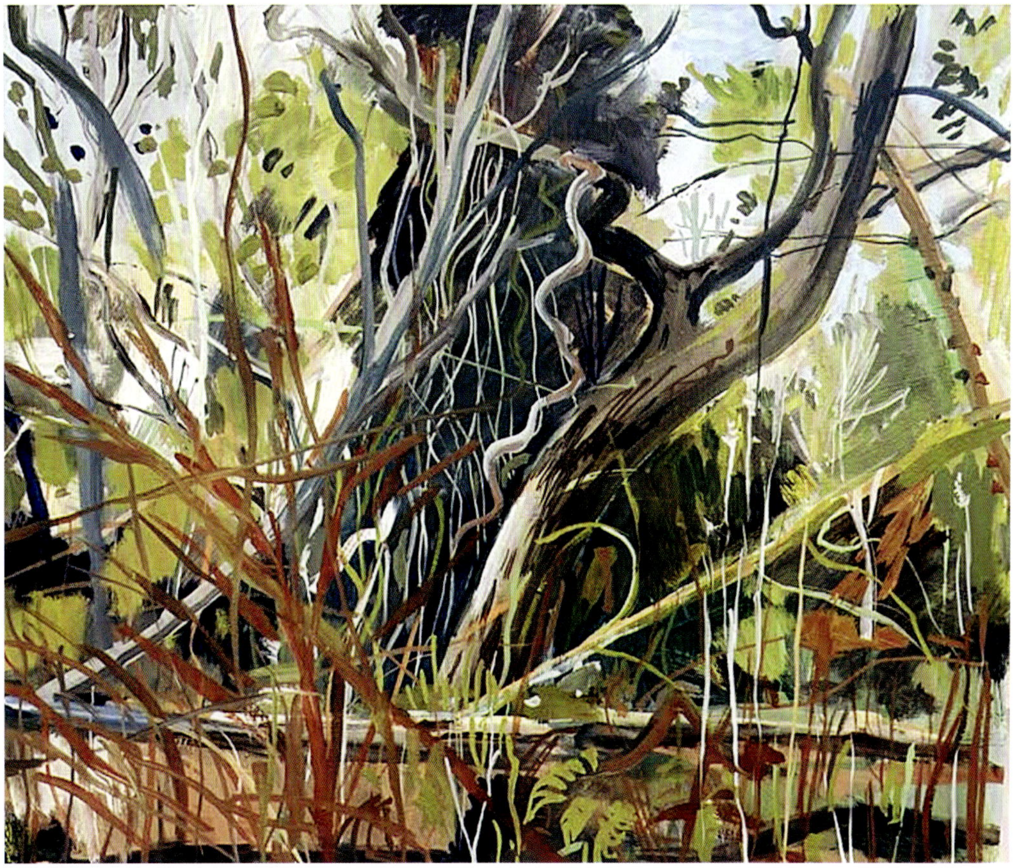

OPPOSITE *Arch*

TOP *Interwoven*
ABOVE *End of Winter*

RIGHT *Almost Lost*
BELOW *Out of Winter*

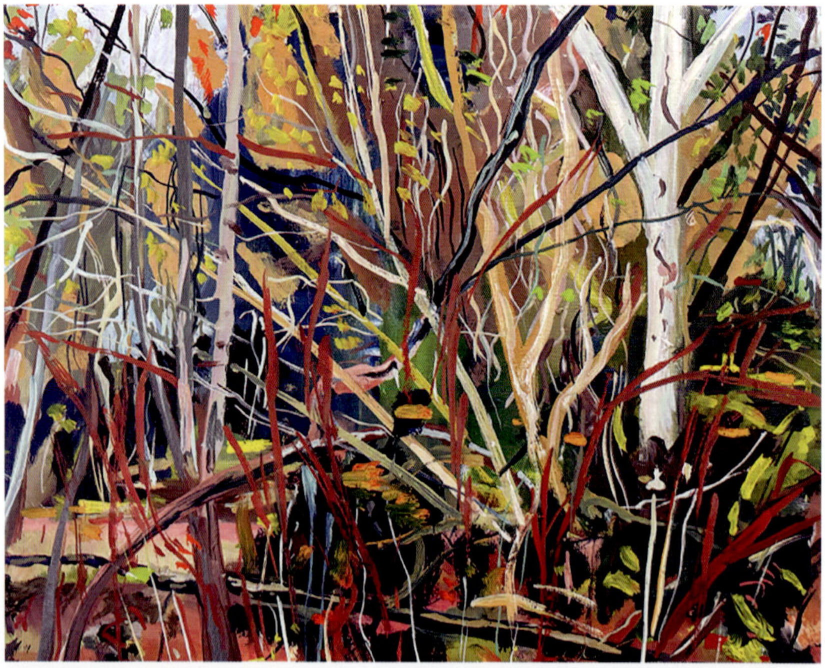

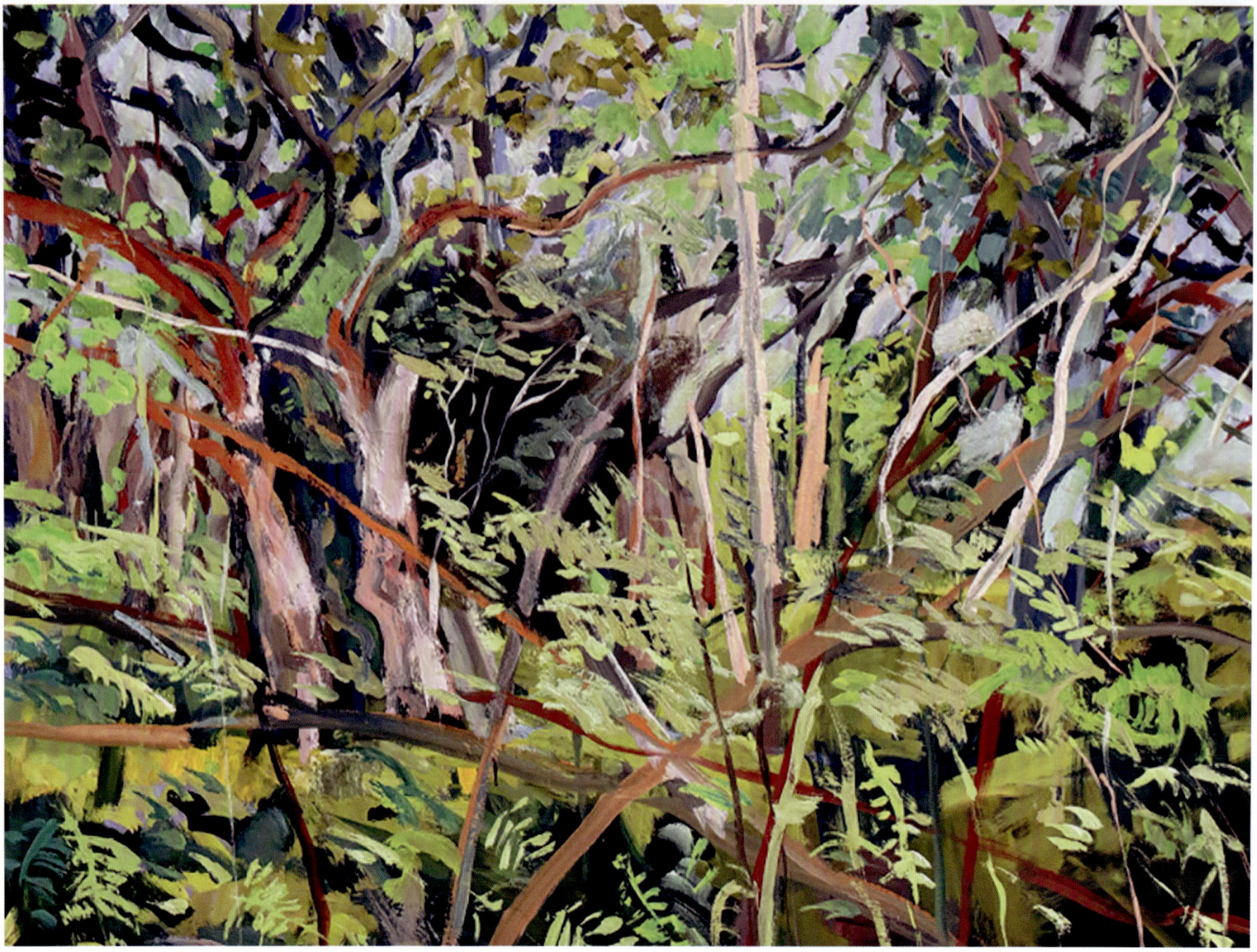

Tom Genders

I paint trees because they are important. I paint them because I feel inclined to, but it feels more of a necessity when it is happening.

I paint in oil and produce on-location sketches to inform my studio pieces. I stretch and prime the canvas by hand, always being fiercely independent. The trees that particularly draw me in are our beautiful natives: hazel, hornbeam, oak and hawthorn. These are magnificent beasts and particular favourites. Still, I love them all, for their individuality of form and varied historical relationships with humankind. They are the backbone of the history of this island, interwoven with everything humans have done since the last ice age. A childhood spent looking closely at birds has given me an eye for detail and identification, and this comes across in the artwork. I enjoy it when the character of a tree is discernible and nameable in the work, even if that piece is quite abstract or subtle. I am currently interested in the transitions through managed landscapes, from wildwood to coppice, orchard, meadow and finally garden. Essentially, I am trying to capture impressions of well-managed natural and semi-natural spaces with a tangled aesthetic.

BELOW *Blackthorn, Hazel, Ash and Oak*, 2021

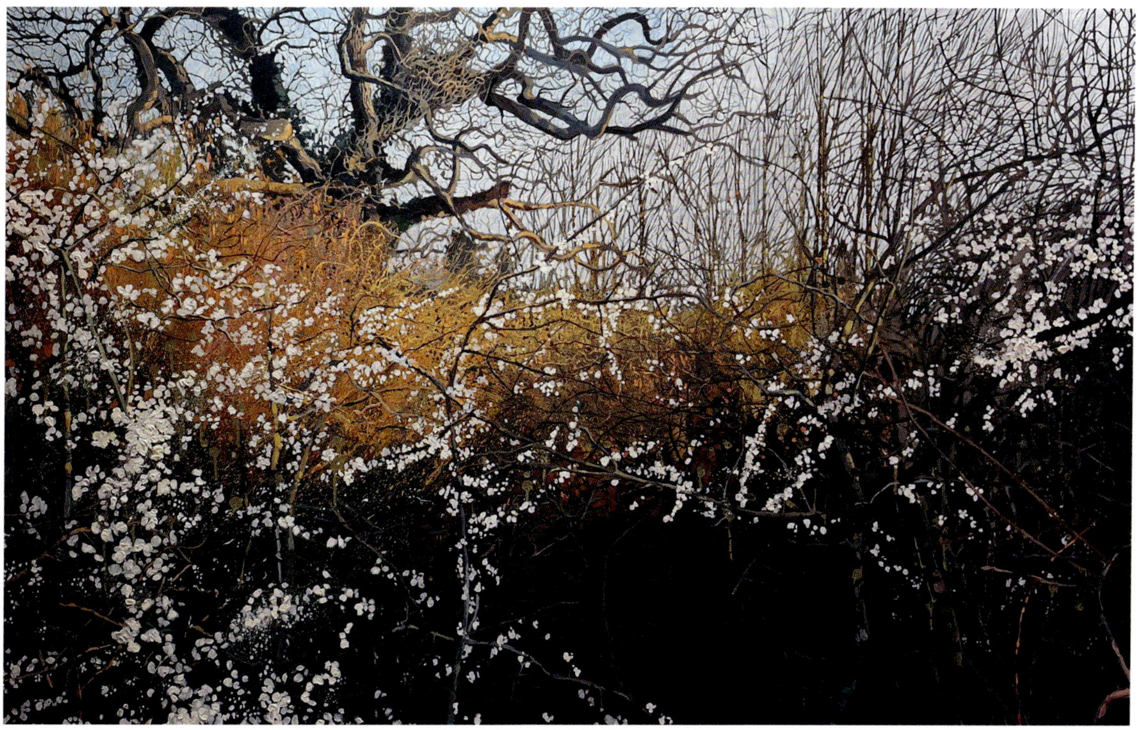

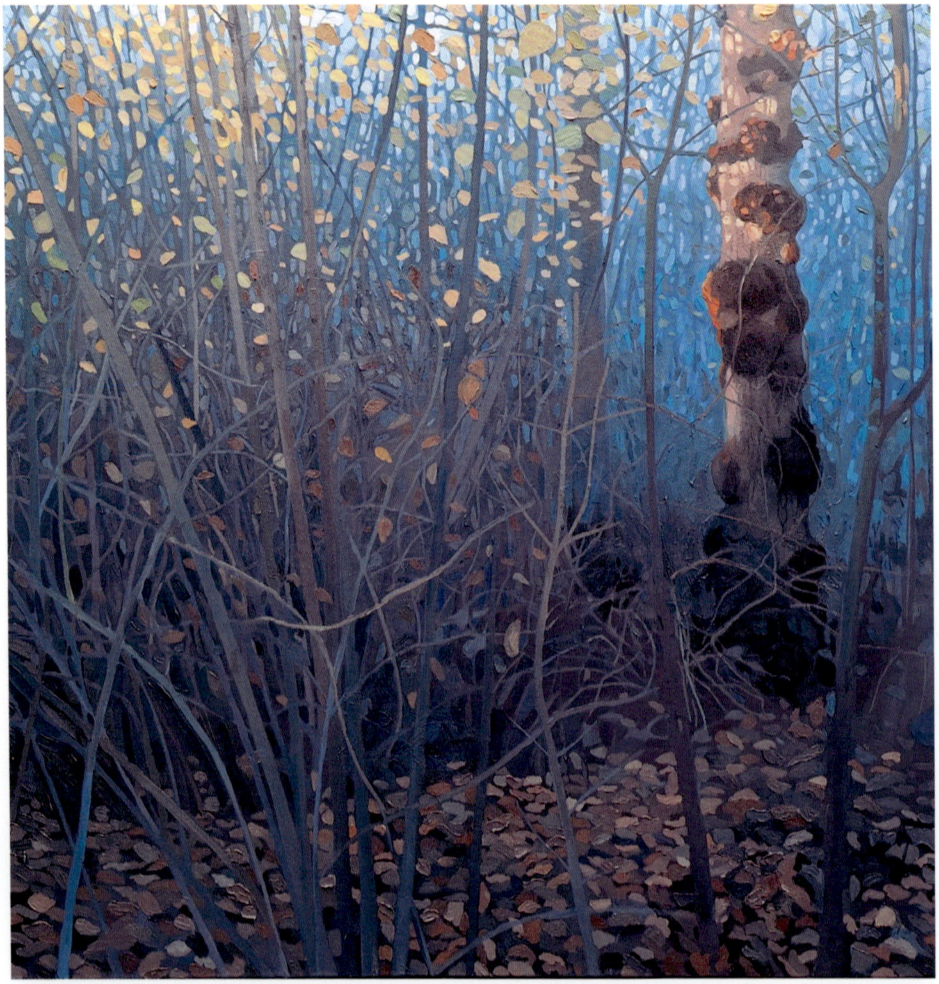

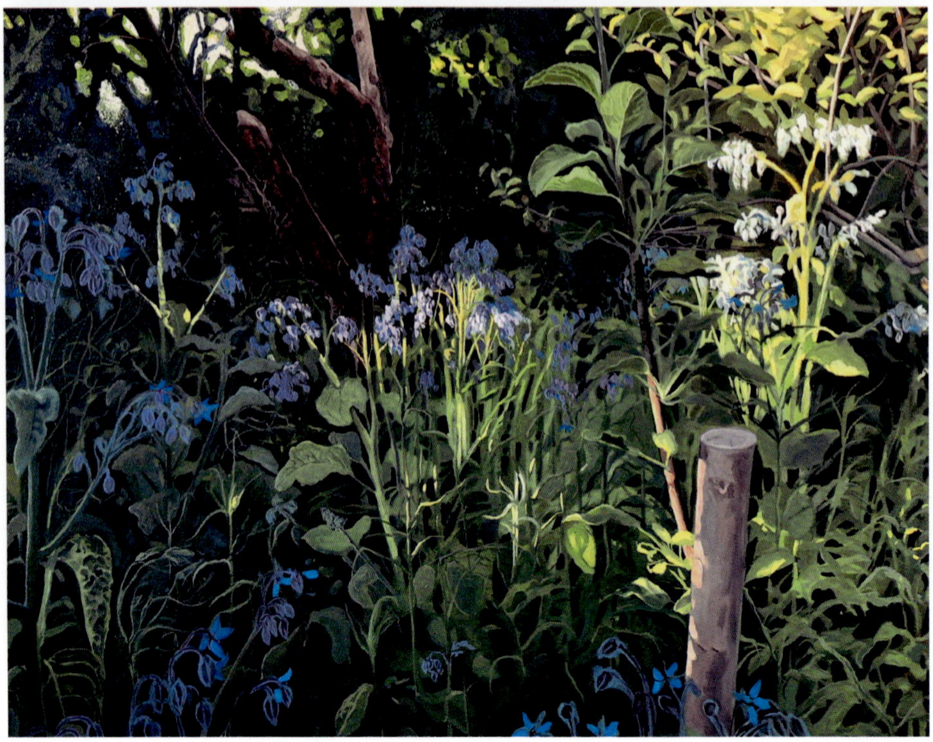

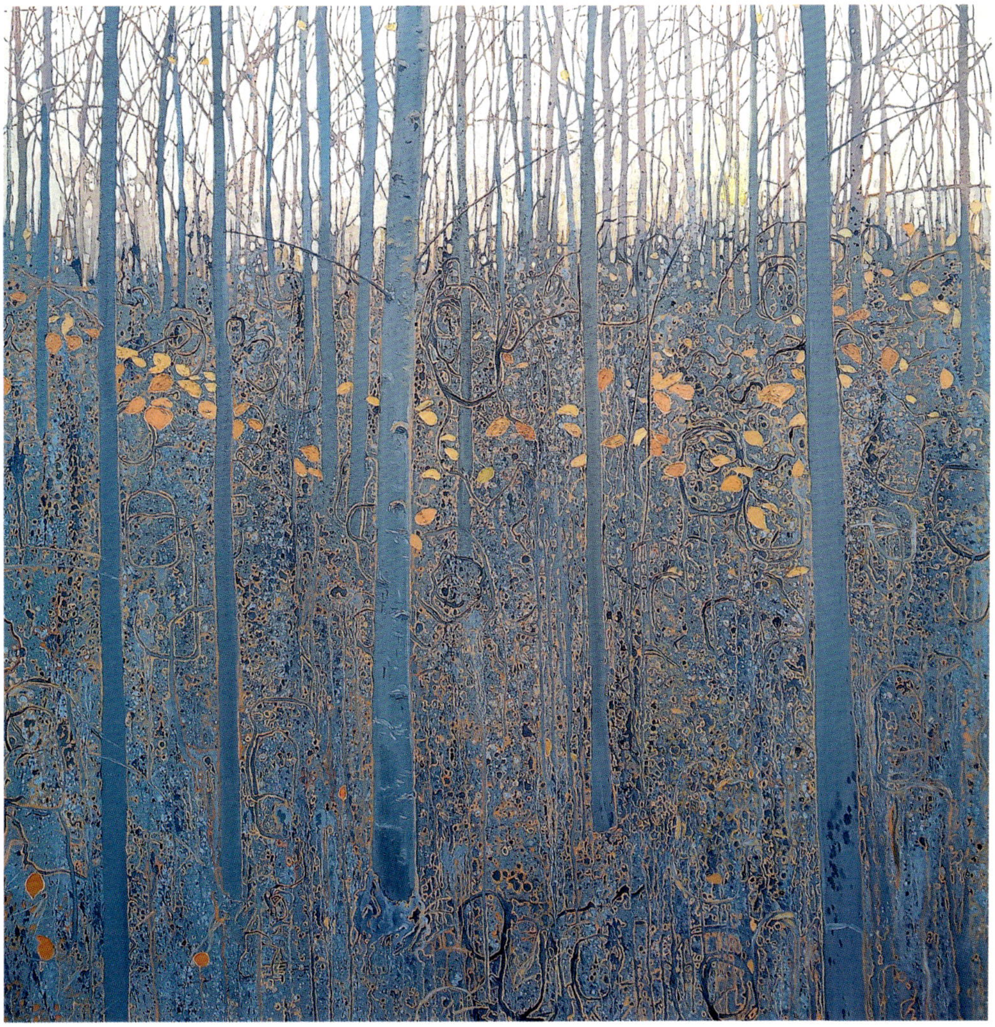

OPPOSITE ABOVE *Grafton Oak*, 2024
OPPOSITE BELOW *Borage, Apple and Plum*, 2021

ABOVE *Aspen and Hazel*, 2022
RIGHT *Hazel in Winter Light*, 2022

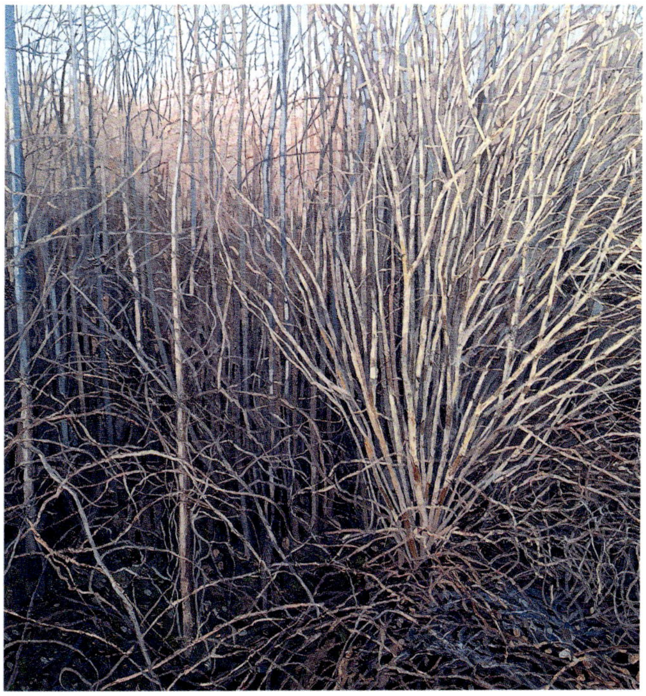

Crispin Heesom

Trees have always been very important to me. As a child, I remember climbing a cedar tree. Getting close to the top, I was staggered when I looked down at the whole panoply. At the time, I had no desire to paint it, but I am sure that impression may well surface!

A few years ago, I moved to a small rural village where I am now living. I was attracted by the remnants of an eighteenth-century quarry, locally known as the 'Hills & Holes': roots burrowing into a knotted surface, tissue-woven branches, and the rotted, discarded wood have all become participants in the creation of a very different landscape. My drawings *From a Diary* show how the place has changed over the years. Due to time and wear, the Bowthorpe Oak is a fascinating tree. It initially gives the impression of four trees rather than just one, looking like an array of dark towers. It cannot be seen from a singular point as it is veiled by broken branches, and conveying its immensity and complexity is a challenge. The image needs to flow to capture the tempo and changing seasons. One needs to get a sense of things falling into place – seeing, absorbing and feeling the place.

BELOW *Bowthorpe Oak*, 2024

OPPOSITE ABOVE *Bowthorpe drawing*, 2024
OPPOSITE BELOW *Fineshade Ash*, 2023

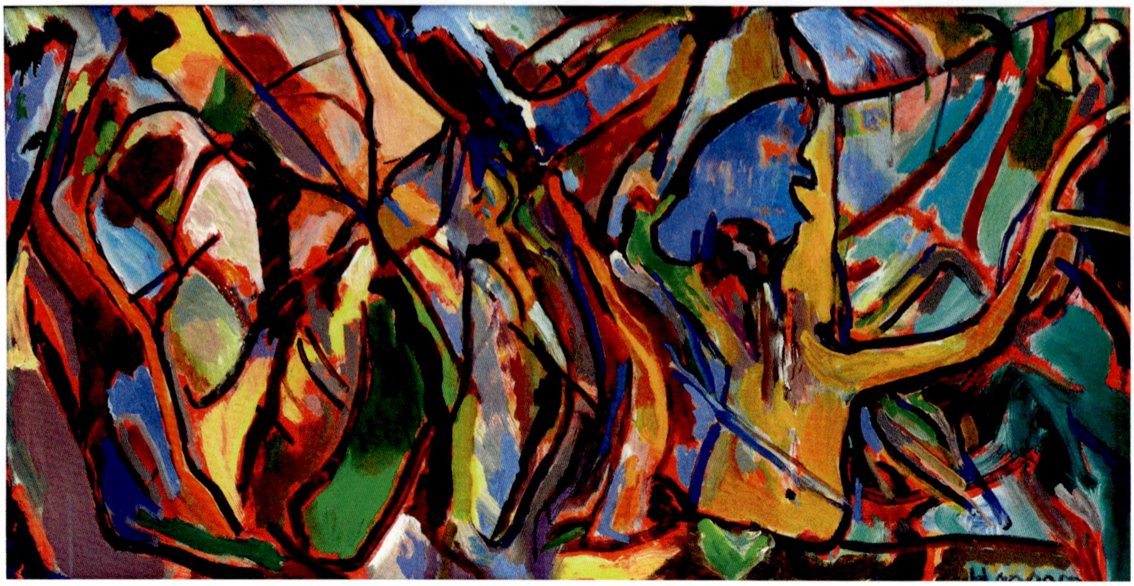

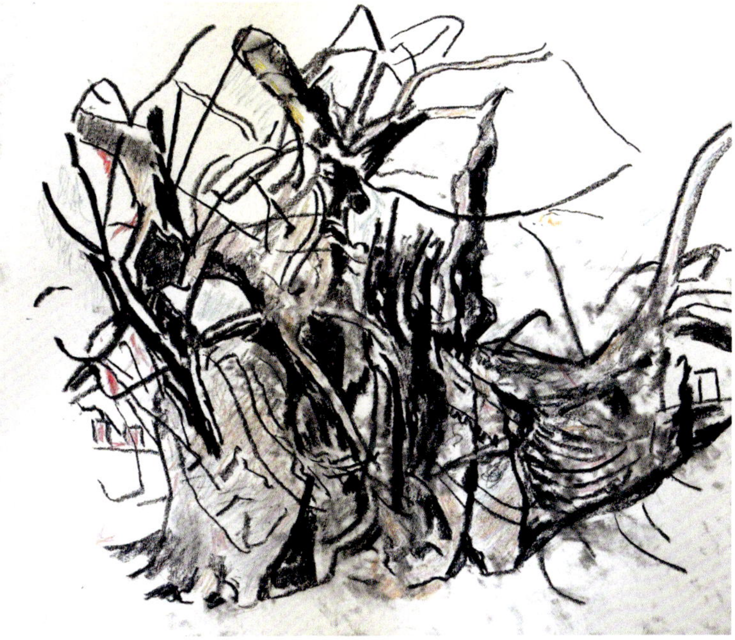

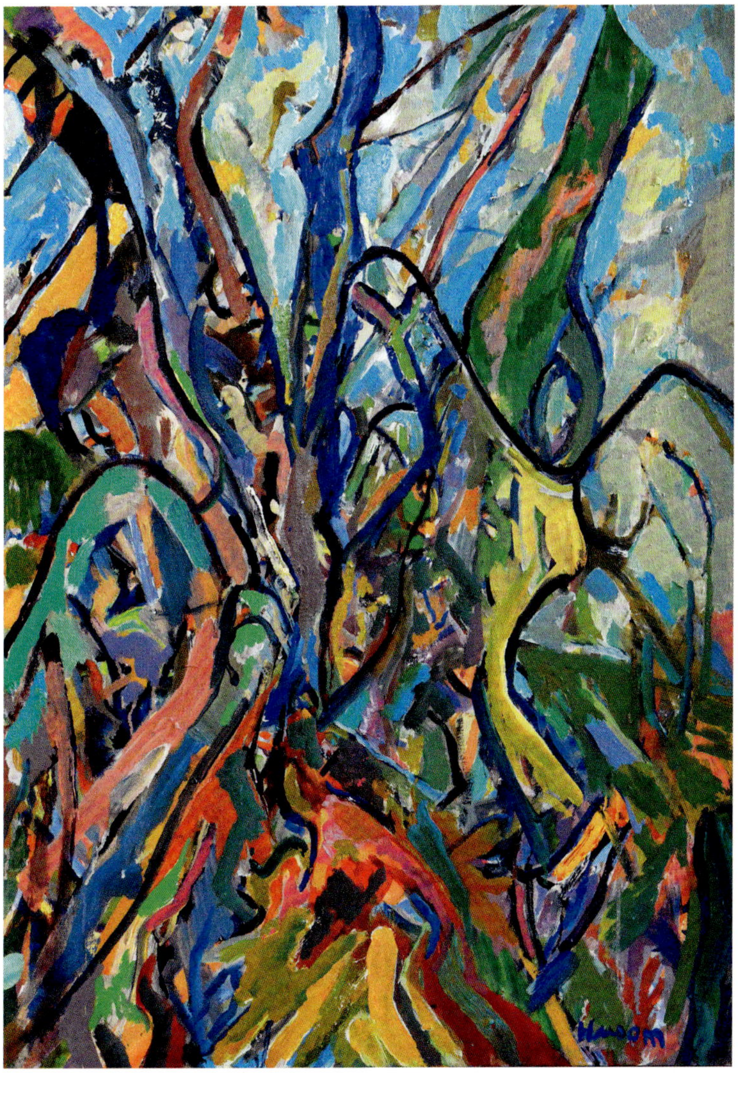

Julie Held LG, NEAC

I look out at my garden daily in awe and delight at the changes I observe, sometimes within an hour. Beauty. But each tree contains history within its trunk. Understanding their complex underground network of roots is also vital. Trees contain not only traces of the past, but are vital in tackling climate catastrophes. I love the thin light of early morning, and the crepuscular light of early evening. These lights remove detail and present a more pictorial landscape. This is what my painting is about. We must understand not only their beauty but also their importance. Maybe, then, we can realise that they are part of livelihoods, ecosystems and much, much more, helping to ameliorate our climate catastrophe.

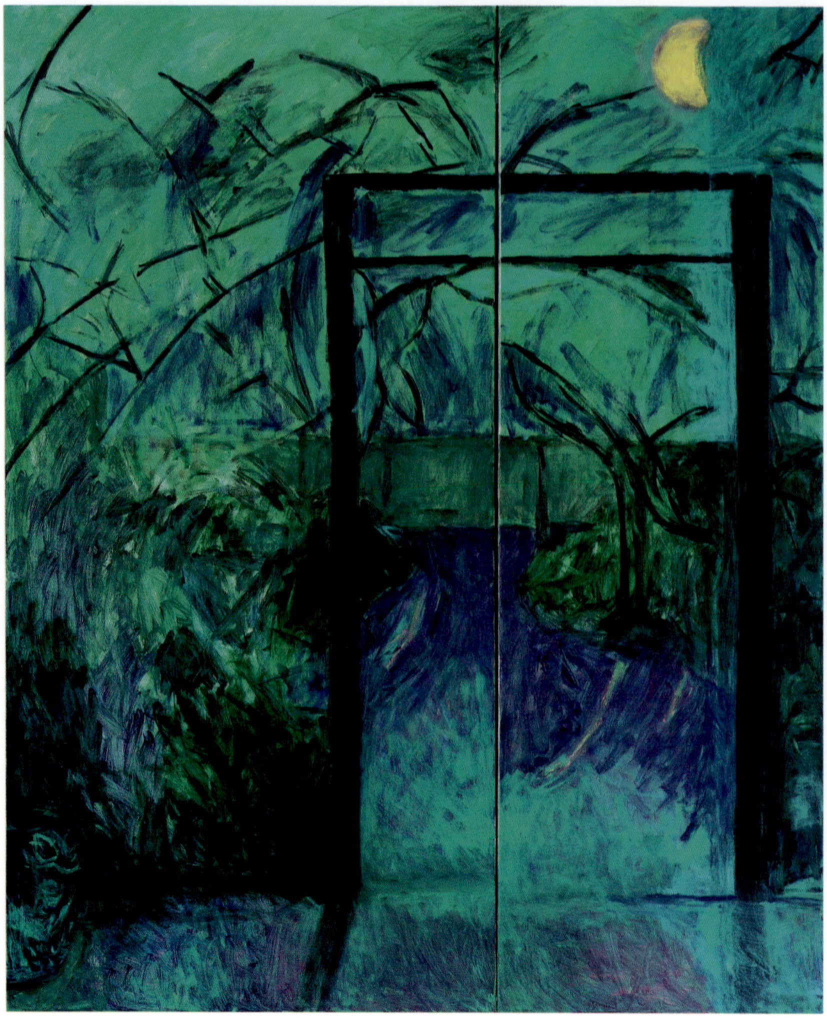

OPPOSITE *Late Summer Night*, 2022

BELOW LEFT *Heat*, 2020–22
BELOW RIGHT *The Garden Autumn Bright*, 2022

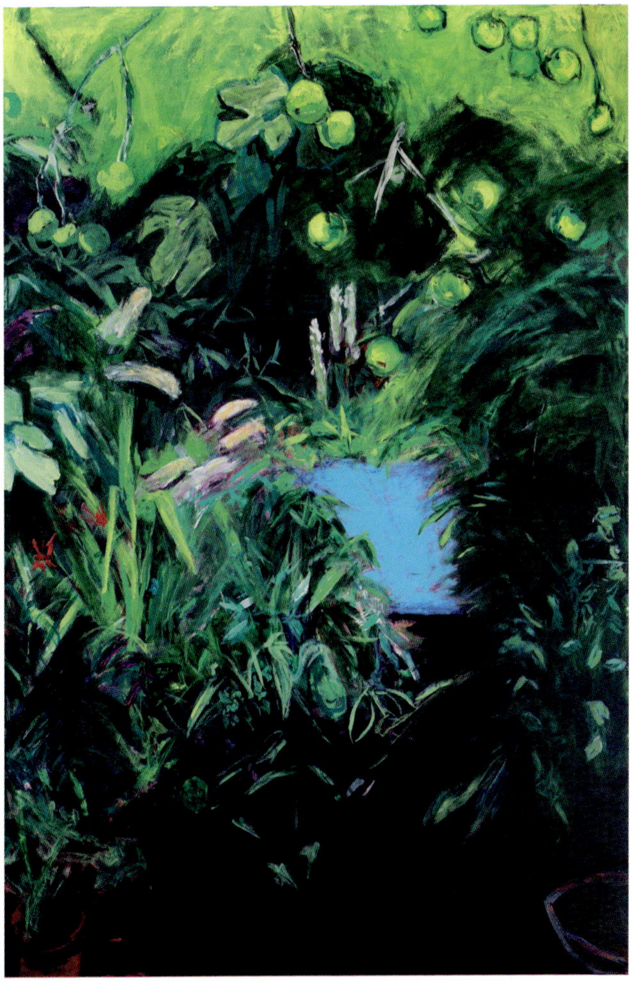

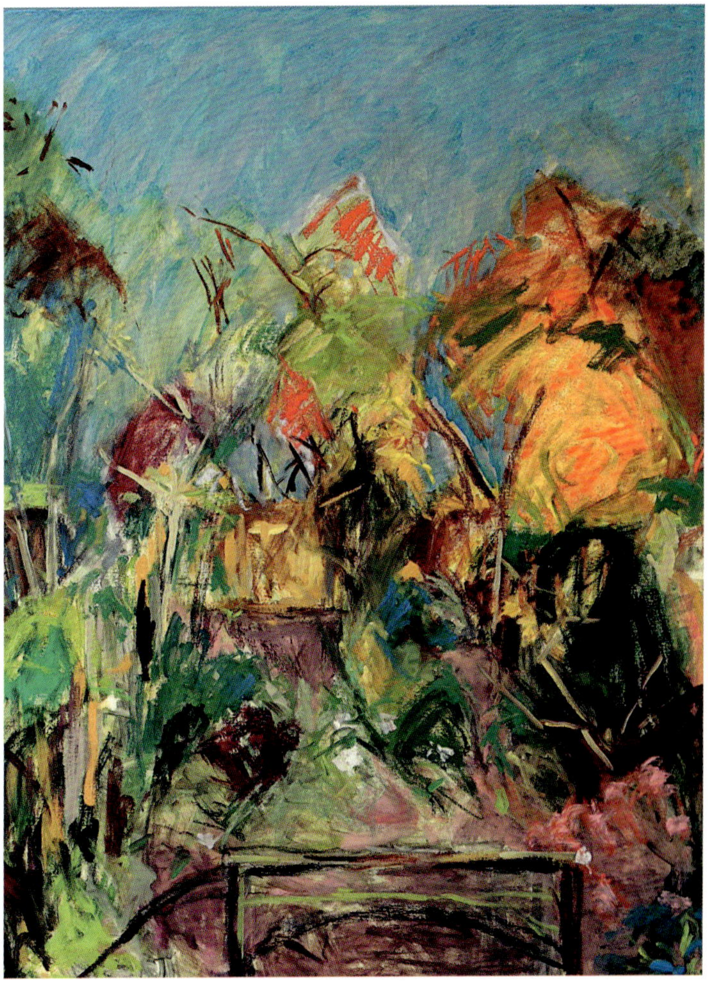

BELOW LEFT *Stormy Weather*, 2024
BELOW RIGHT *Autumn Bright*, 2022

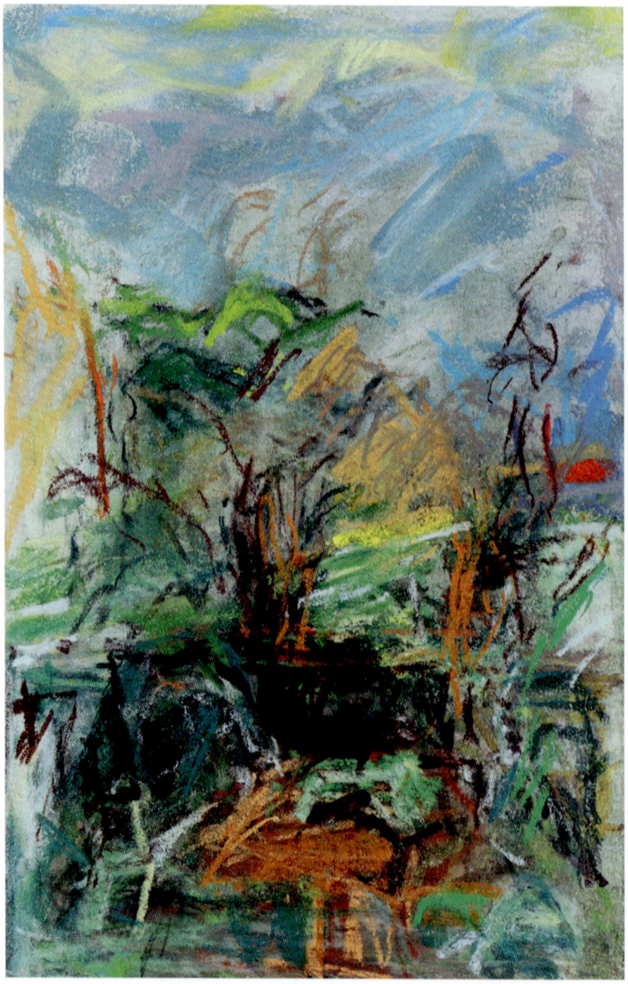

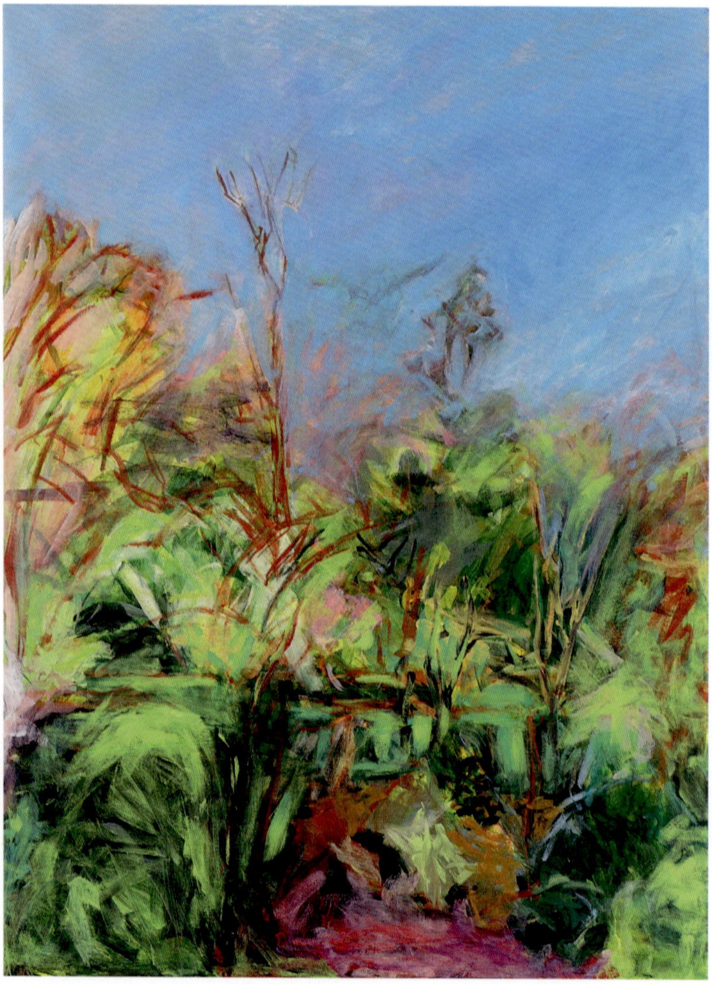

Tilia Holmes

I was named Tilia after the lime tree. My parents have planted some fifteen hundred trees and built their livelihoods on promoting the importance of trees and working in woods, inspiring me to do the same. After drawing all my life, I have spent the last seven years developing my artistic style and building a portfolio, focusing on trees and nature. To me, trees signify life, our ability to breathe and the environment's preservation. I aim to enhance the natural beauty of the material, by using the ancient art form 'pyrography' to burn marks and textures into sustainably sourced wood. Working with the grain to let each design emerge through pyrography, burning and scorching, I then bring the artwork to life using oil paints and gold and copper metal leaf.

BELOW *Pine Tapestry*, 2024

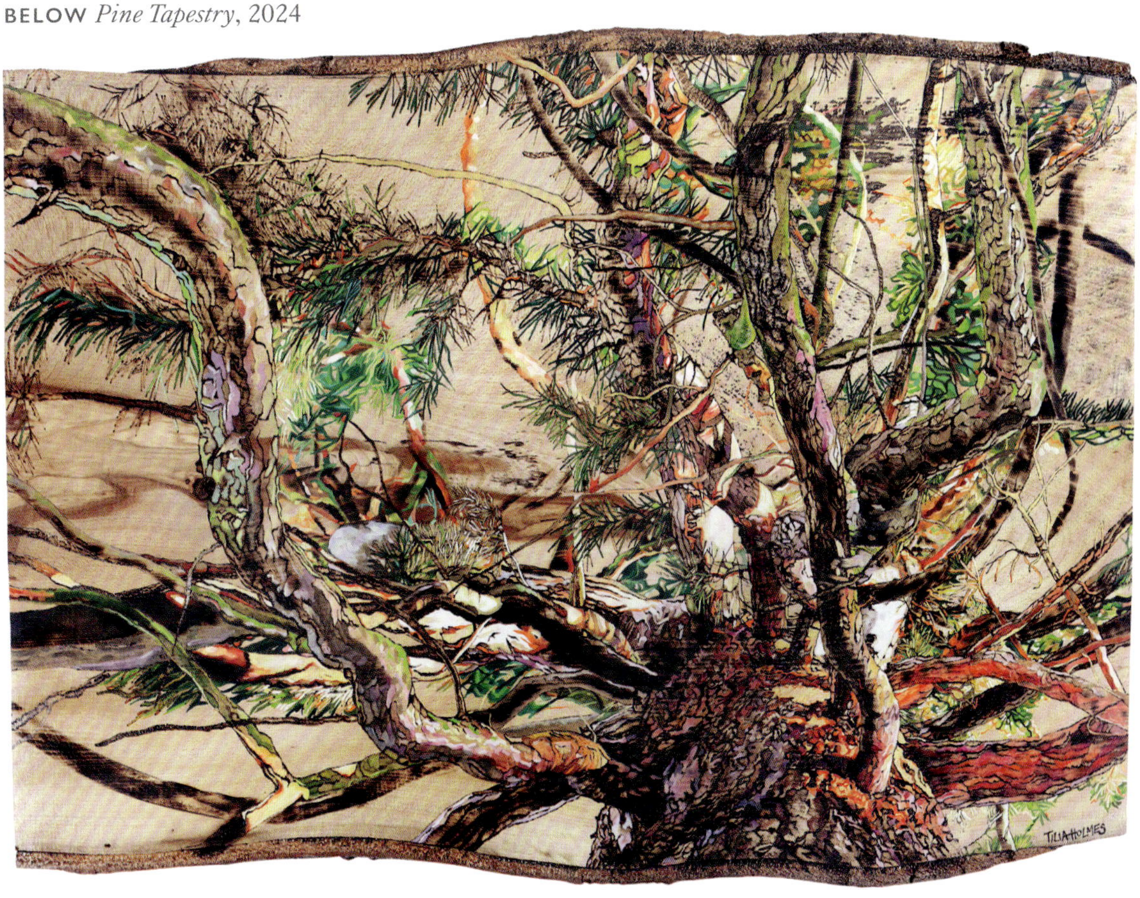

BELOW *Pine Canopy*
BOTTOM *Golden Hour*, 2023

OPPOSITE ABOVE *Entwined*, 2020
OPPOSITE BELOW *Red Emperor Maple*, 2024

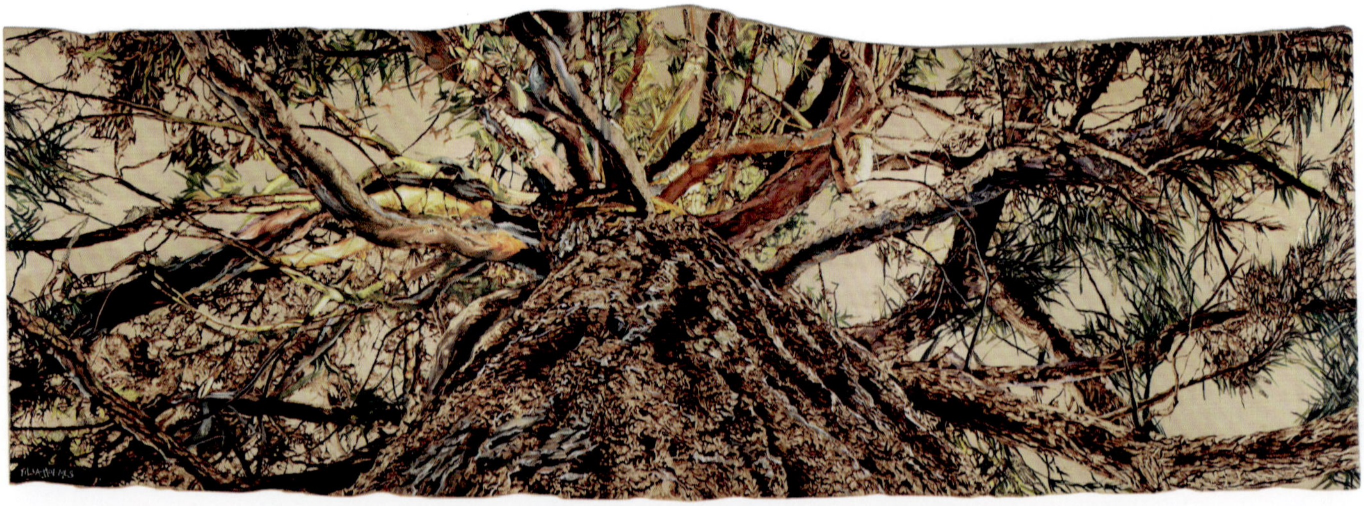

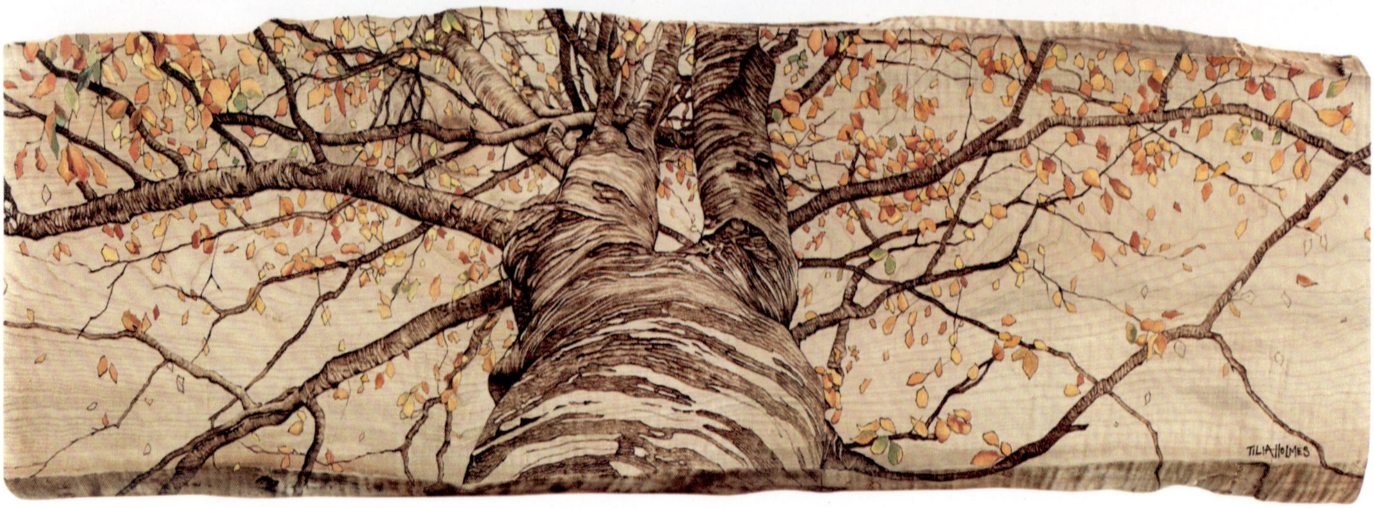

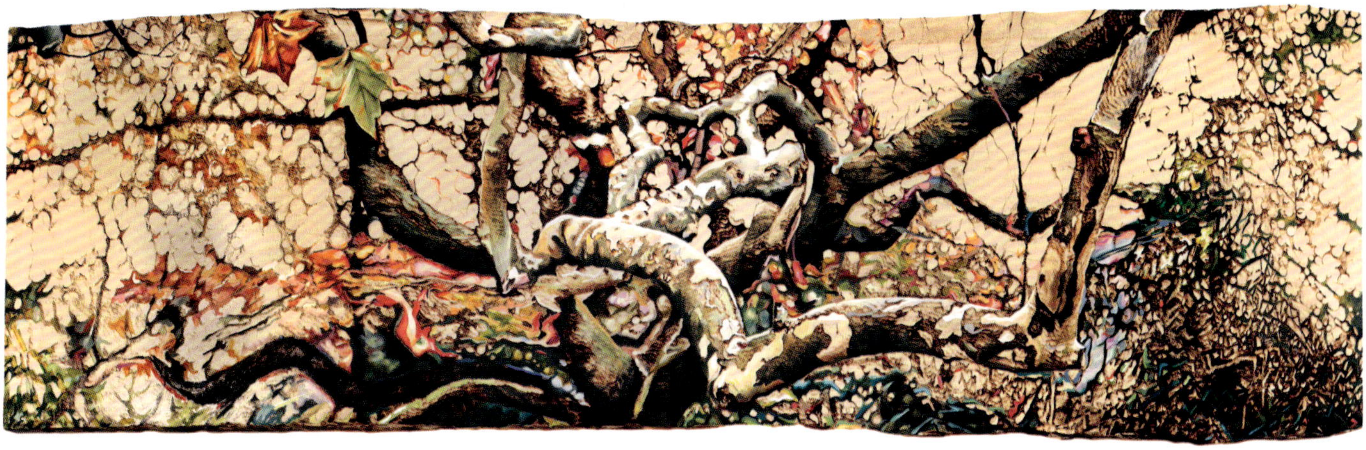

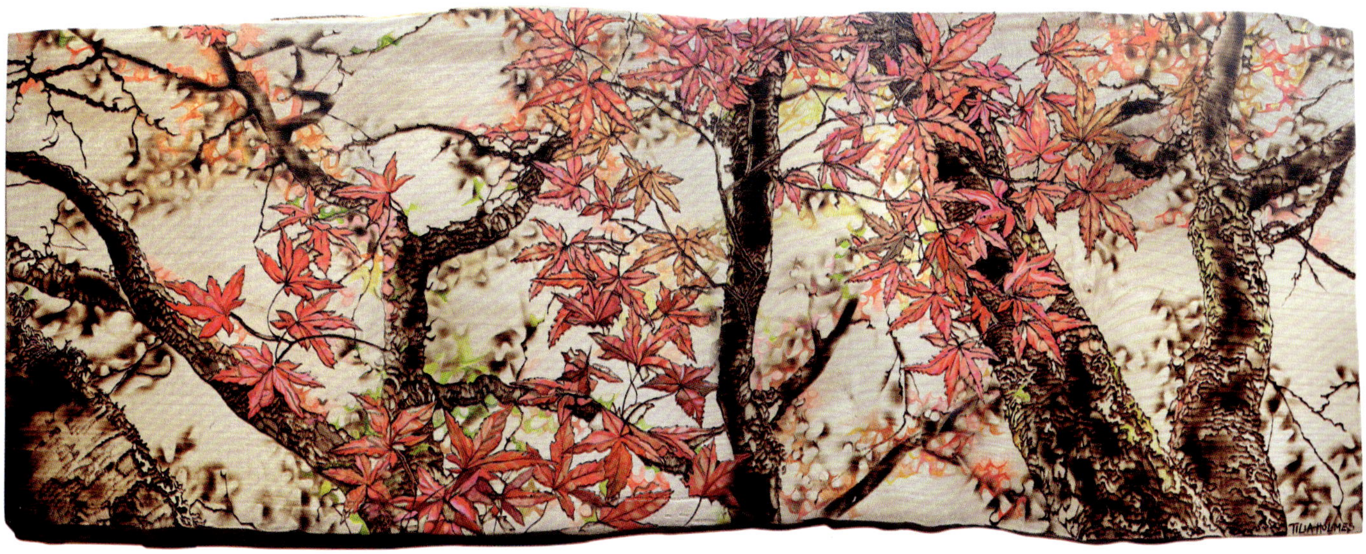
TILIA HOLMES

Abi Kremer

As I enter a woodland, there is a magical feeling, an energy that captivates me. The first place to enthral me in this way was a Dorset woodland, which generated a five-year site-specific project for which I received an Arts Council grant. Subsequently, on becoming a founding member of the Arborealists, I have become immersed in a range of projects, taking me to France, the Welsh borders, Dartmoor, and most recently, an ancient tree, which is more like a walk-in habitat. I endeavour to document the diverse forms and structures through a highly experimental watercolour practice, letting shapes emerge. This organic phenomenon continues to address the subconscious, creating a surreal visual language inspired by Eileen Agar. Colour is the key to expressing mood, and the transparency of this medium, the layering and spontaneous developments, synergises with nature. I admire the qualities of light in Winfred Nicholson's art, as well as the thrilling colour compositions of Bridget Riley. Another inspiration is my work with contemporary dance companies, in which the charge and rhythms created by live performances parallel my feelings when in nature. For me, trees become animated, like dancers on a stage.

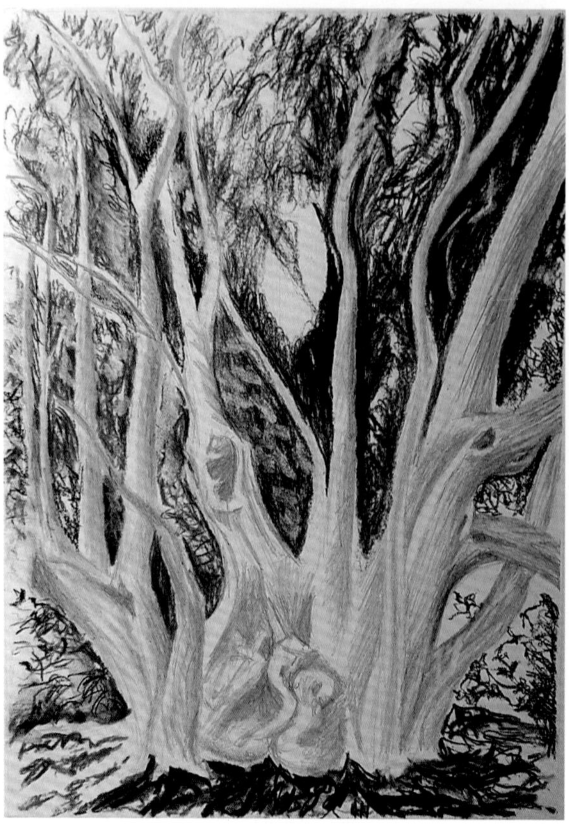

LEFT *Canford Sweet Chestnut 1*, 2023

OPPOSITE LEFT *Remembering Wistman's Wood*, 2022
OPPOSITE RIGHT *Canford Sweet Chestnut 3*, 2024

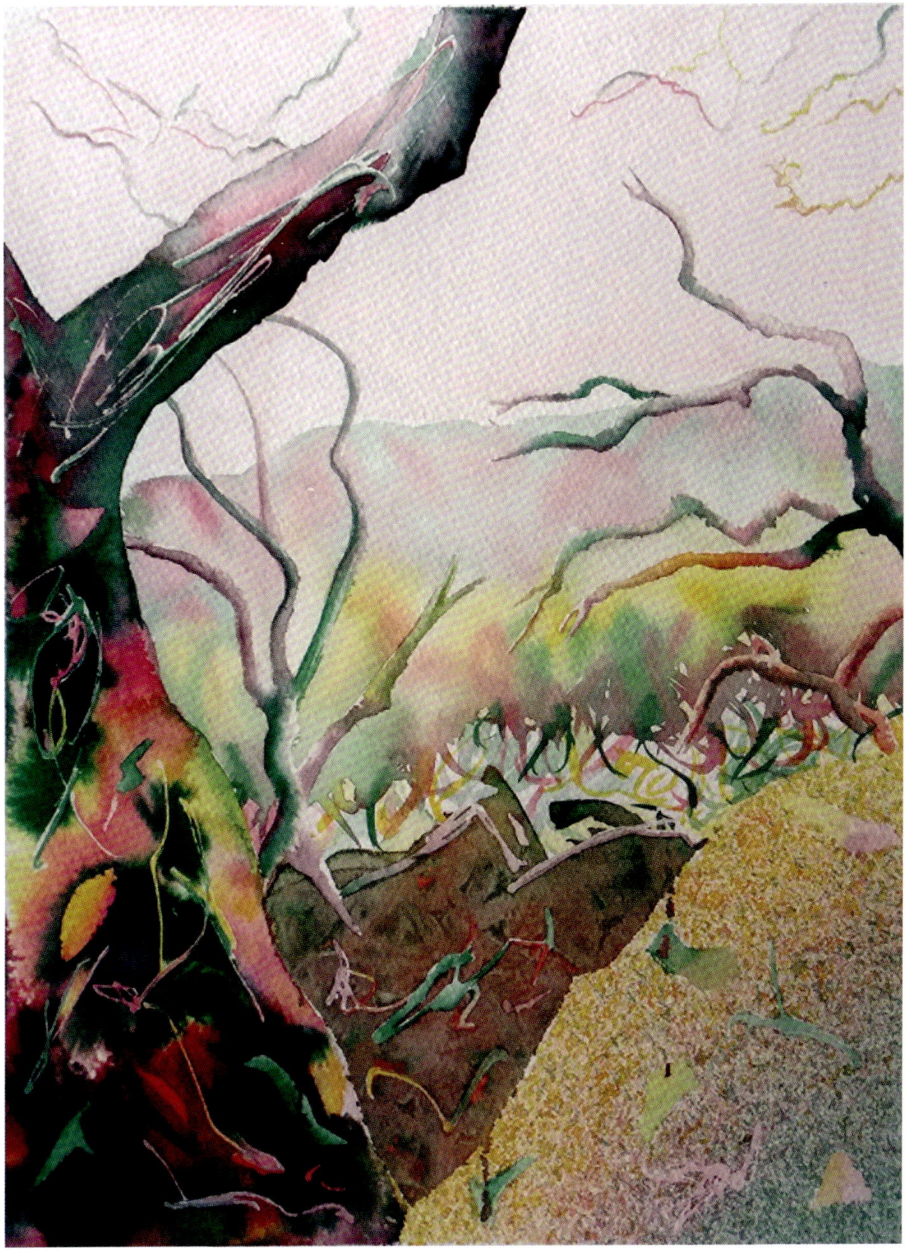

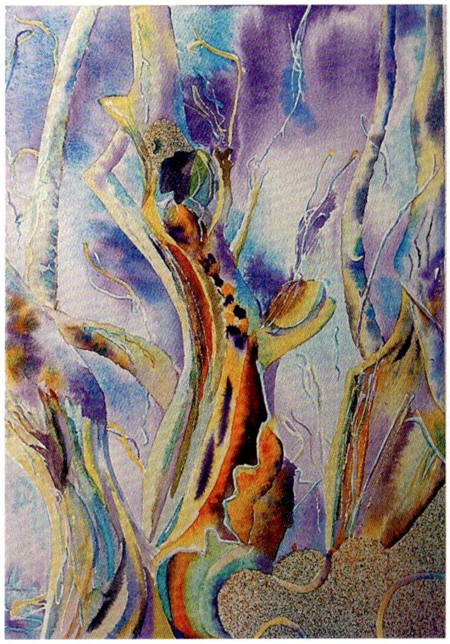

BELOW LEFT *Lady Park Wood 2*, 2018
BELOW RIGHT *Remembering Wistman's Wood 4*, 2022

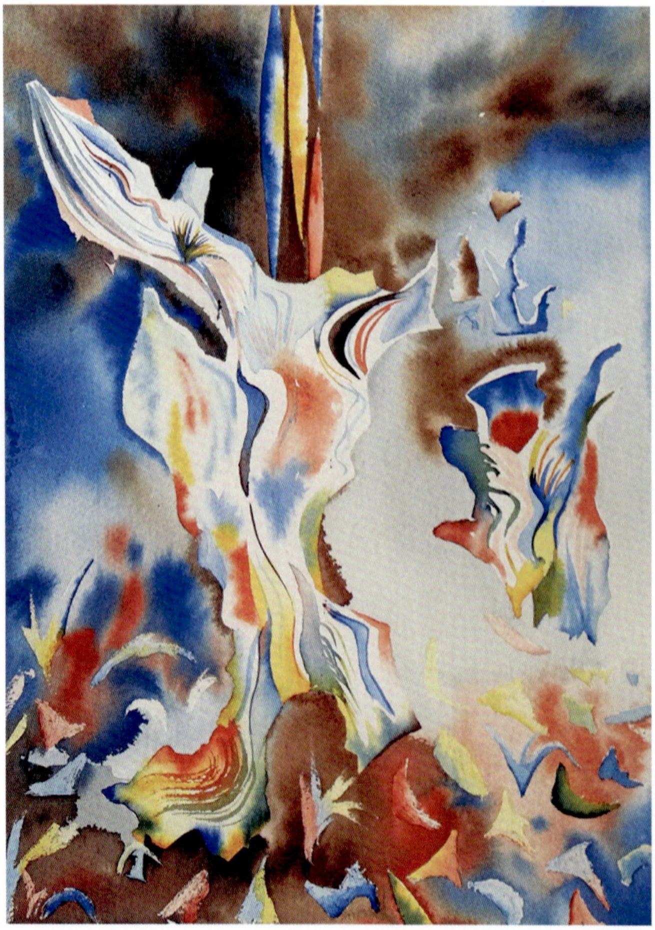

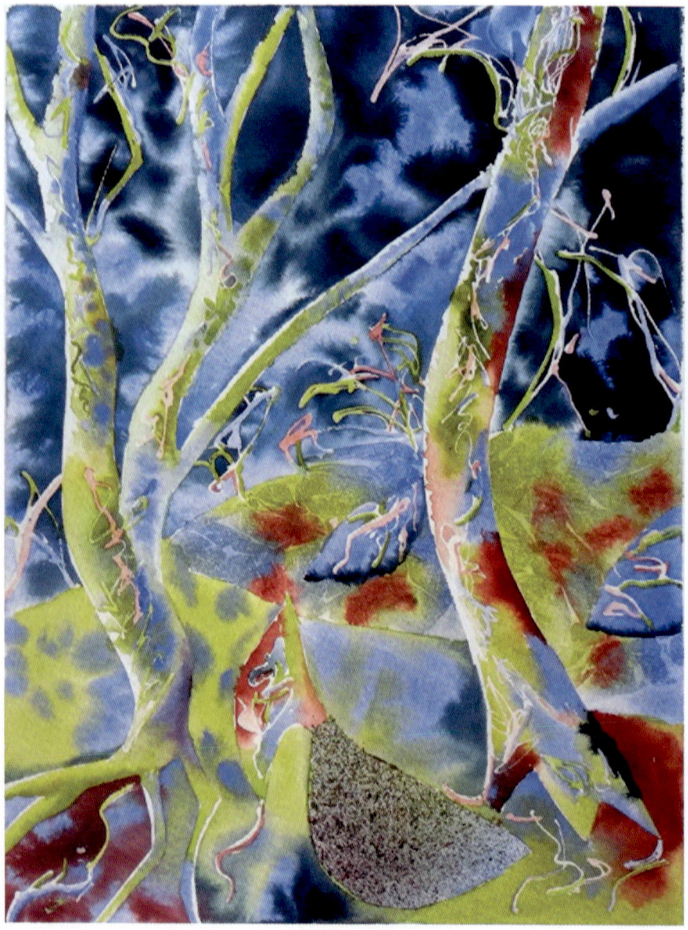

Ursula Leach RE

I make images of trees as part of the landscape where I live and am immersed. I walk and draw almost daily. It is a mainly agricultural landscape where trees are either scattered, sidelined or solitary. There are not many large woodland areas, so certain trees or copses stand out.

I am a colourist, and trees offer a broad range of colours as the seasons change and the weather alters their appearance. Colour is used in a way that is not necessarily realistic, but intended to evoke a parallel to the atmosphere of the subject and recreate the intensity of a visual experience. Space within the image is manipulated away from the literal to imply distance, height and mass. Things placed on the edge of an image indicate possible disappearance or fragmentation. Large areas of one colour imply bareness, aridity and erosion. My response to trees is not particularly romantic, but as I look closely, beauty can be found. Although I am a formal artist, I'm also concerned with the subject and, as with colour, the liminal area between the abstract and the figurative. The work is intended to be a document as well as an expression.

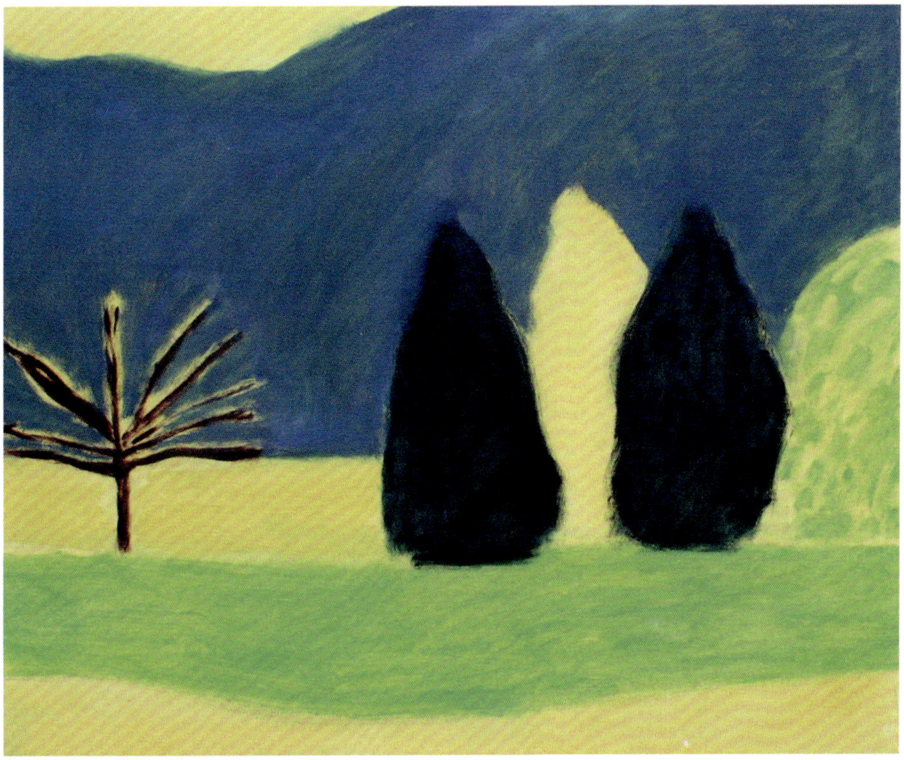

LEFT *Yellow Spring*, 2024

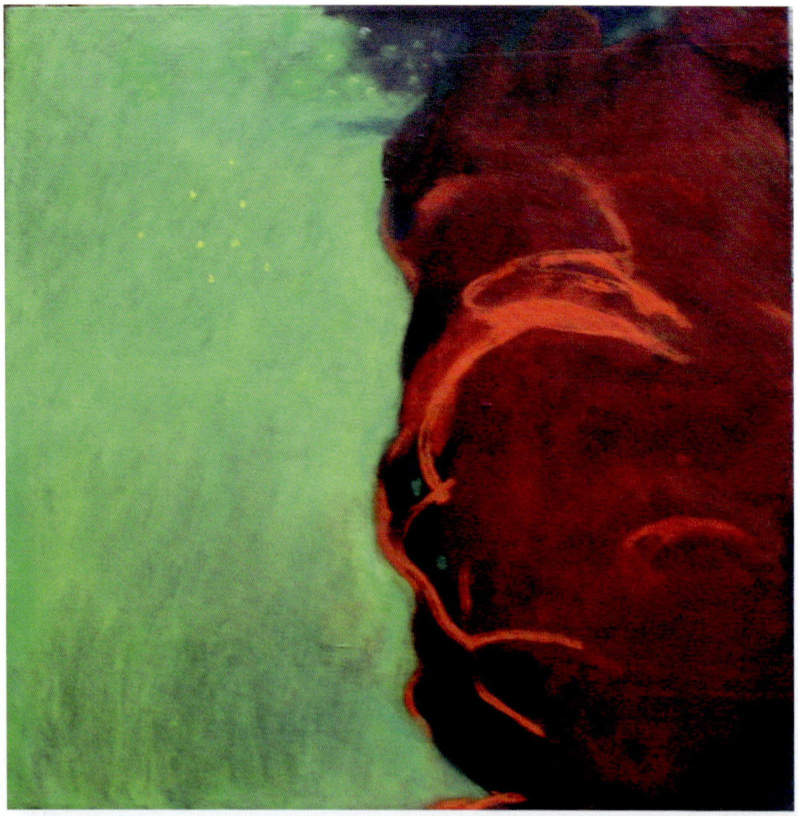

LEFT *Steep I*
BELOW *Solitary Tree*, 2024

OPPOSITE LEFT *Fall II*
OPPOSITE RIGHT *Glimmer*, 2022

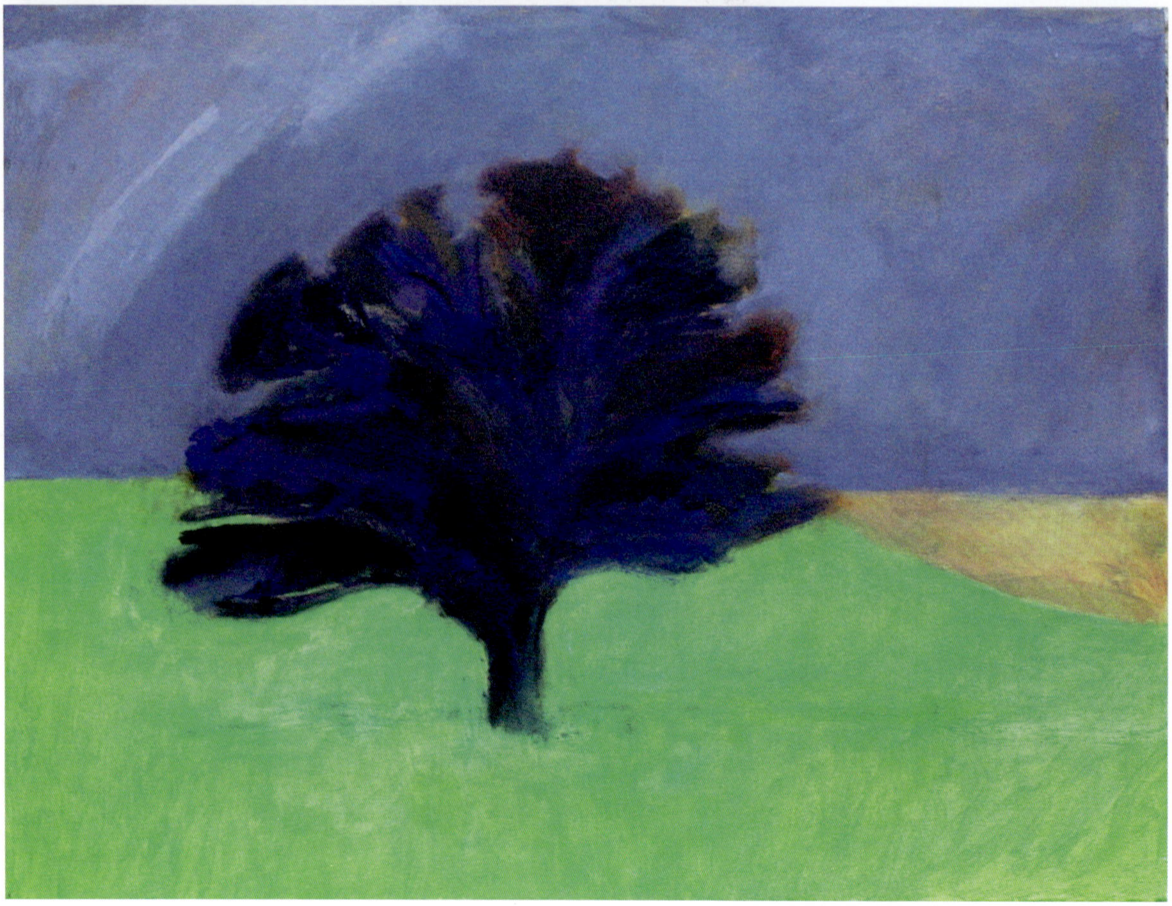

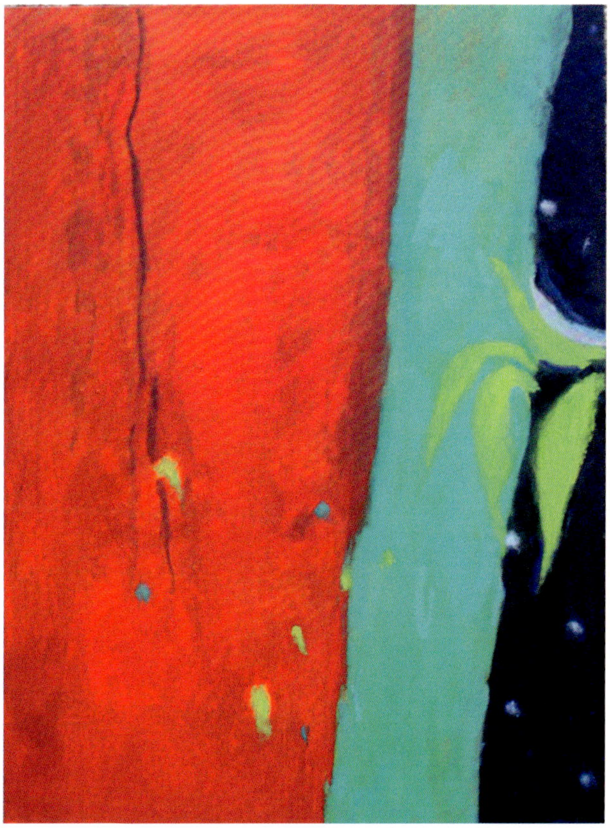

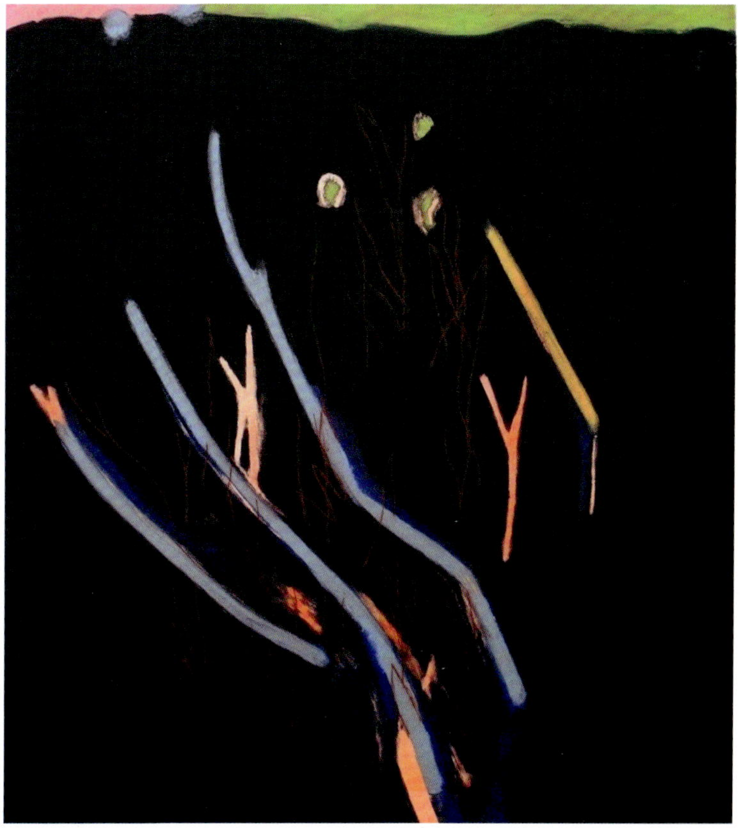

Natasha Lien

I was brought up walking my dogs daily in the nearby National Trust woodland, where I experienced the changing seasons; the different colours and the contrasting structures of the trees (with and without leaves) that came with change. I want to share their life-enriching experience in my work. I am passionate about drawing, painting and creating etchings of trees all over the world (including Greece, Jordan and Morocco). My mission is to depict trees in various forms, from rhythmical group compositions to the individual textures of each particular tree and structure within.

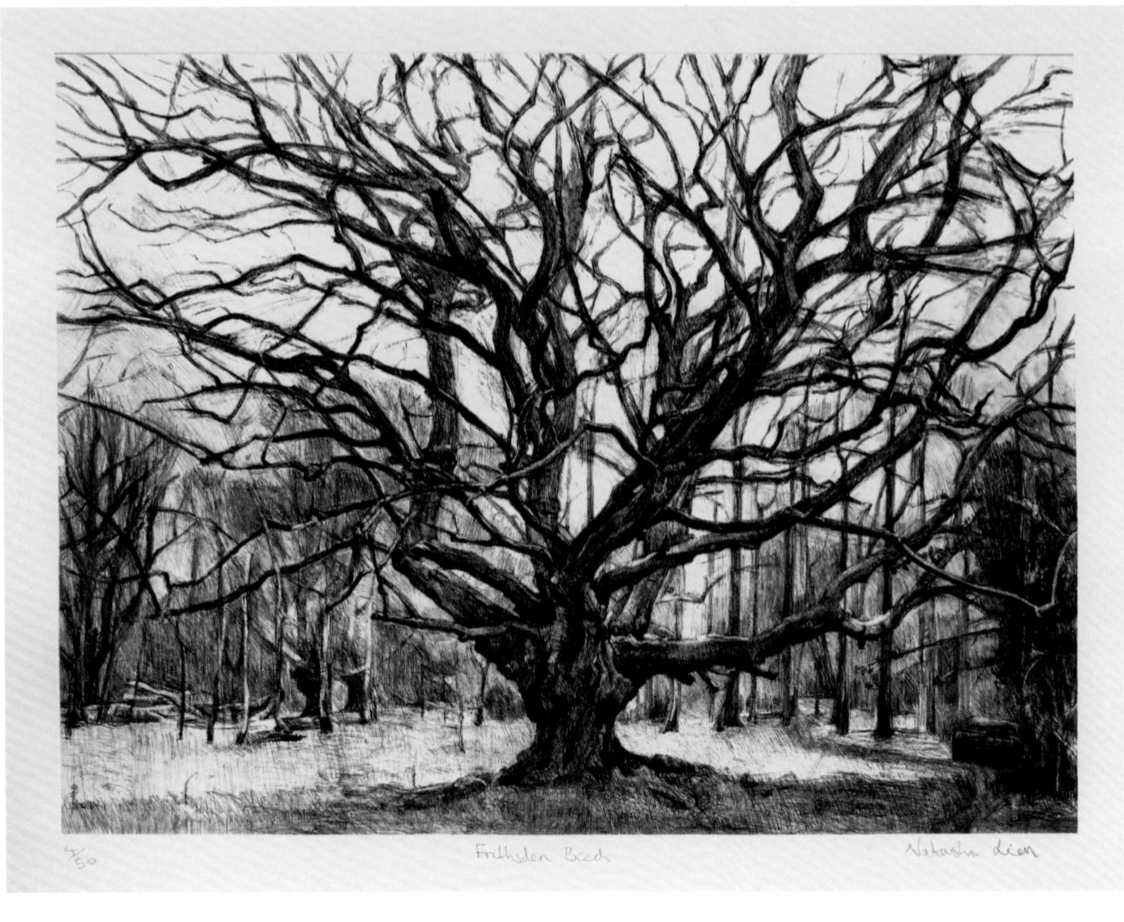

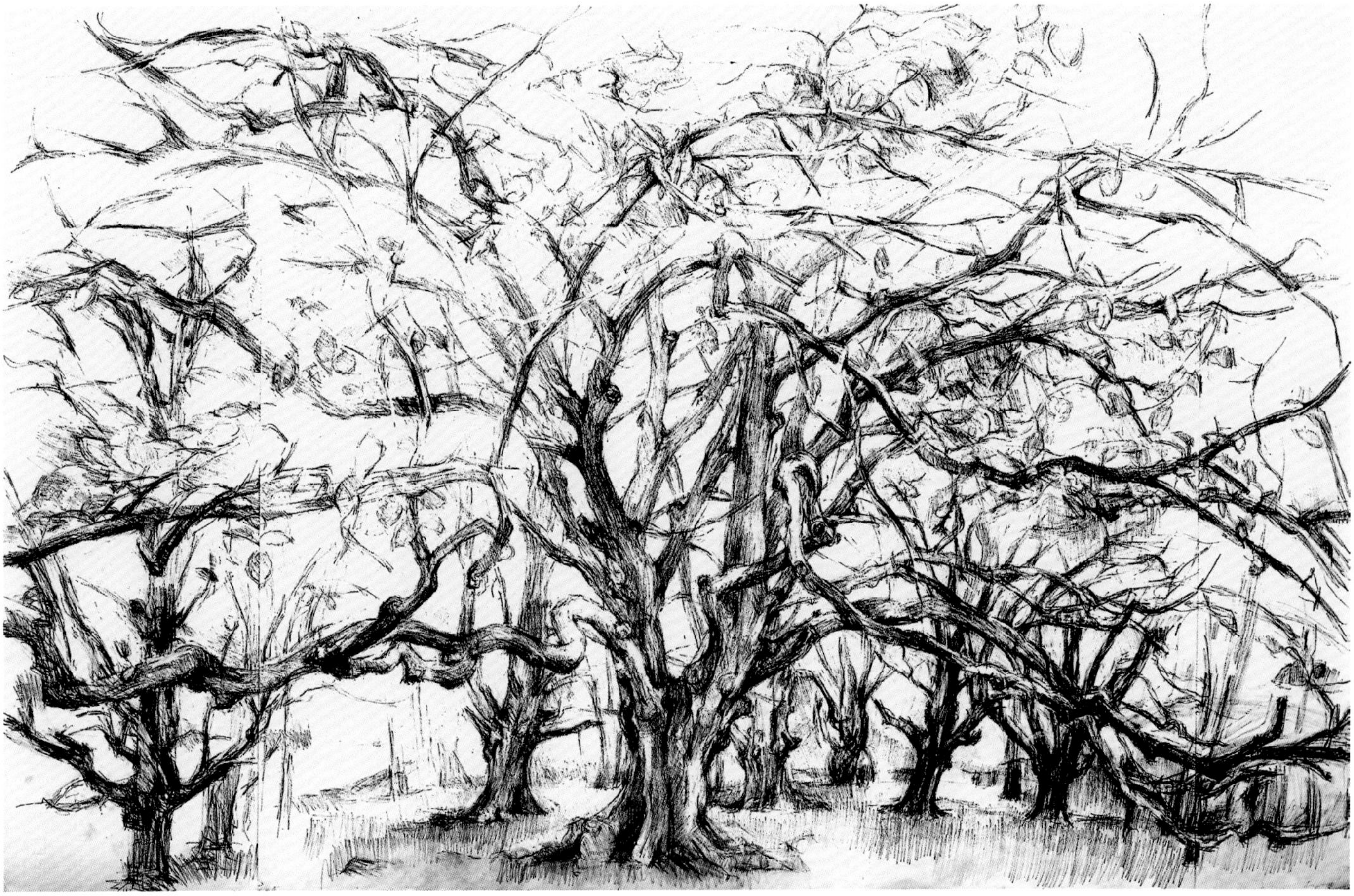

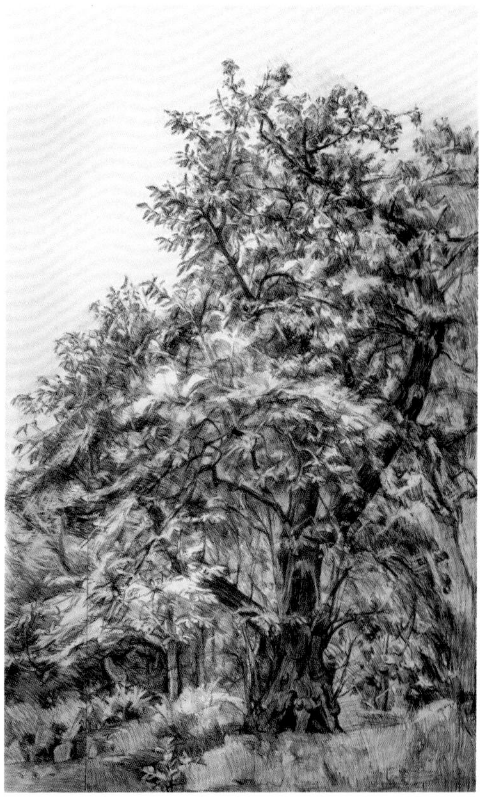

OPPOSITE *Lockdown Beech, Frithsden*, 2020

ABOVE *Frithsden Beech*, 2023 from a drawing c.2010
RIGHT *Hampstead Sweet Chestnut*, 2012

RIGHT *Staverton, Suffolk*, April 2024
BELOW *Greece Refugee Island*, 2021

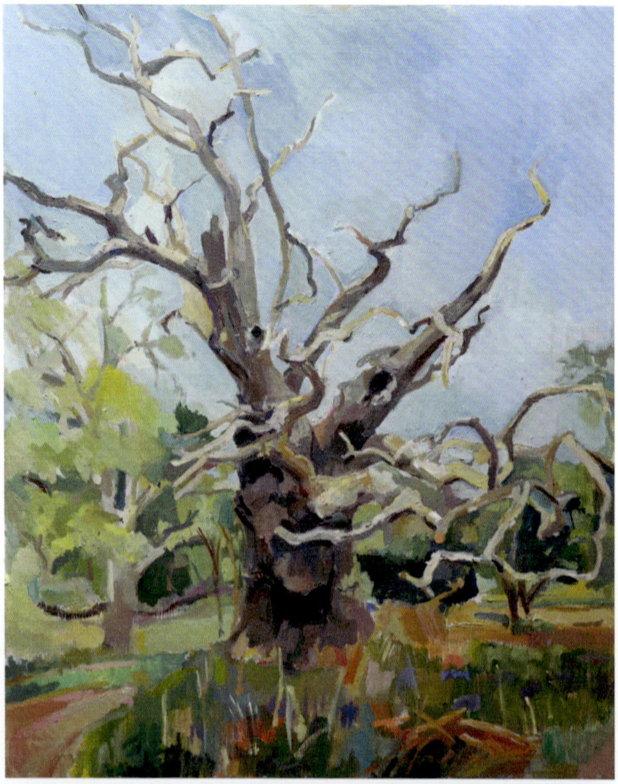

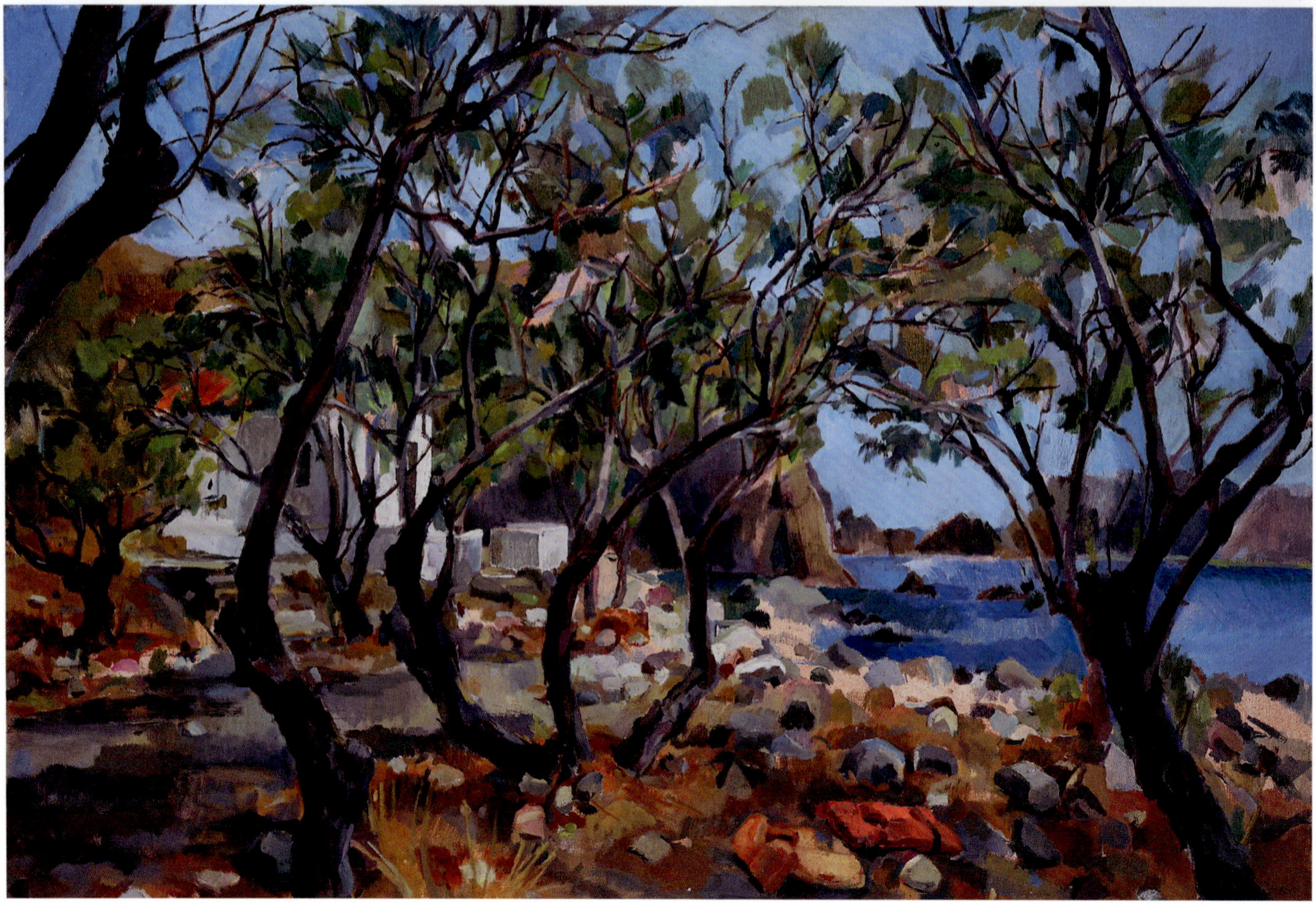

Rosemary Mafrici

An important element of my artistic development includes my background in animation; between 1987 and 1994, I worked on *Raggy Dolls* for Yorkshire Television and *Victor and Hugo* for Cosgrove Hall Productions. Although I have produced paintings on a wide range of subjects during my lifetime, I have an appreciation and affinity with nature, which is reflected in much of my work. I am often inspired by wild, less-manicured areas and ancient trees. A reminder that we are ephemeral, and many of these trees have seen countless generations of us pass by. I am obsessed with the delicate and subtle changes of colour, which help create a unique mood. I aim to capture exactly what I saw and felt at that precise moment in time, using high realism, allowing the viewer to experience and appreciate the moment with me. I capture nature with sensitivity and a strong sense of urgency to protect it.

BELOW *Oak Tree*

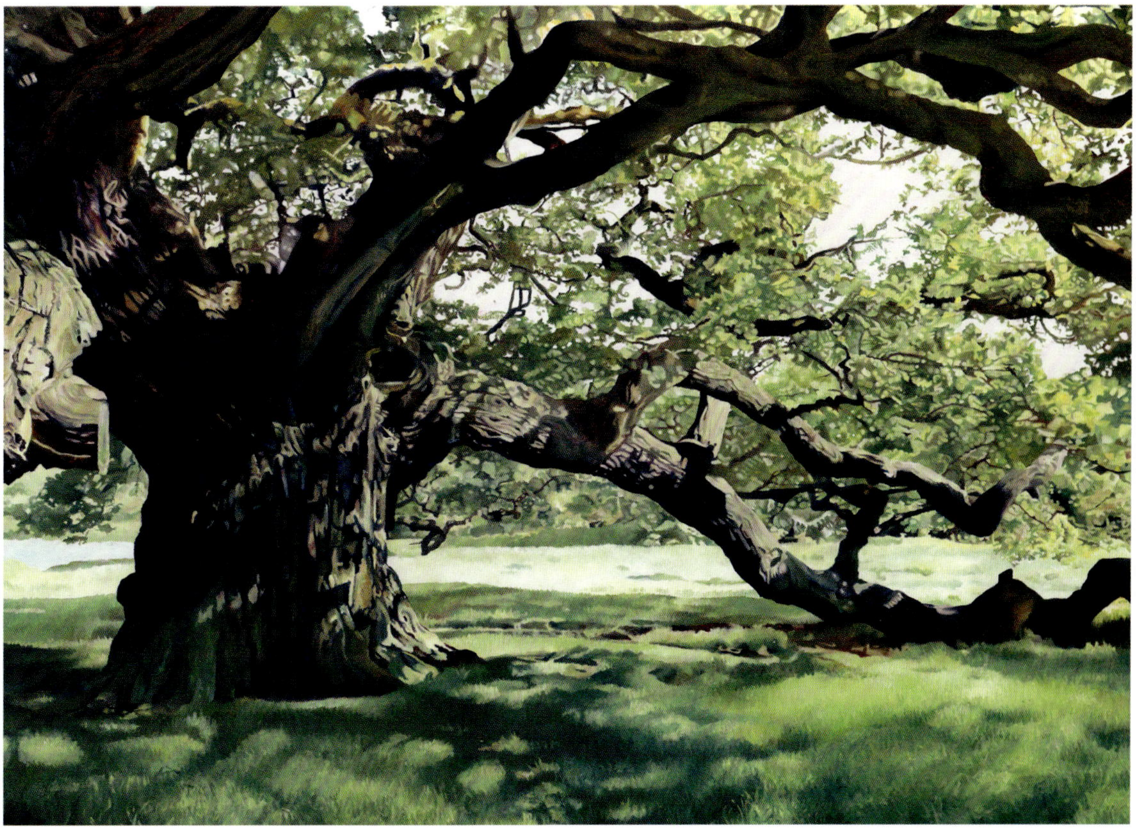

BELOW LEFT *Wistman's Wood*
BELOW RIGHT *Pathway*

OPPOSITE LEFT *Winter Sunlight*
OPPOSITE RIGHT *Olive Tree*

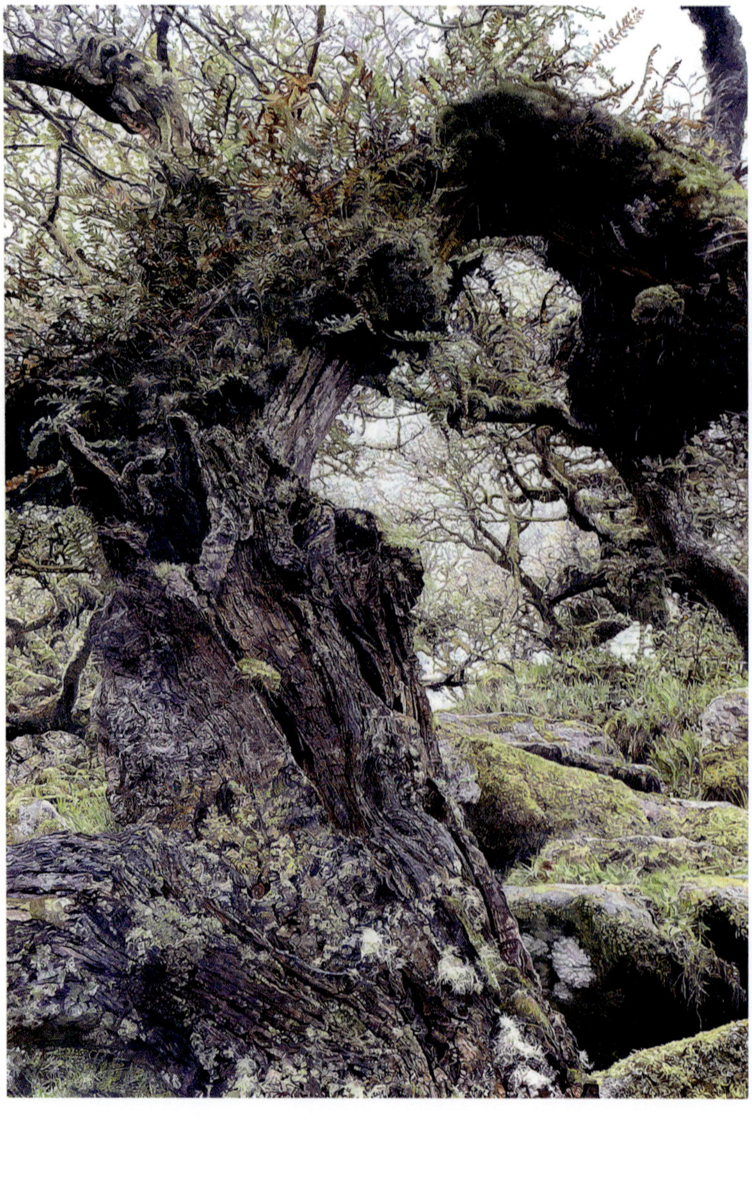

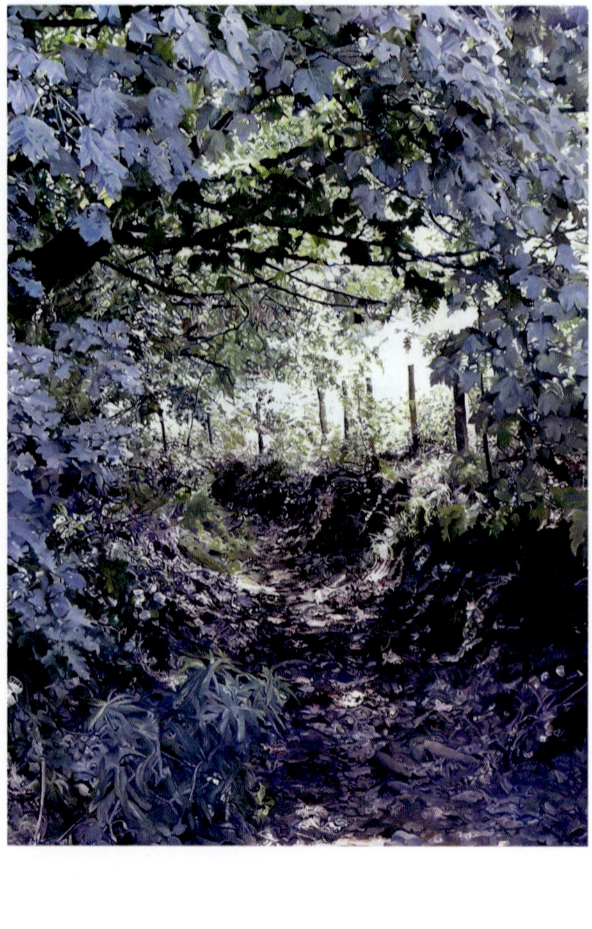

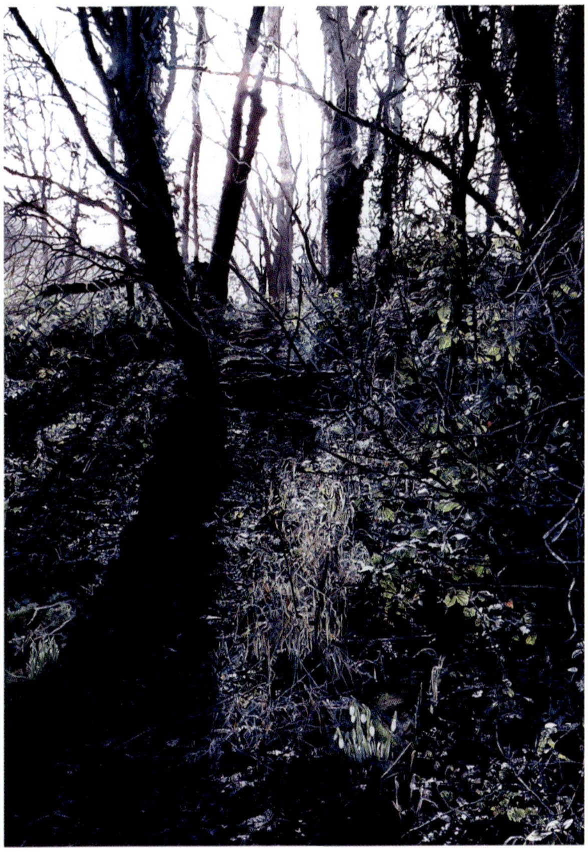

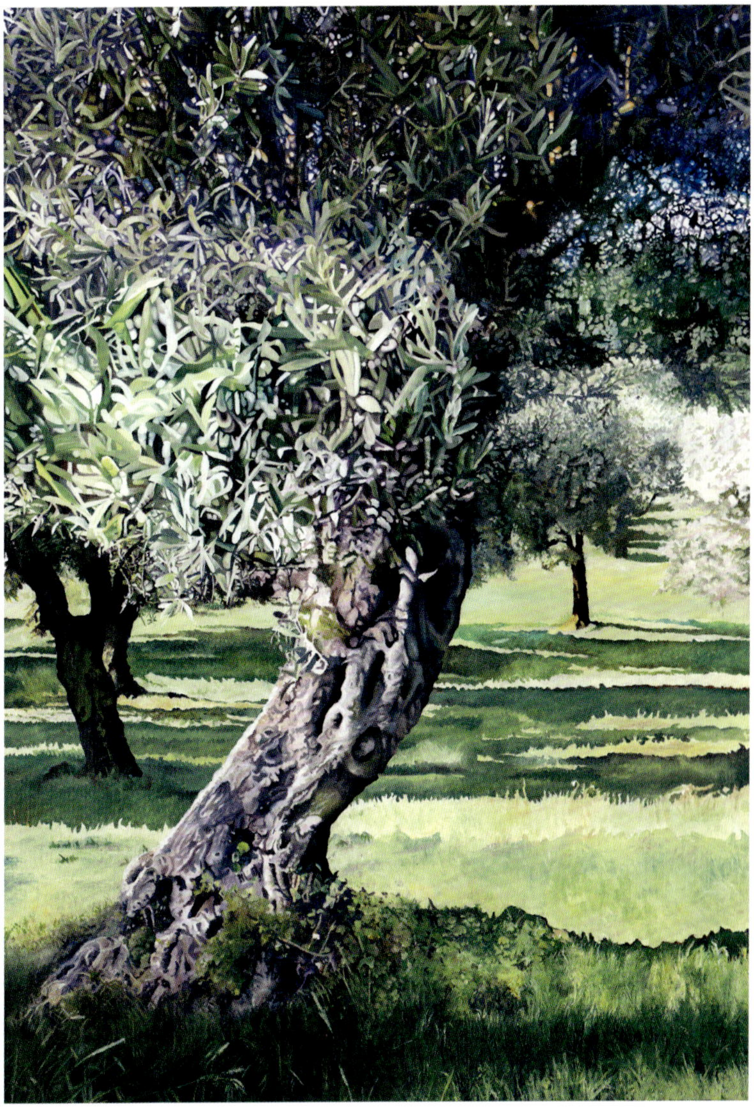

Fiona McIntyre ARE

I am a painter-printmaker with a love of colour and raw materials. I translate this into drawings, paintings and copper etchings with a focus on trees, wilderness, creation myths and the alchemy of natural materials into paint. I work with modern oils as well as earth pigments and foraged tree materials, turning them into inks to connect more directly to specific landscapes. Recently, I spent seven weeks in Clifford Chambers on the River Stour, observing and drawing ancient willows in all weathers, which had a huge effect on my understanding of the time-continuum and my perception of reality and our place within it. The Tudor hamlet and surrounding countryside have barely been touched for hundreds of years and the hamlet is mentioned in the Domesday Book. These timeless willows reminded me of mythological creatures with wizened bodies of gnarly eyes and limbs. Since conducting an earlier residency at the Sidney Nolan Trust on the Welsh/English border, I have been attracted to pareidolic and anamorphic figures seen within natural forms of trees and rocks. In another location in Exmoor's Horner Woods stands 'The General', an ancient oak at least 500 years old like a wise old man covered in moss and plants growing from its massive branches, and human-like forms emerging from its limbs. Trees are my place of sanctuary where I developed new ideas in peace and tranquility.

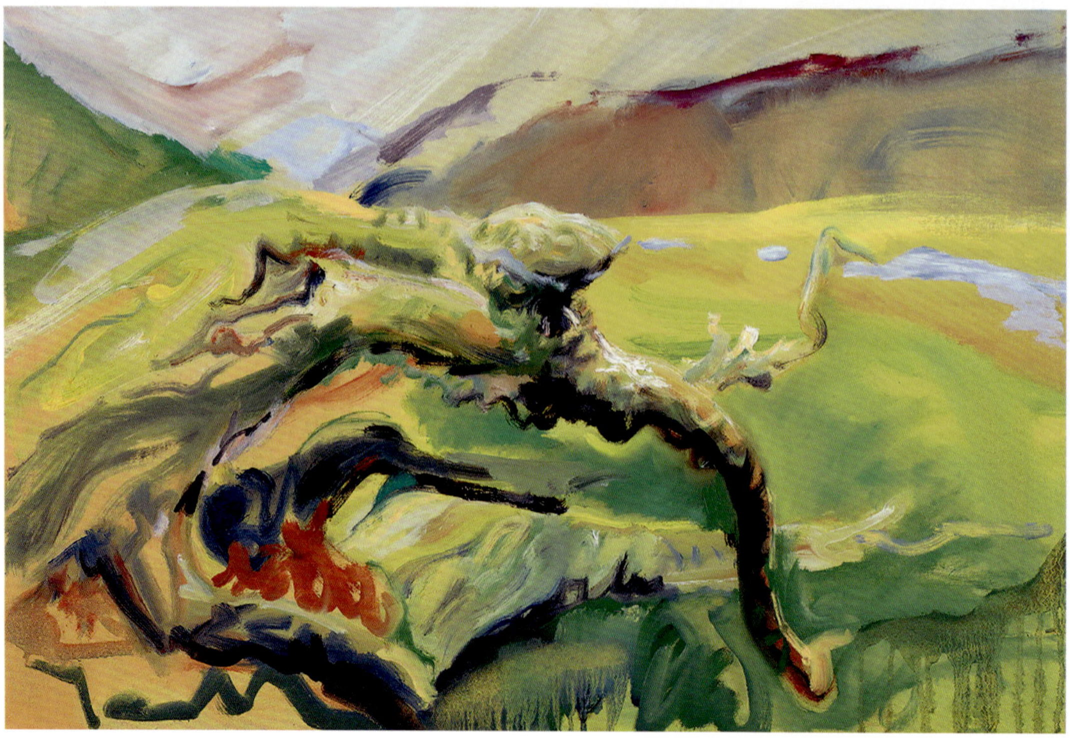

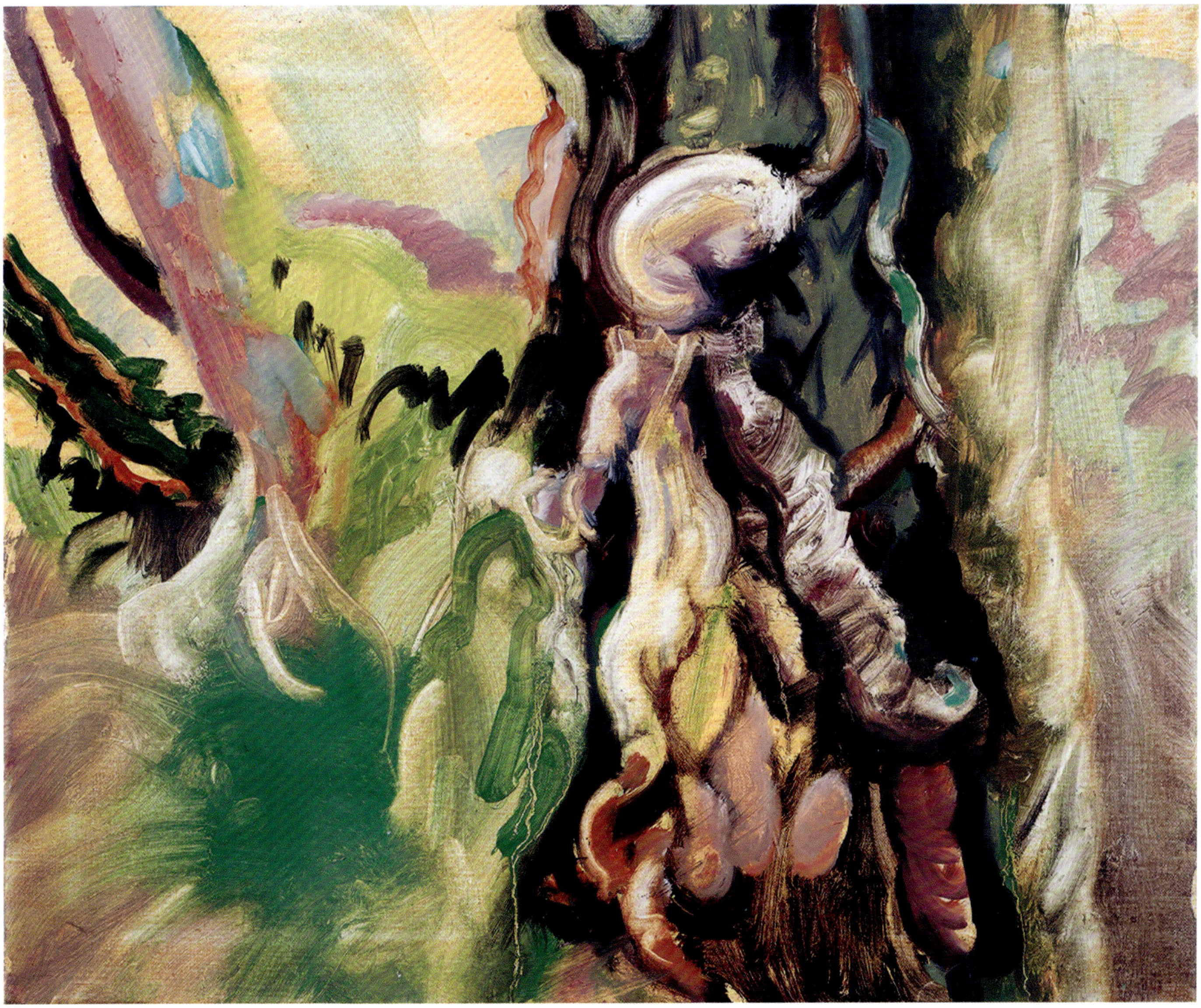

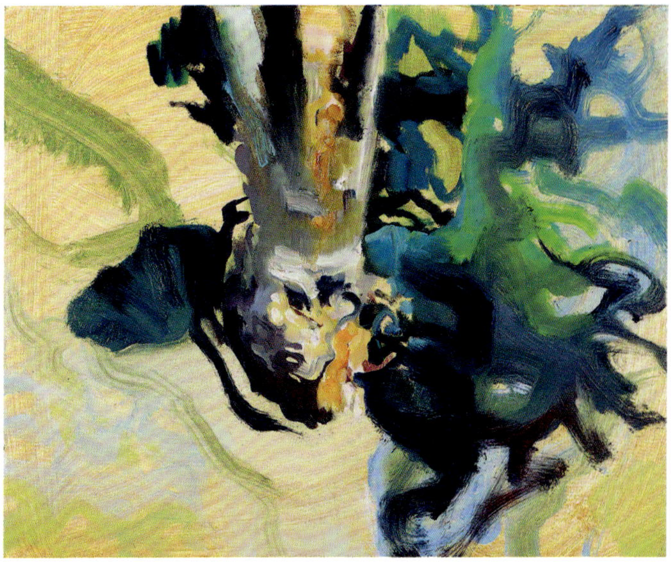

OPPOSITE *Pareidolic Creature*, 2022

ABOVE *Anamorphic Tree Person*, 2022
RIGHT *Pareidolic Oak, Horner Woods*, 2022

RIGHT *Willow No. 1*, 2023
BELOW *Willow No. 3*, 2022

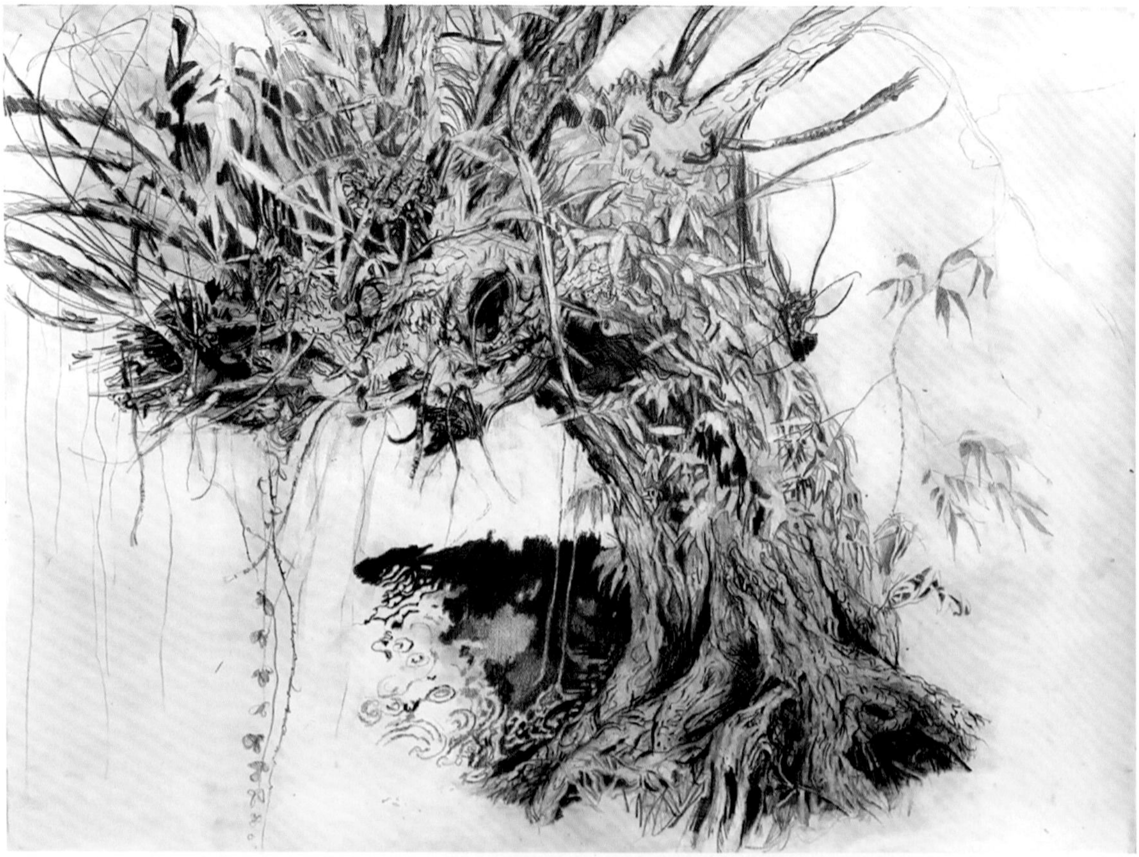

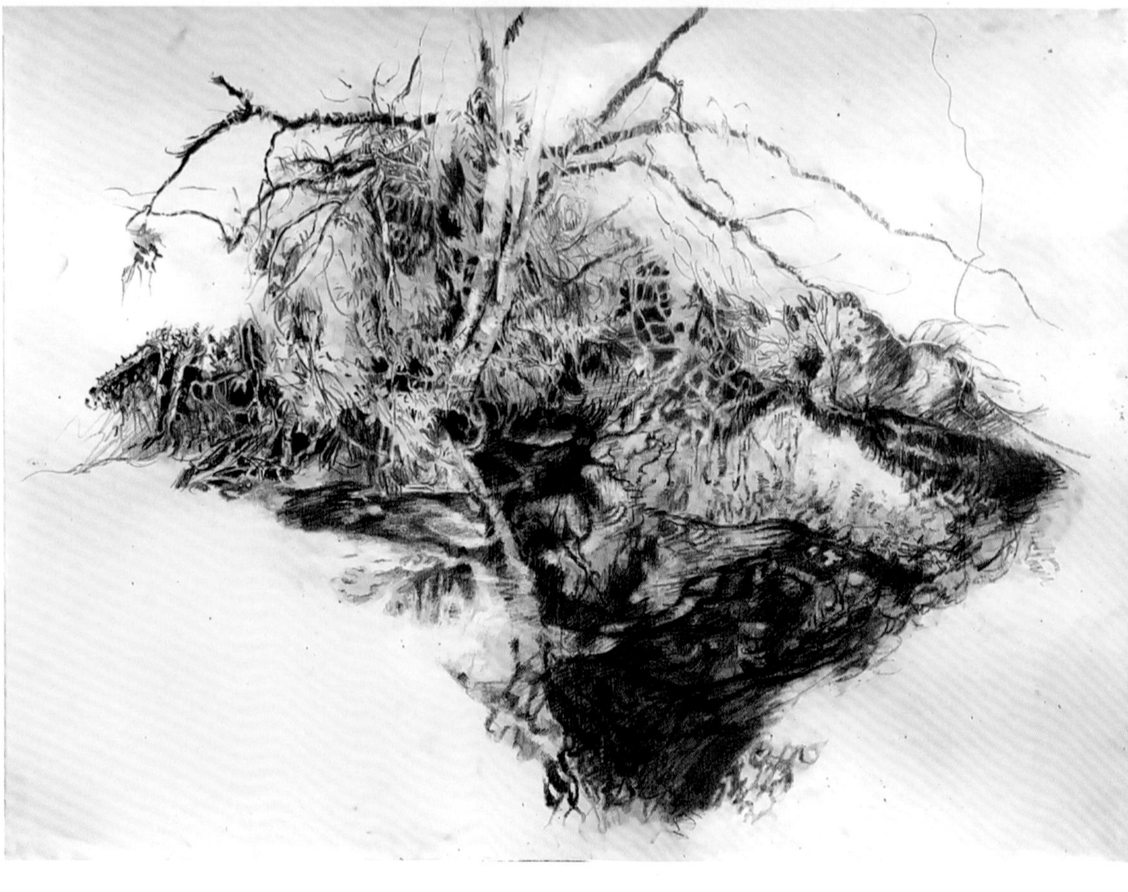

Władysław Mirecki

Even before I became a painter, trees have been as essential to my world as the beasts of nature. In my earliest works, my trees were amorphous blobs wrapped in greenery. I had to truly analyse them as objects in the round to get them right. This has given me a preference for naked trees. Then, in winter, they reveal themselves and their surroundings so much more.

I am unaware of the names of the trees I paint. I tried learning their Latin names and making botanic studies of them. But I found this to be distracting. Their colour, shape and texture, together with mass, is what awes me, and I have tried to capture this. The context in which they lie is also of importance; the space around them, and the leaf mould at their base. They do not exist in isolation; other trees live with them, and creatures live upon them, and while I'm making the picture, I, too, become almost tree-like, still and silent.

BELOW *River Colne*, 2022

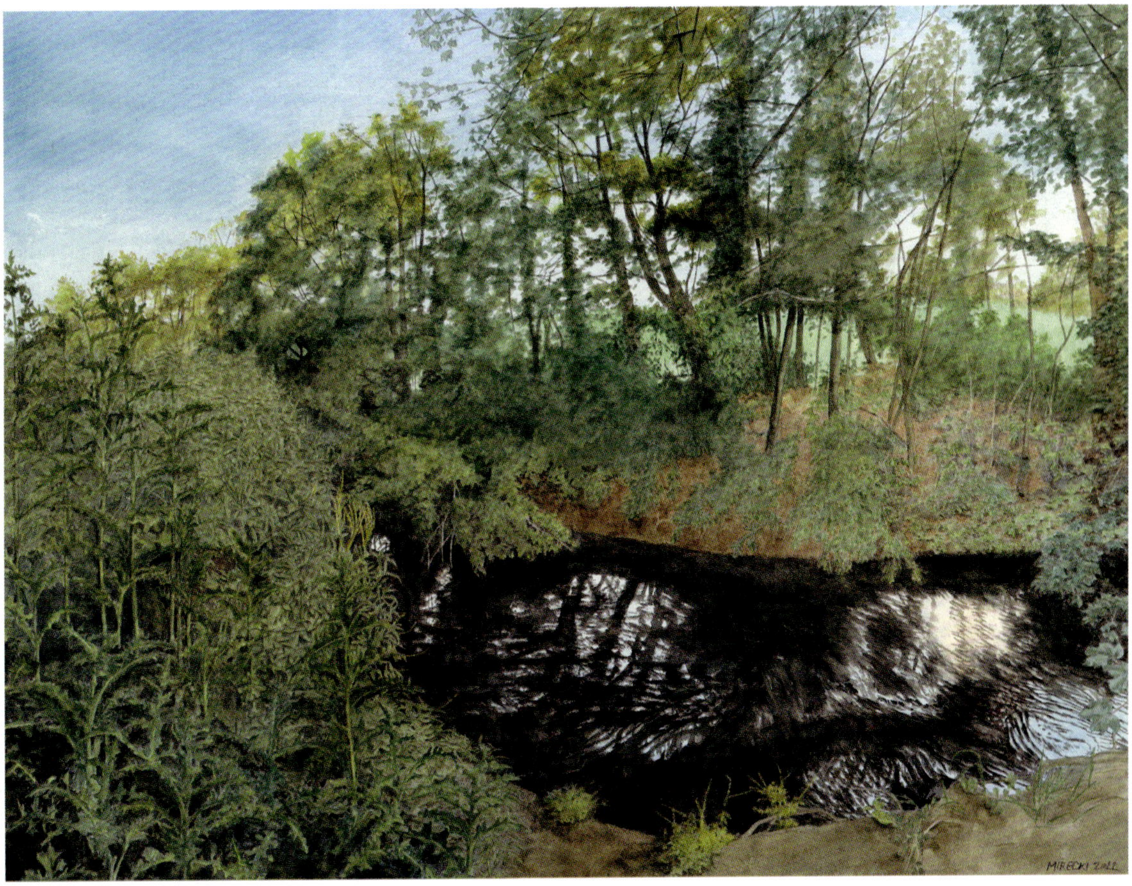

BELOW LEFT *Winter Wood*, 2023
BELOW RIGHT *Footpath to the Sea, Dunwich*, 2022

OPPOSITE ABOVE *Country Road*, 2022
OPPOSITE BELOW *Ploughed Field and Phone Mast*

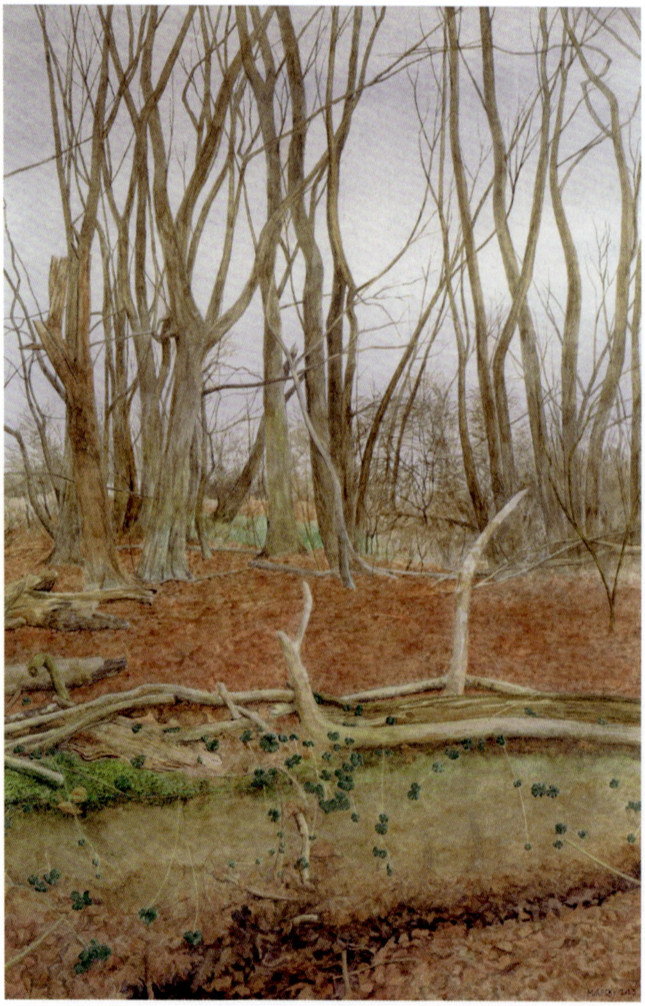

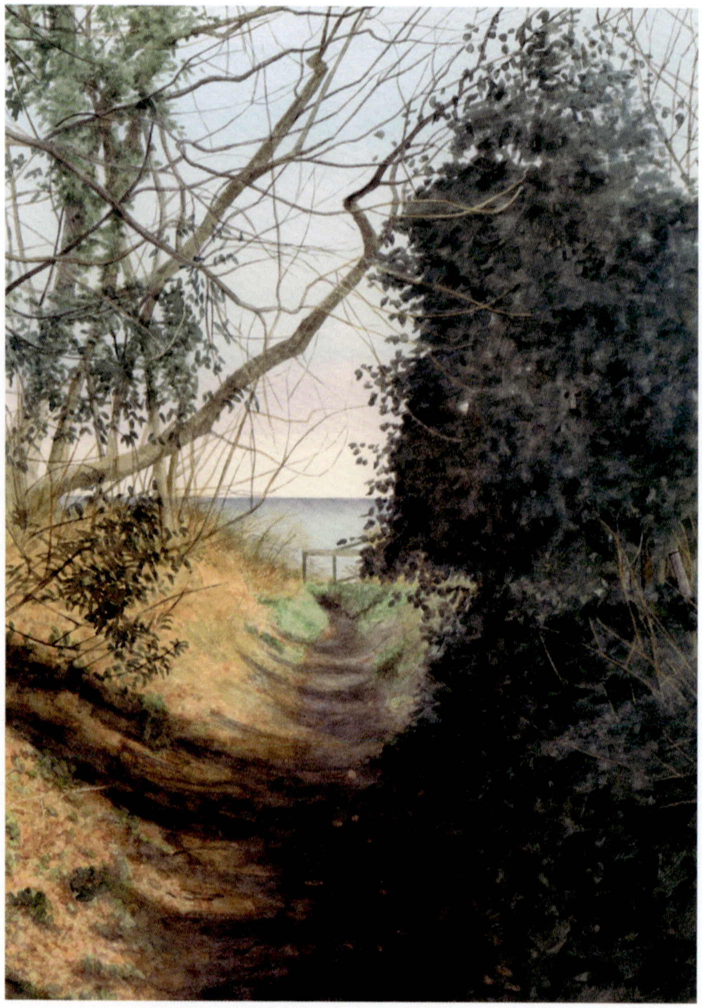

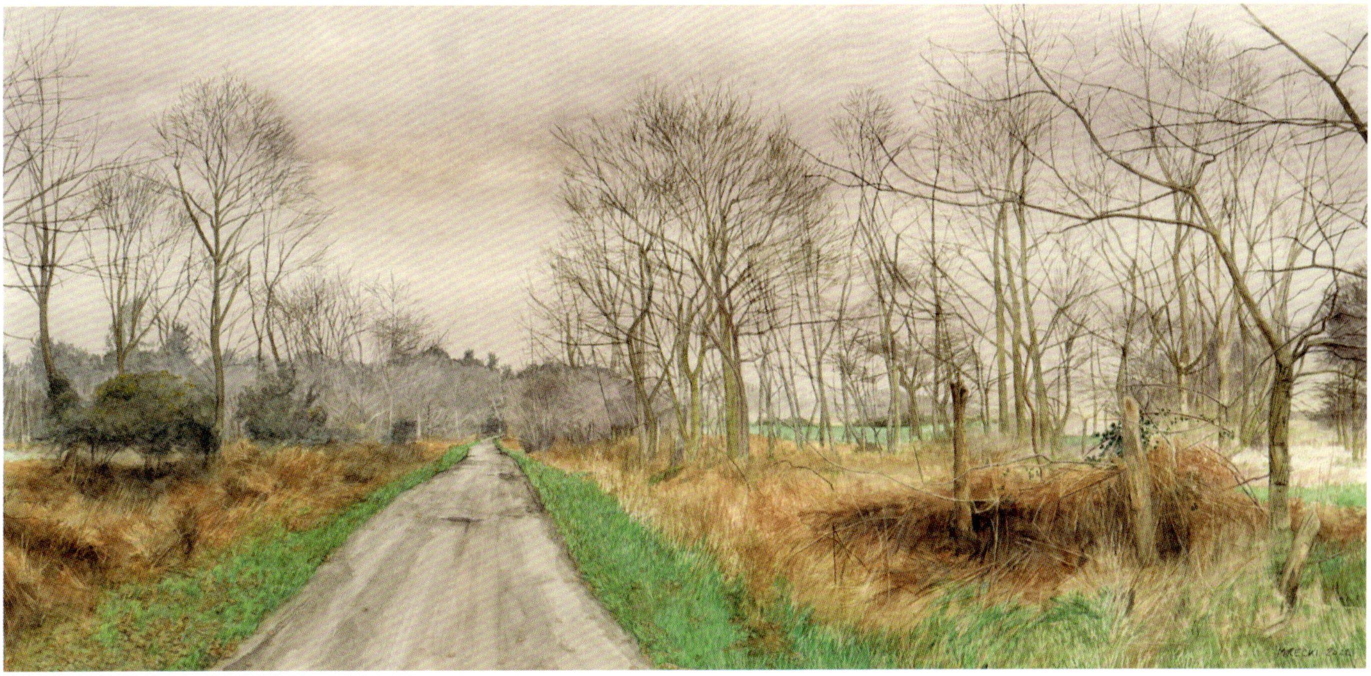

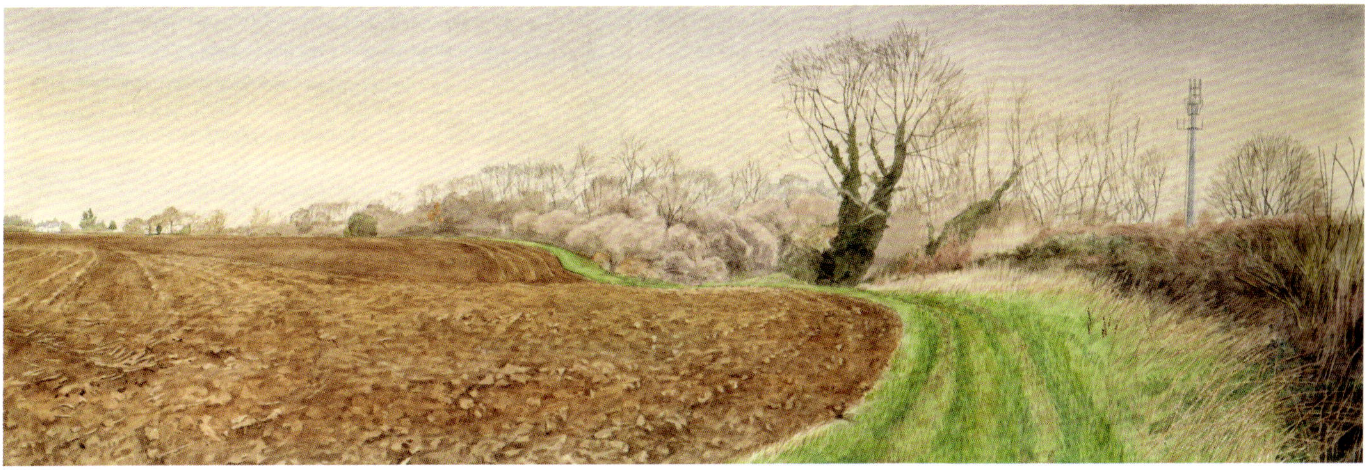

Paul Newman

Living and working on the Dorset and Somerset border, Paul is a graphic fine artist intrigued by nature. He works almost exclusively in graphite and is interested in detail, texture and tone, inspired by elements of the ancient landscape and stories of Wessex. His work is created by researching the nature and history of places: geology, ecology and sometimes interaction with human activity. Walking is an important part of the working process. It helps one understand the character and distinctive atmosphere, as Paul Nash referred to as the 'genius loci'. Much of Paul's work comes from places that have been explored and returned to repeatedly, with an ingrained personal significance. The work is a response to being affected by memories or experiences over time, in those places. He is keen to link the places he finds and the stories that fashioned them. His influences are maps and writers, geologists and legends, songs and poems. Drawings and photographs taken in the field are turned into finished pieces in the studio. In particular, Paul is drawn to their shapes and individual textures, their place in regional folklore, and their gift of allowing us to collectively connect and think about our relationship with nature.

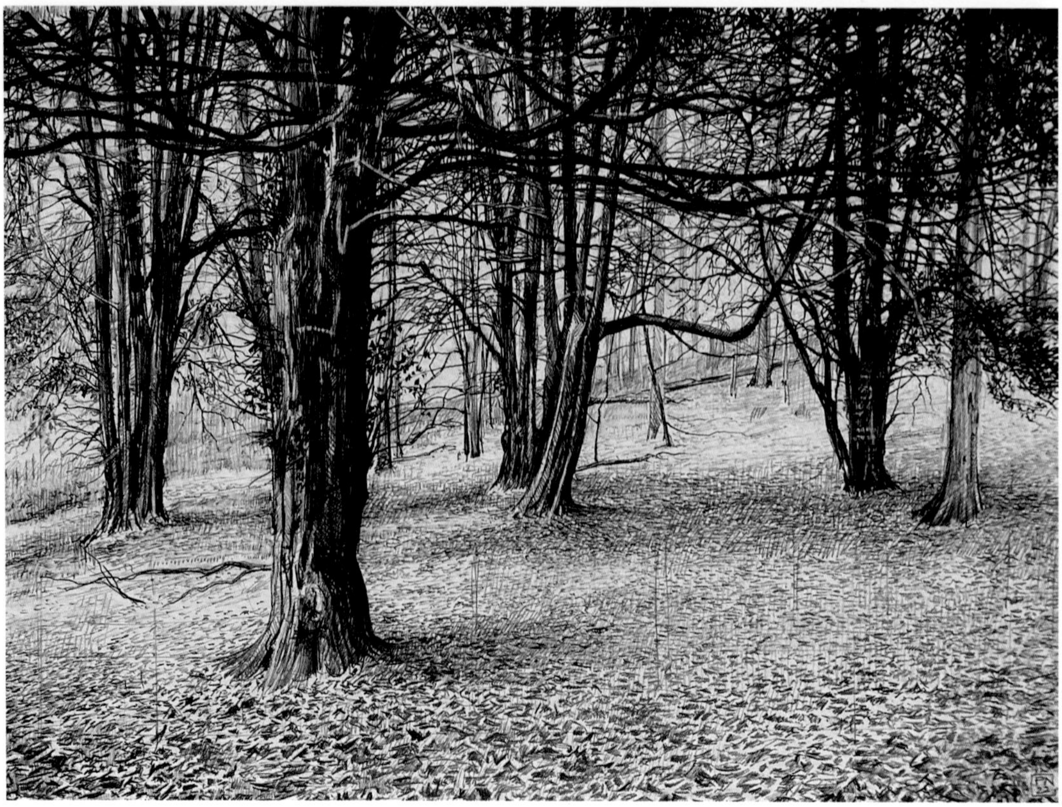

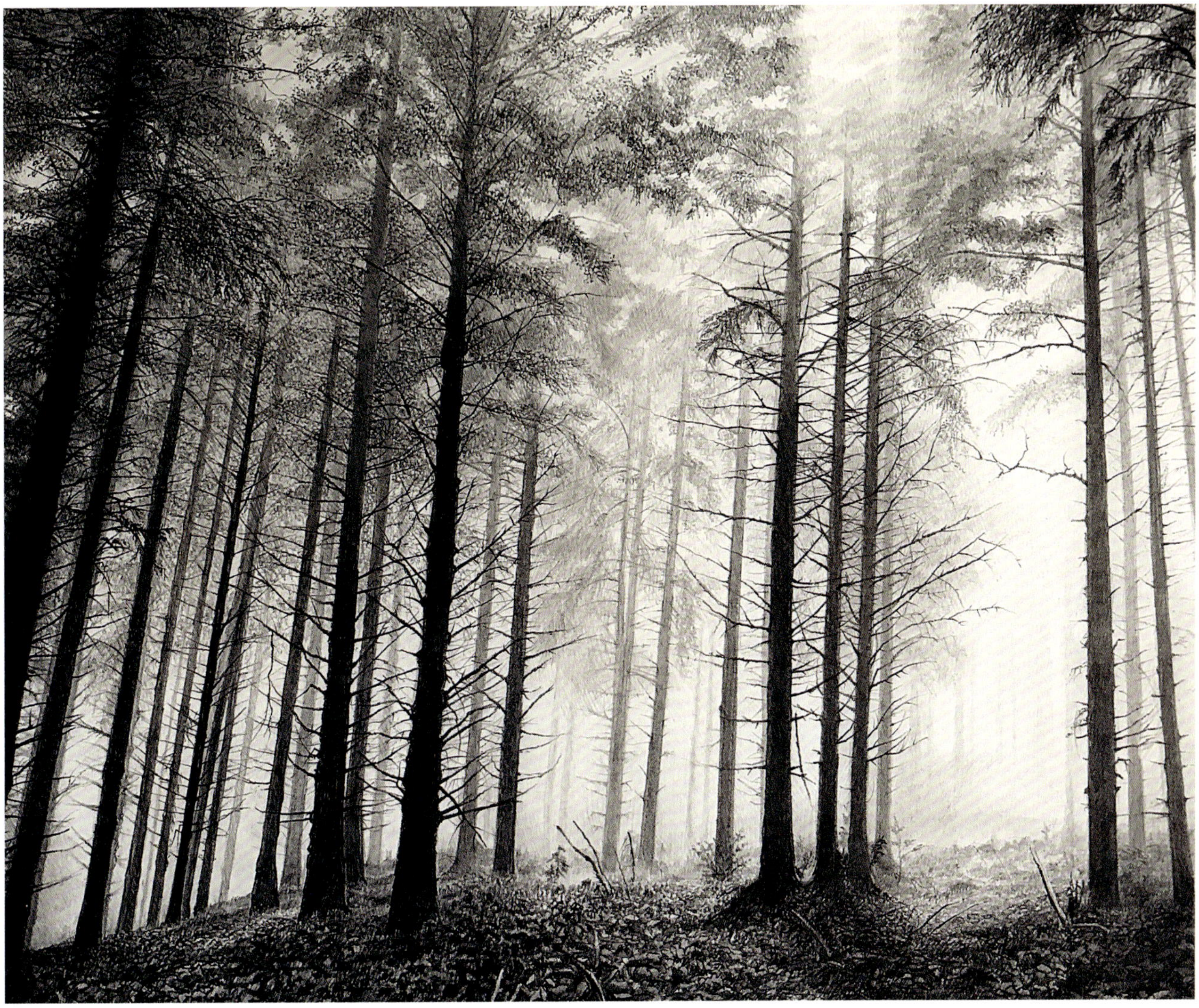

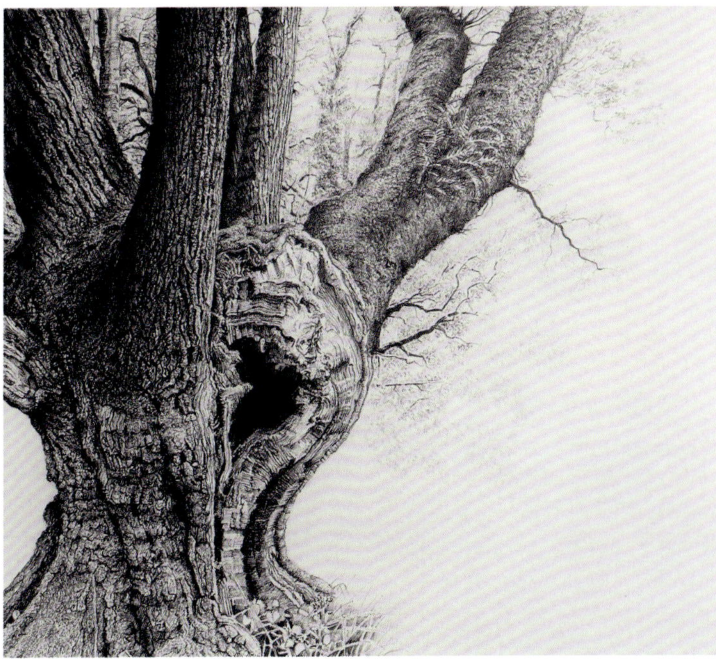

OPPOSITE *Yew Grove, Hanover Wood, Somerset/ Dorset Border*, 2022

ABOVE *Netted in a Silver Mist*, 2019
RIGHT *Cloutsham Ball Oak*, 2020

RIGHT *Near Bellever Tor*, 2010
BELOW *Silton Oak*, 2005

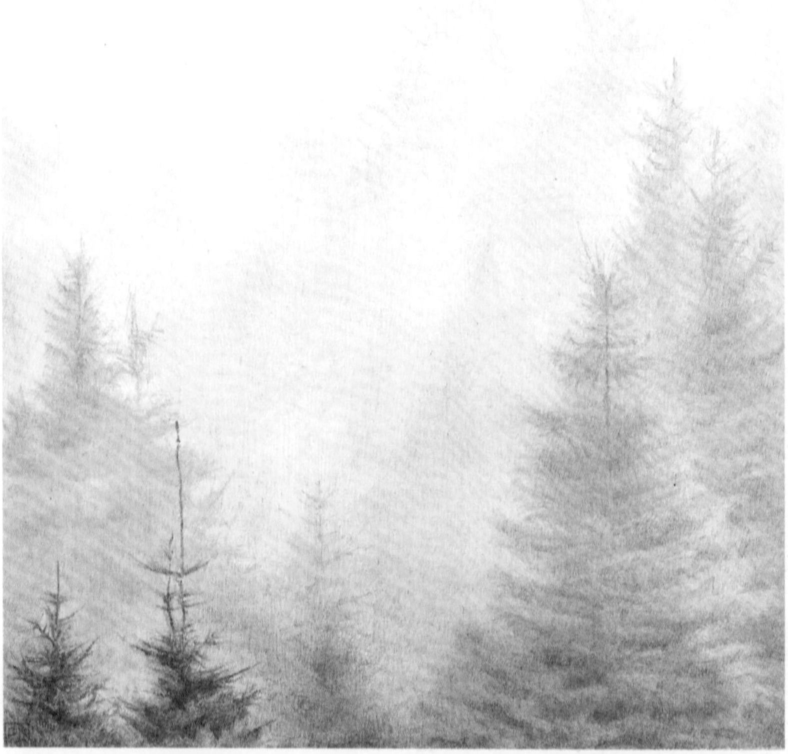

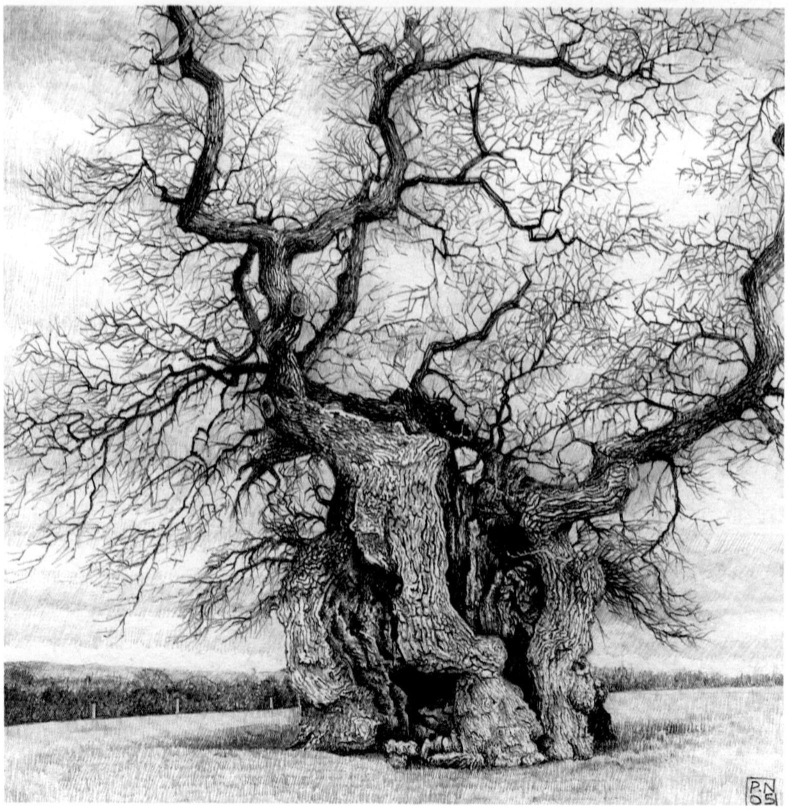

Howard Phipps ARE, RWA

Much of my work is concerned with landscape, in particular the chalk downs of Wiltshire and Dorset, close to where I live. I like to make drawings or paintings on location over numerous sessions. I frequently use these drawings as the basis for wood engravings, a method of relief printmaking where the polished surface of a block of end grain boxwood is engraved using traditional tools with names such as spit-sticker and graver. On completion, the surface is inked using a roller, and an impression is taken on paper using an Albion hand press, dated 1862.

BELOW *Lewesdon Hill Beeches*, watercolour

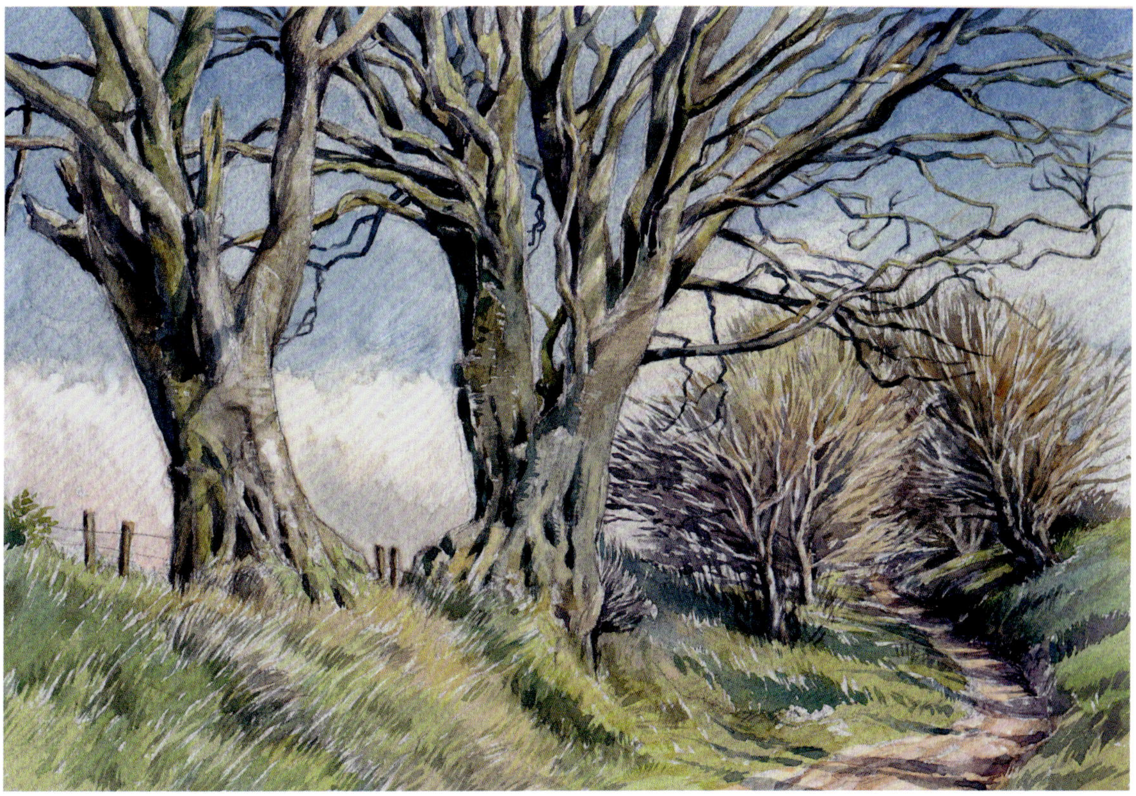

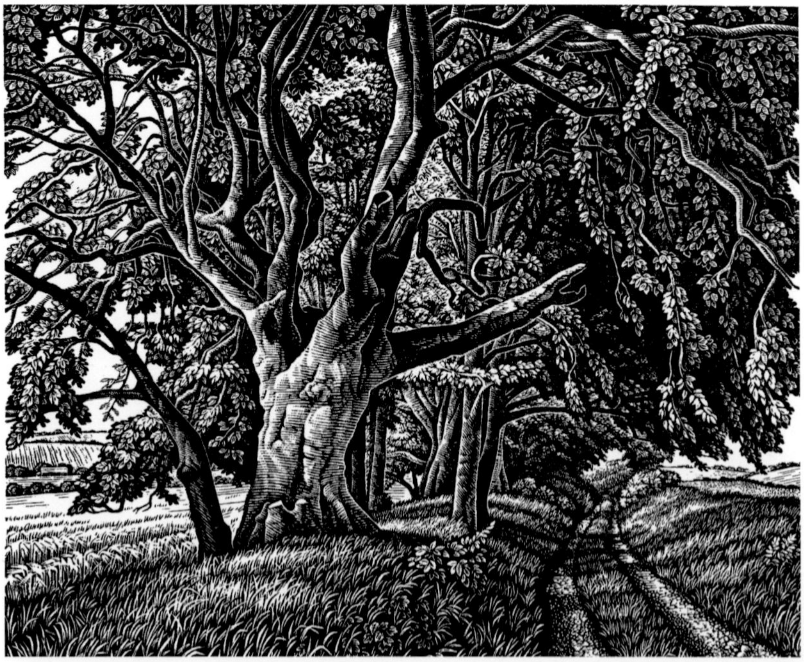

LEFT *Ox Drove*
BELOW *Lewesdon Hill Beeches*, wood engraving

OPPOSITE ABOVE *Wistman's Wood*
OPPOSITE BELOW *Melbury*

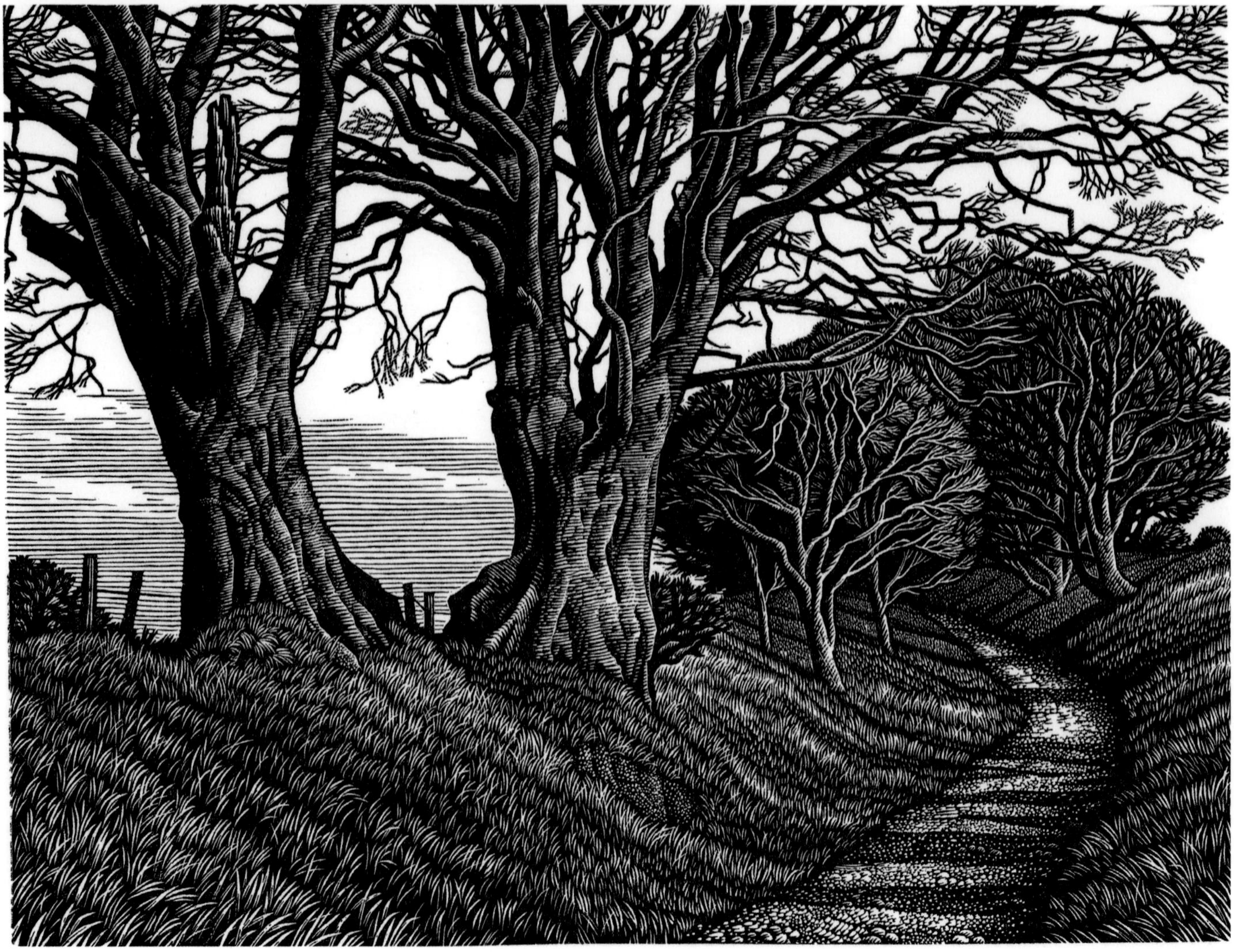

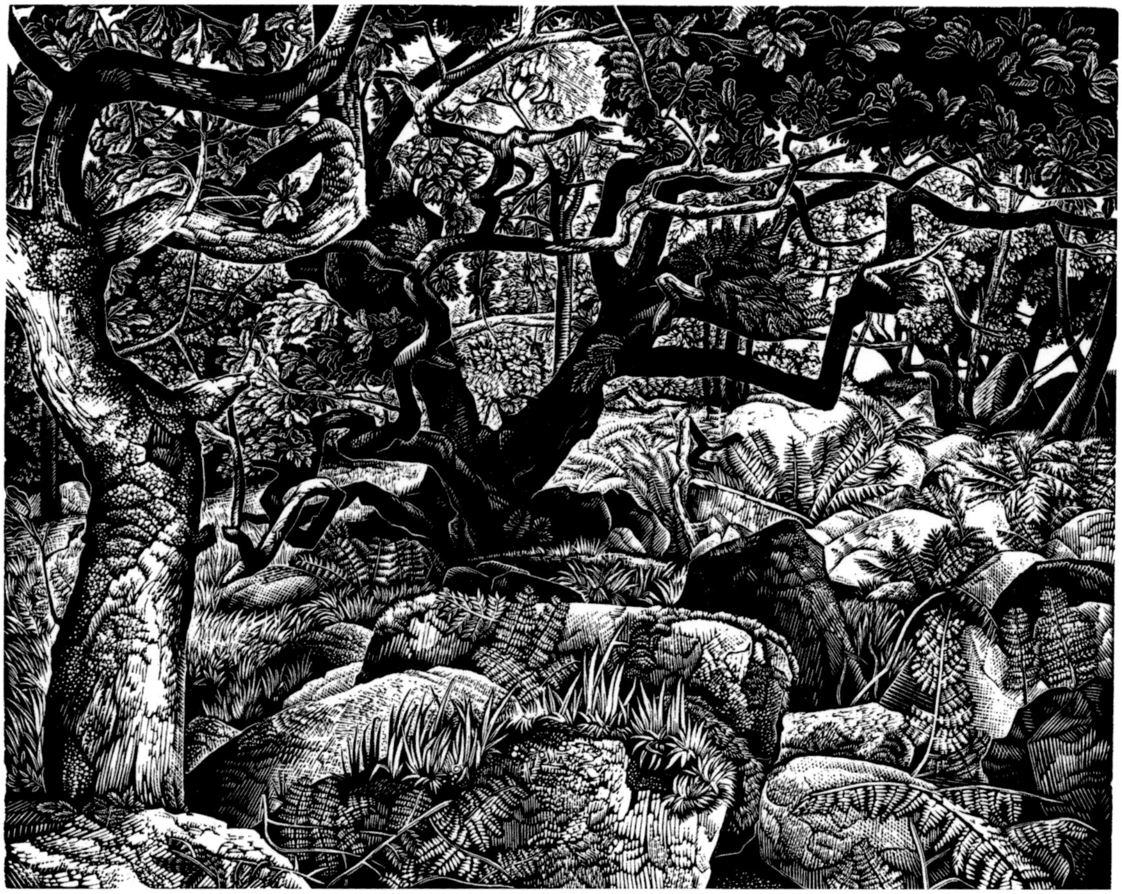

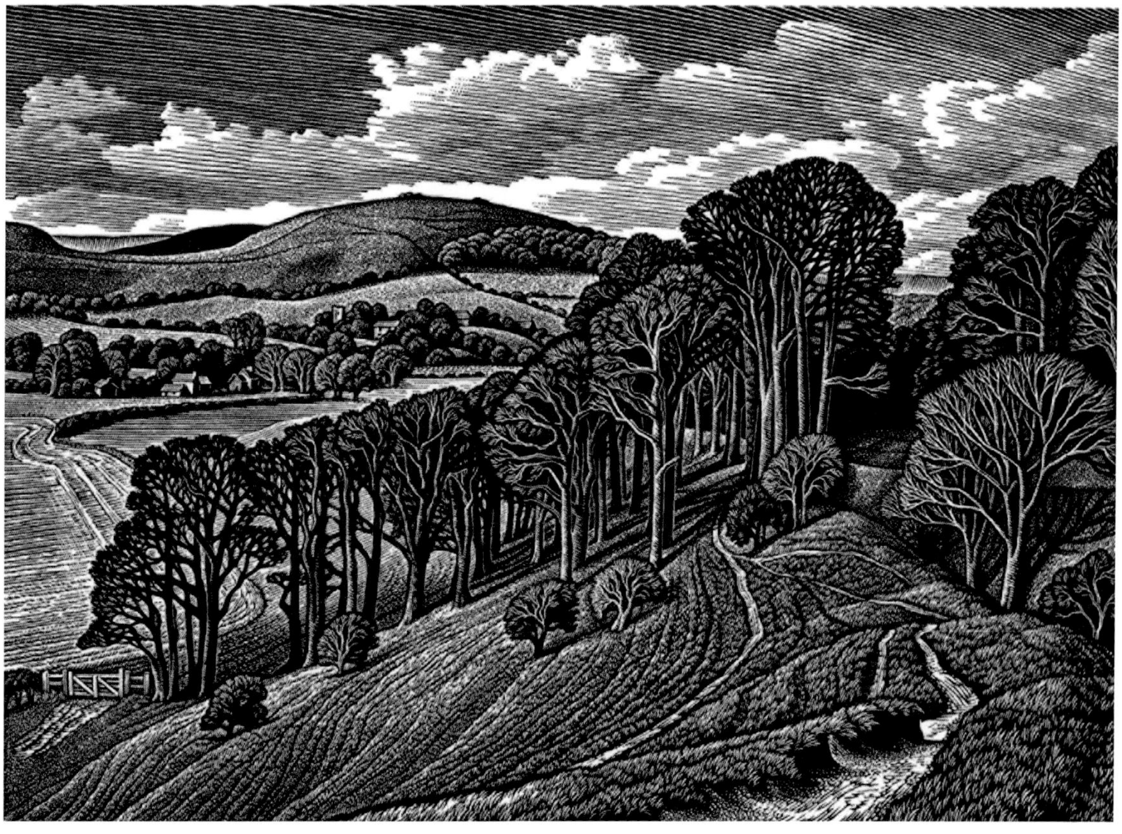

Alan Rankle

I began to have an interest in landscape art and depicting trees, after seeing paintings by Jacob van Ruisdael and Salvatore Rosa at the National Gallery, as a student. The landscape paintings of the seventeenth century appeared to represent 'the art at the beginning of modern times', when the influence of religion in Europe began to wane. An existential enquiry into our relationship to the natural world became the crucial subject of art, and when the spiritual aspect of the presence of nature again took precedence. The link between these ideas and their affinity with early pagan myths and folklore (often focused on trees and the culture of the woodland grove) became increasingly an area for artistic study in the Baroque period, particularly at the beginning of the Industrial Revolution with the rise of Romanticism as a painting movement. In my work, the relationship between painting Romantic landscapes and the landscape paintings of the Far East became a stylistic influence. Drawing and painting trees is crucial to understanding the ideas of conceptual artists such as Joseph Beuys, where landscape art embodies the spirit of nature. As Alighiero e Boetti said: art for the collective psyche of nature.

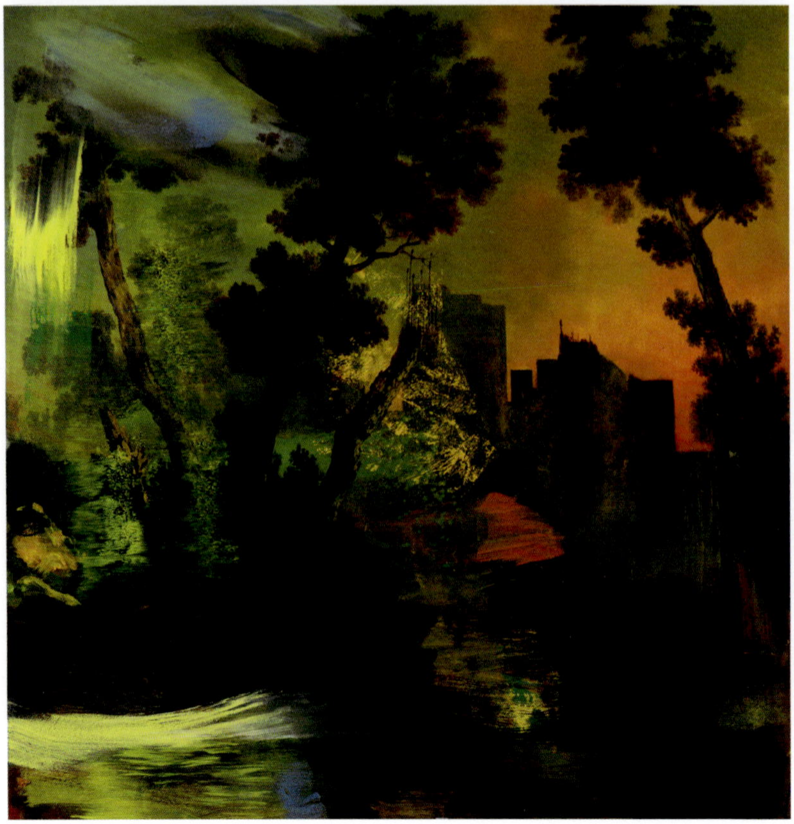

OPPOSITE *Untitled Painting XXVI (Bodiam)*, 2018

BELOW LEFT *Fairlight from the Watermeadows V*, 2018
BELOW RIGHT *Fairlight from the Watermeadows IV (Goya)*, 2018

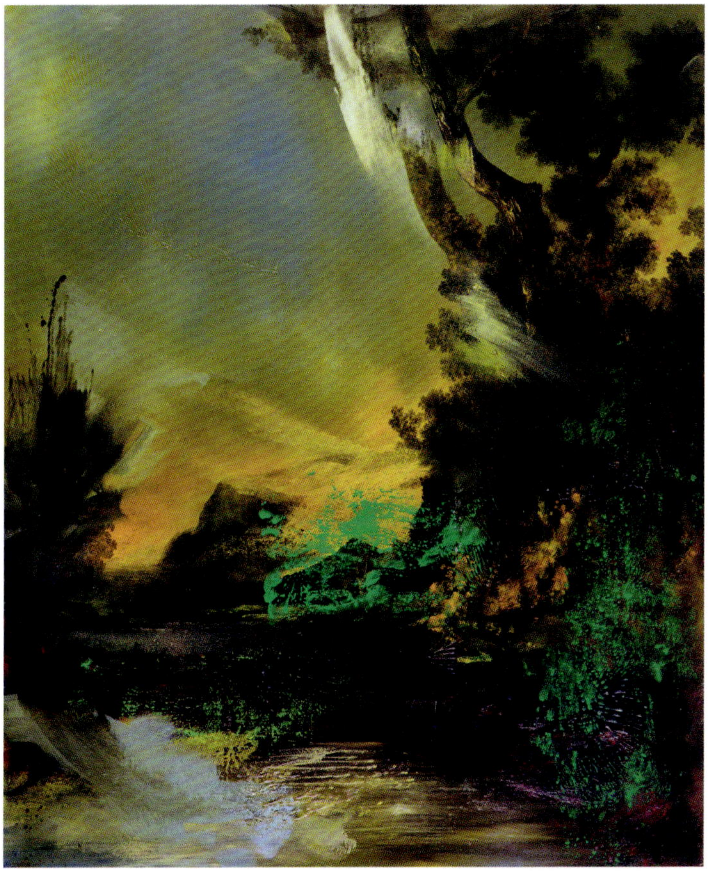

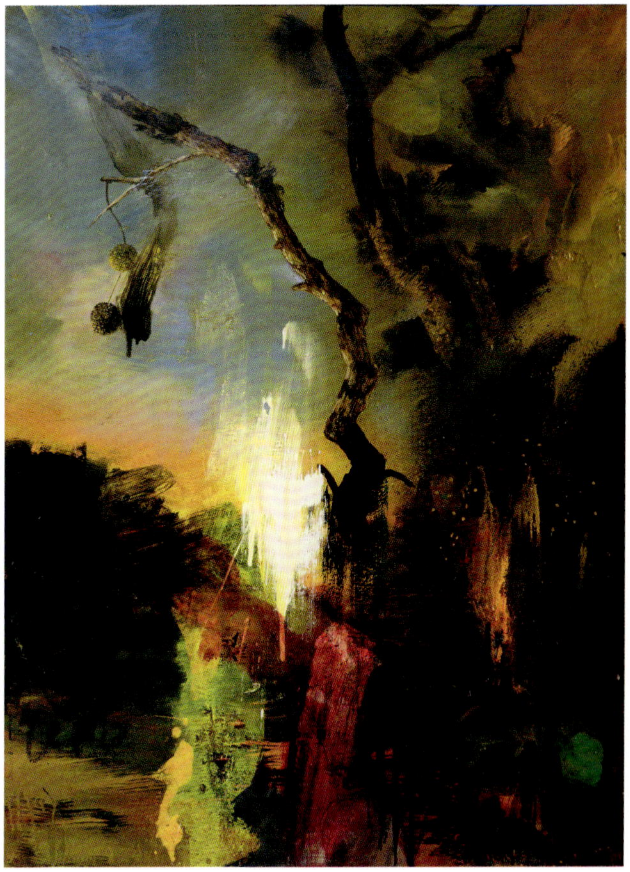

RIGHT *Study for Edge of Arcadia*, 2016/21
BELOW *Untitled Painting XXVII (Montsegur)*, 2020

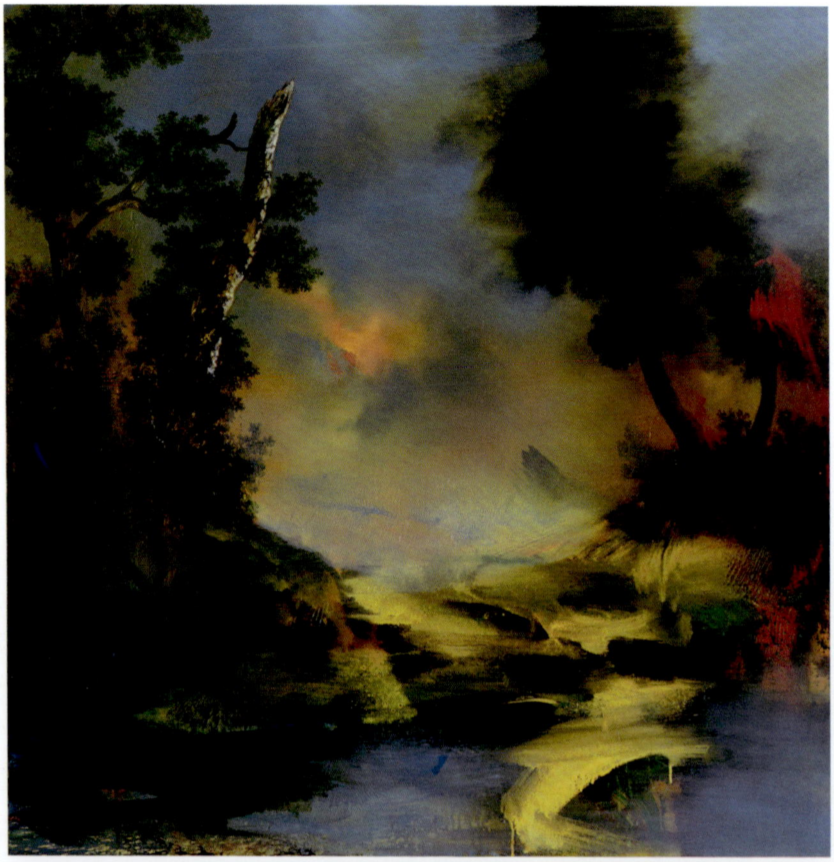

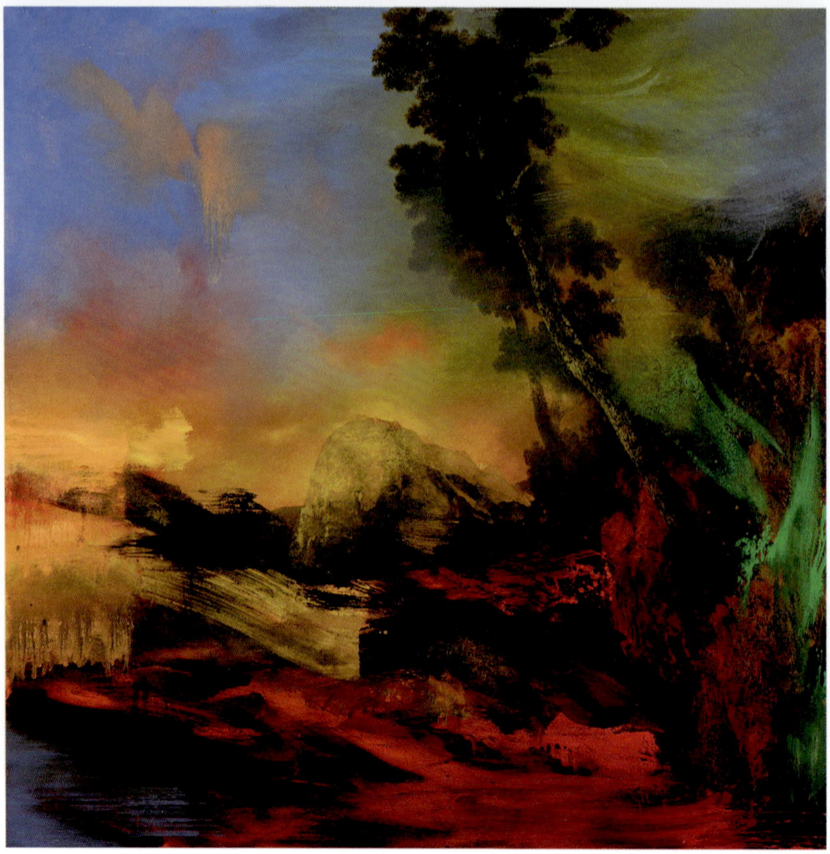

Angela Rumble

When I studied at art school in the 1990s, it was expected that all artwork would be about 'issues'. I spent years bogged down in theory and working from old medical photographs. The results were frequently, and intentionally, unsettling. As time went on, I discovered that these feelings could be engendered in work that gradually excluded the medical material and the issues that arose and, ultimately, any trace of the human. What always remained were the trees. I now find that trees have all the qualities that I look for in a subject. There is layering, light and shadow, linearity and texture. I work in oils and print, sometimes in combination and using a limited, often unnatural, colour palette. They can give atmosphere, unsettling or calming, by turn. Trees enable me to go far into abstraction without losing them as recognisable objects, to evoke feelings without any visual trace of the human. The Arborealist projects have taken me to previously unfamiliar sites around England. Working from sketches and photographs, fragments are broken down into more abstract elements that are worked to give obsessive, and often confusing, detail but with the individual character of the specific area filtering through.

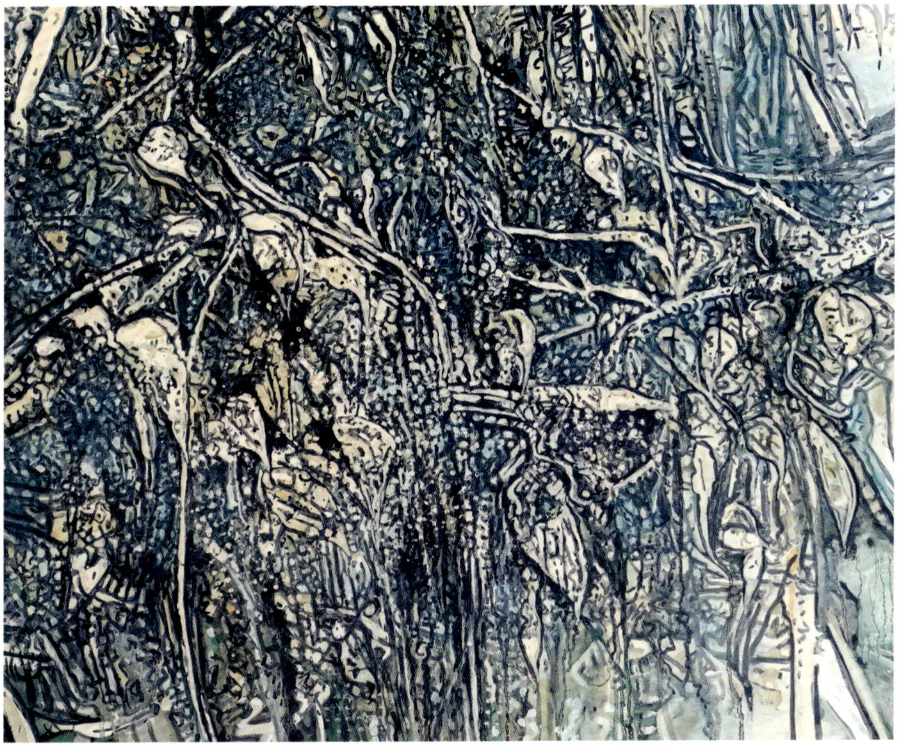

LEFT *Reflections 2*, 2023

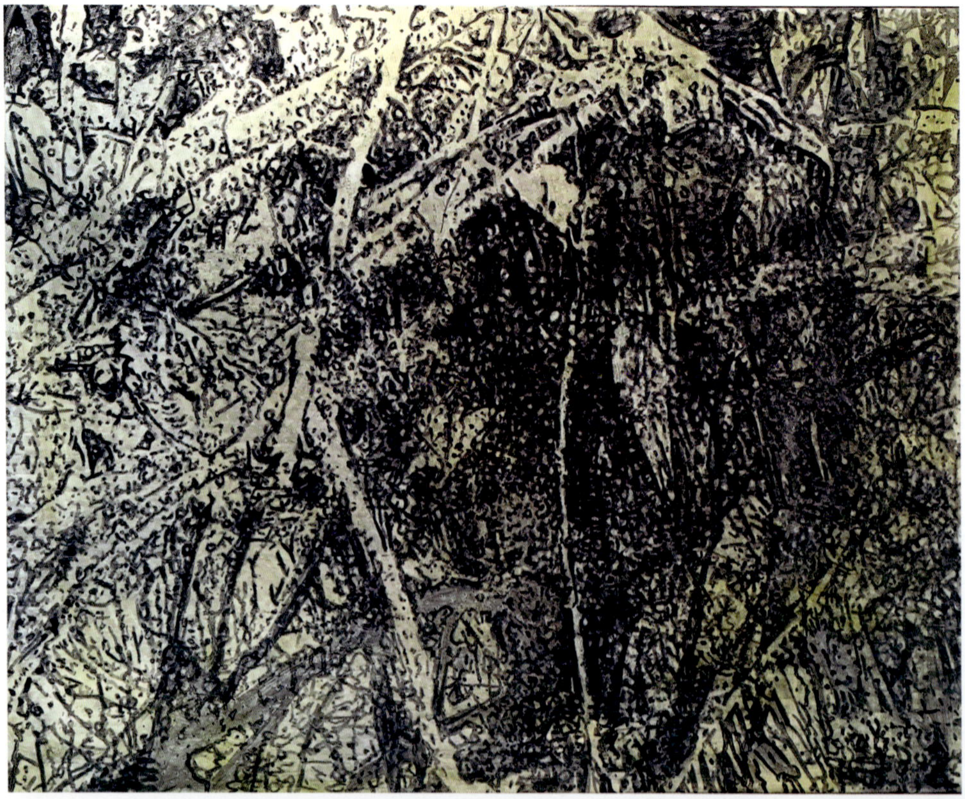

LEFT *Reflections 1*, 2023
BELOW *Reflections 3*, 2023

OPPOSITE ABOVE *Exmoor*, 2022
OPPOSITE BELOW *Blue Yew*, 2020

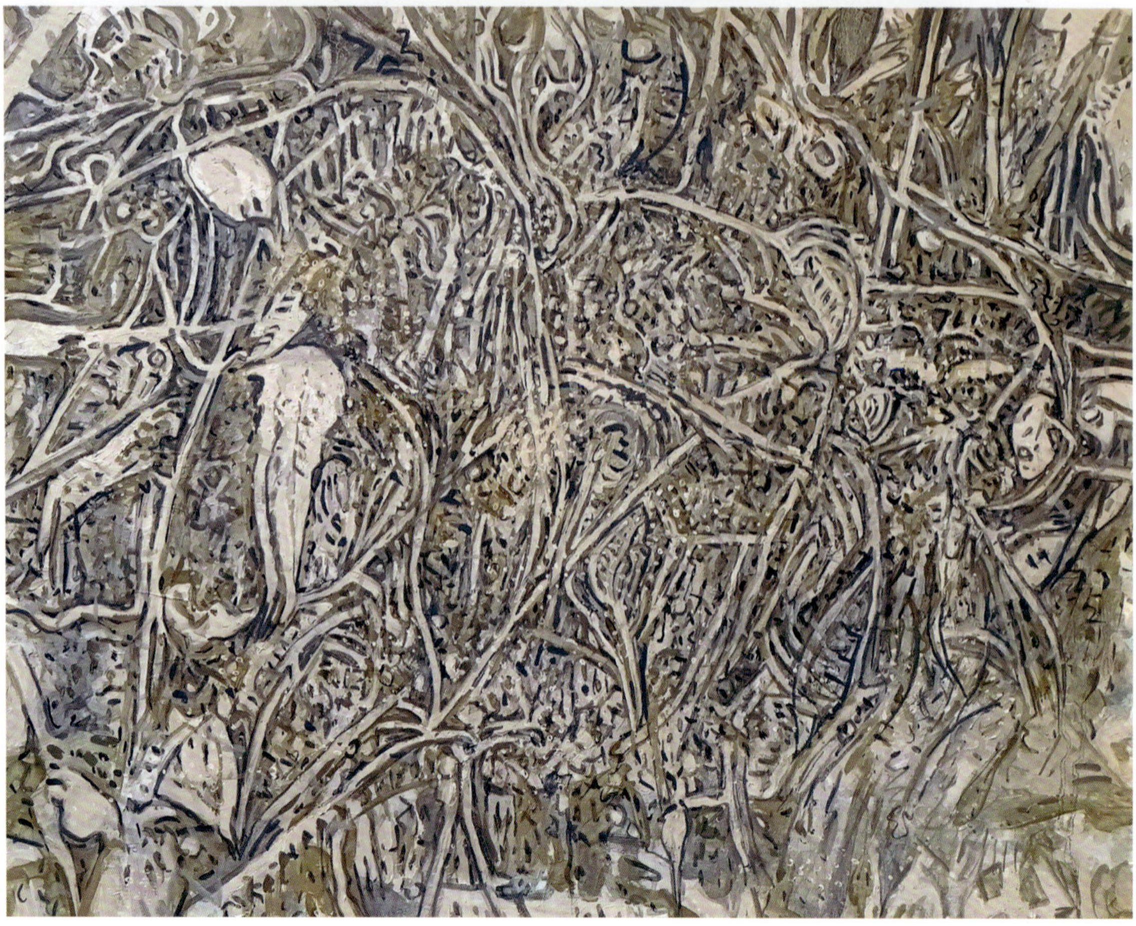

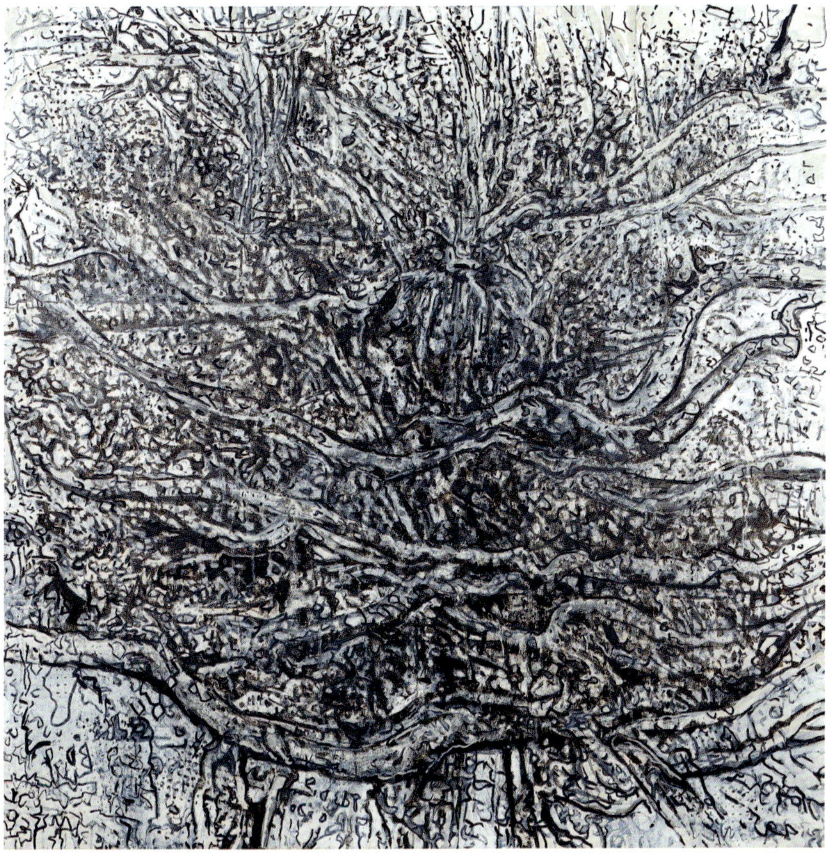

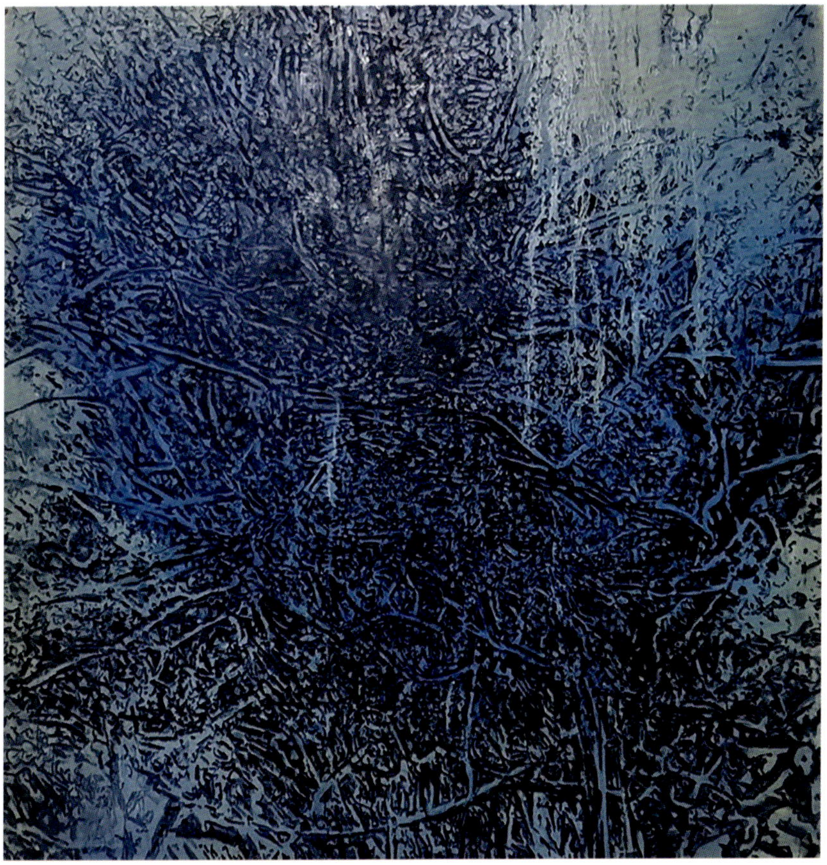

Celia de Serra

I draw in charcoal and pencil, primarily landscapes featuring woodlands, hillsides, waterways and scrubs. Some are forgotten places, others are well-known beauty spots, and some I reinvent from accumulated ideas. My work is very involved and takes a long time to resolve in the studio. Although I spend about half of my working time exploring, sketching and photographing, I revisit places again and again, to get a proper sense of them – looking for compositions with 'something about them'. Trees are the central characters in the search for beauty in our landscapes, whether they stand defiantly alone or are gathered in groups. For me, woodlands are crammed full of visual ideas; they are dynamic spaces broken by chaotic forms, shifting light, a curious sense of stillness and movement, and space and enclosure. When I come across a piece of woodland, place or tree that has that 'something' about it, I draw it to get to know it intimately. It becomes something else for me: a personal experience and endeavour, and a hope that, somehow, this moment will be preserved.

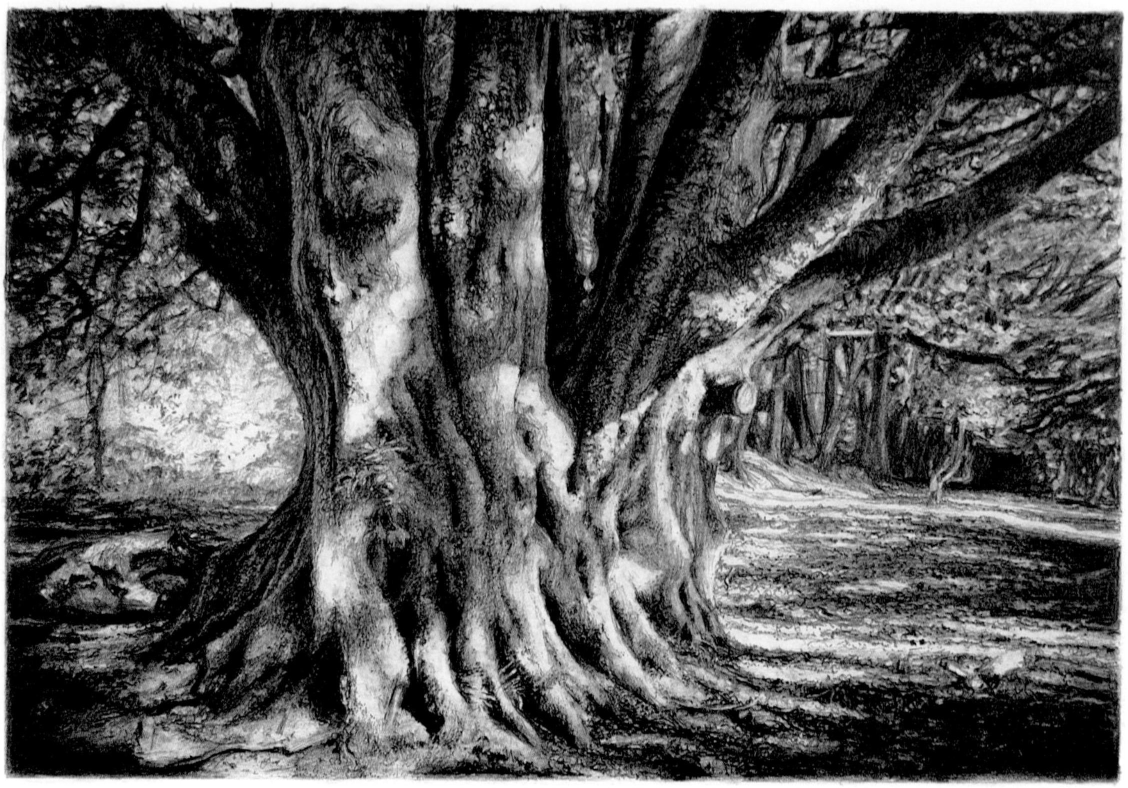

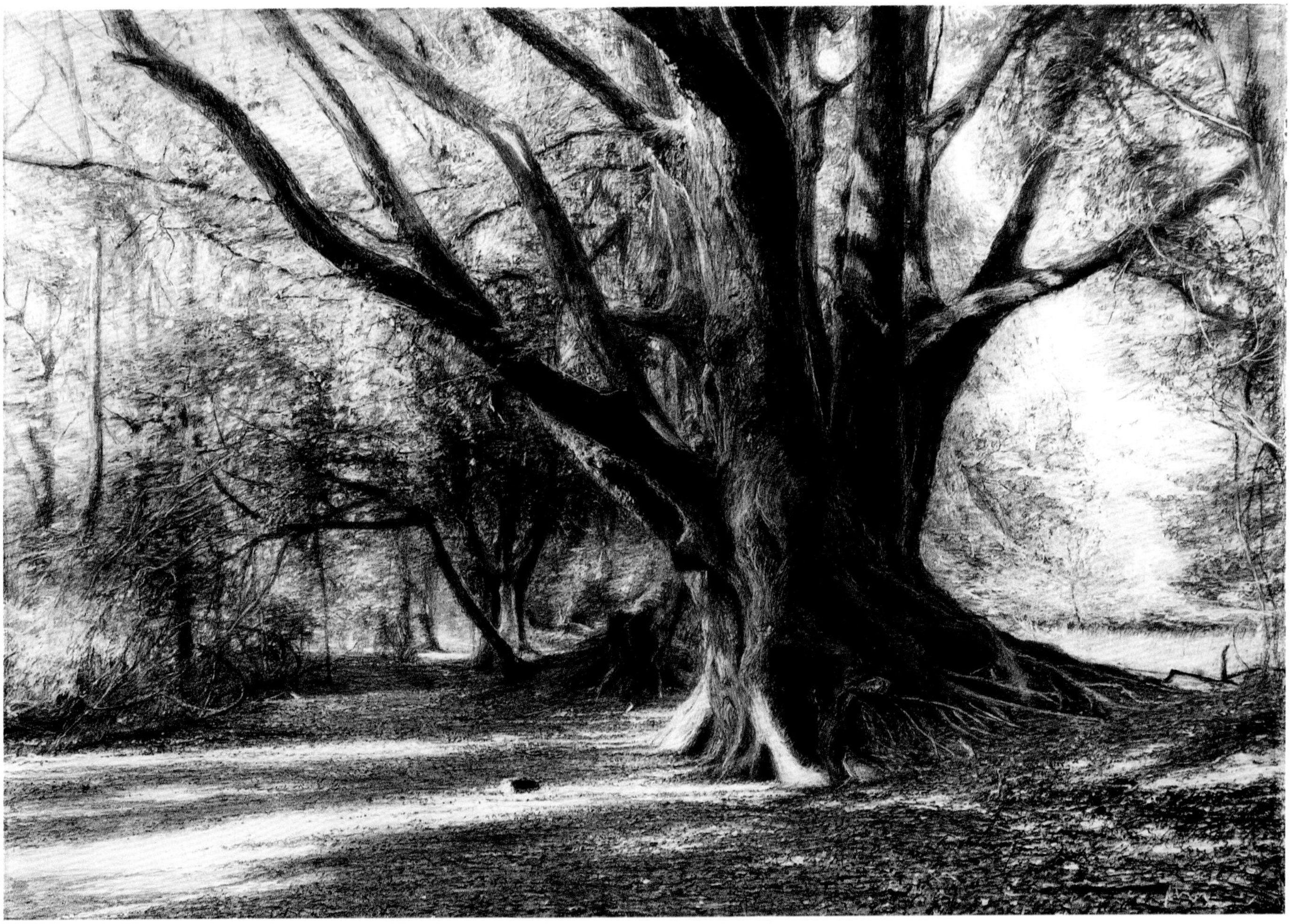

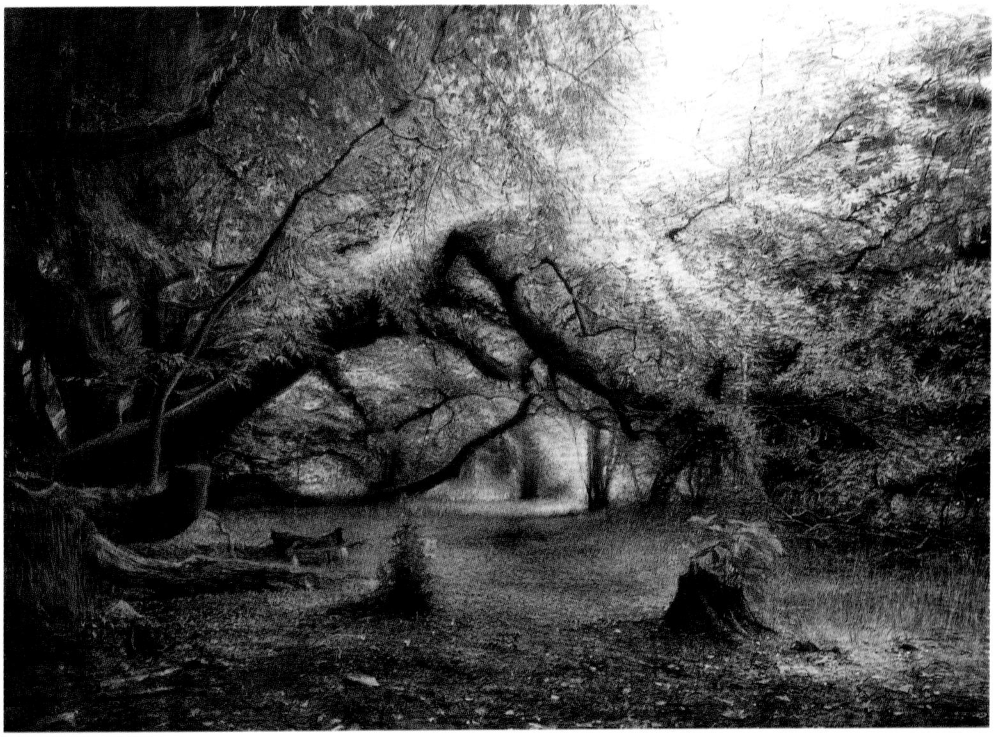

OPPOSITE *Still Here*, 2012

ABOVE *Still Here Too*, 2019
RIGHT *Towards This Place Lightly*, 2024

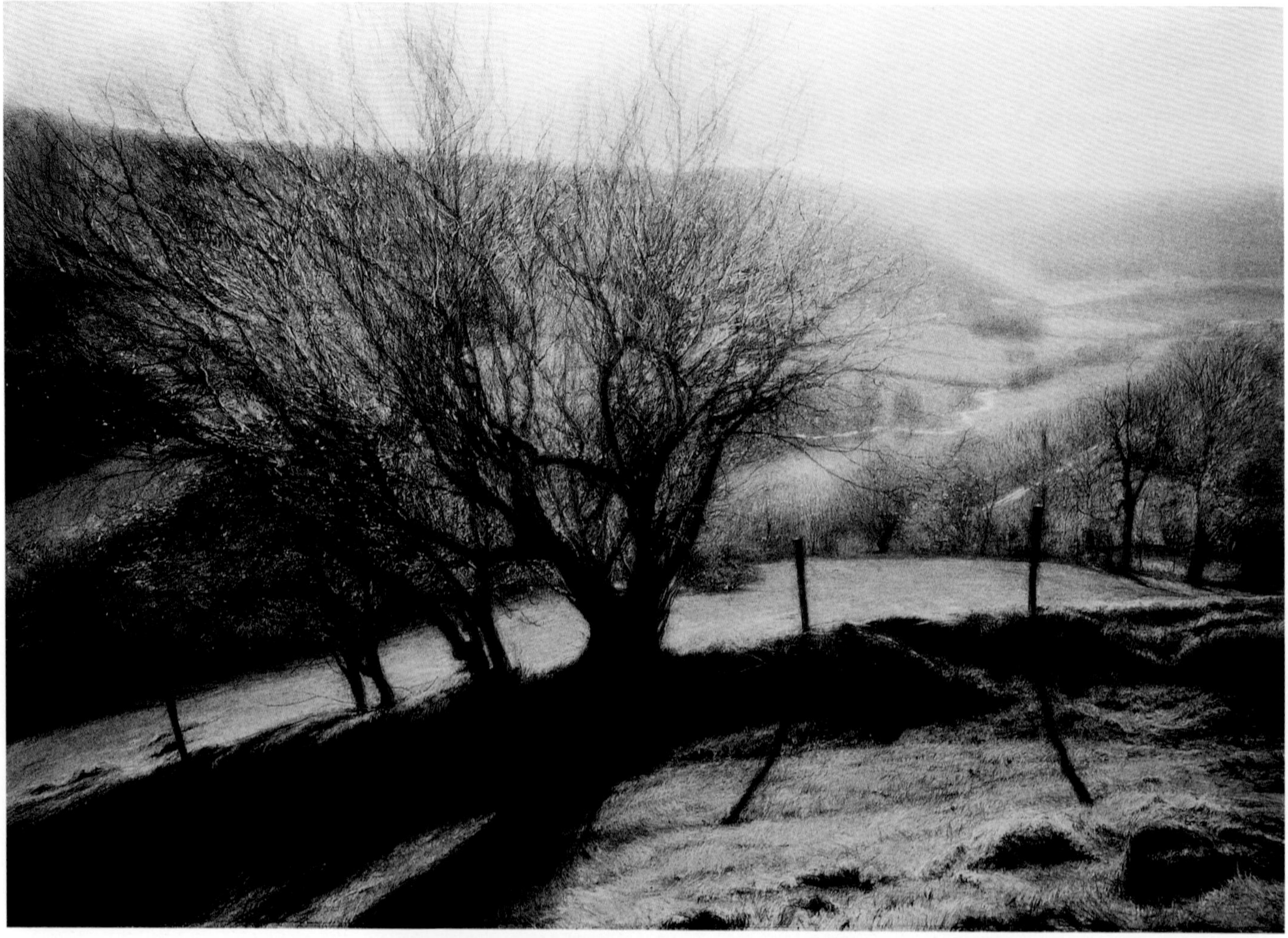

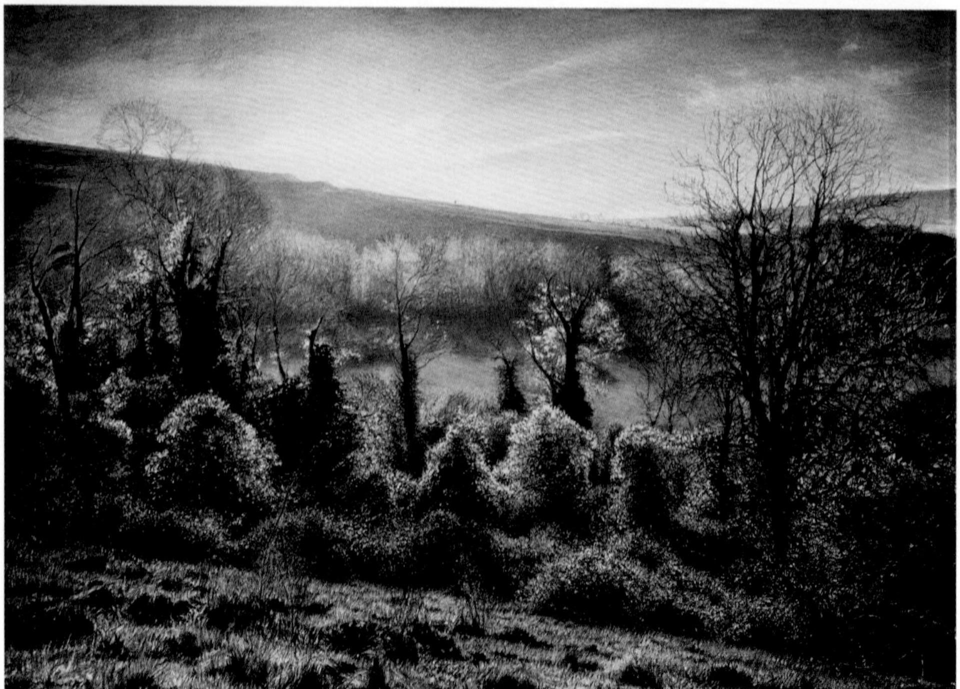

ABOVE *River Valley*, 2018
RIGHT *Fall*, 2024

Nahem Shoa

I have been drawing trees for almost 40 years, painting their portraits, spending whole summers capturing a penetrating likeness. Something about their ancient presence haunts my imagination. I am a well-known figurative painter who has created a large body of work on race and identity, which has led to many museum exhibitions; at the time of writing, my work is on display in 11 museums across England. I never paint from photos, needing the person or tree in front of me, so I can capture their inner and outer likeness in a profound way. I don't want to copy something but discover something through the act of seeing. I have developed my art over time, often making forest paintings from imagination inspired by the studies of people and trees. Right now, millions of trees are burning in forest fires, causing diseases, killing off ancient oaks and olives. Our relationship with nature is fragile. I am making paintings that highlight this, and address global issues about climate-change, nevertheless always attempting to find the poetry I see in every tree. I want to push the possibilities of art, through new areas of painting. Trees are my symbiotic vessel for exploring these aims and ideas. Rembrandt said 'My art is guided by one rule, and that is nature', and I have followed his advice.

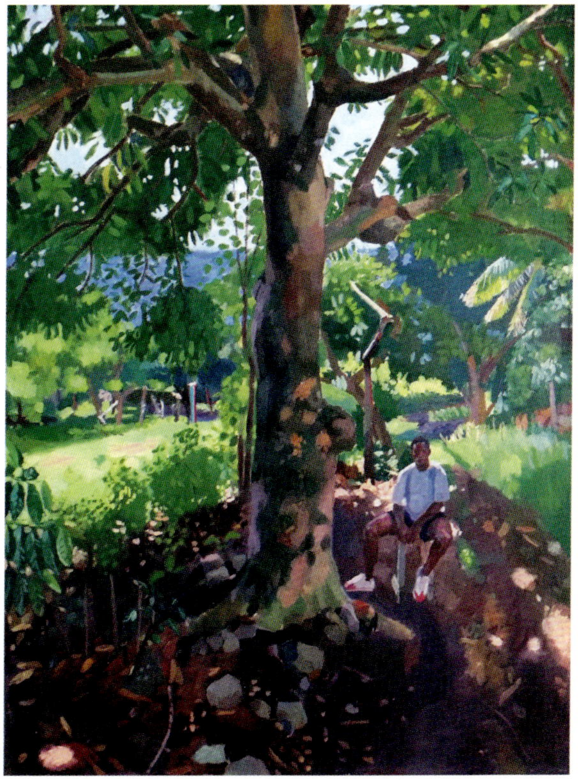

LEFT *Scotts Head, Dominica with Antoine*, 1999

BELOW LEFT *Ancient Olive*, 2019
BELOW RIGHT *Holland Park Oak*, 2018
BOTTOM *New From Nowhere*, 2020

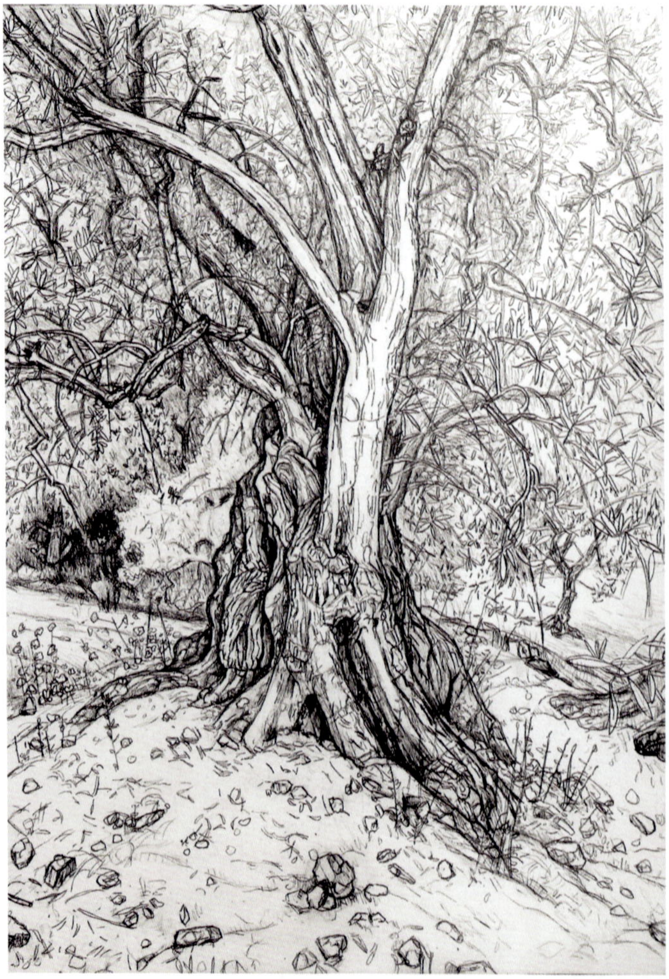

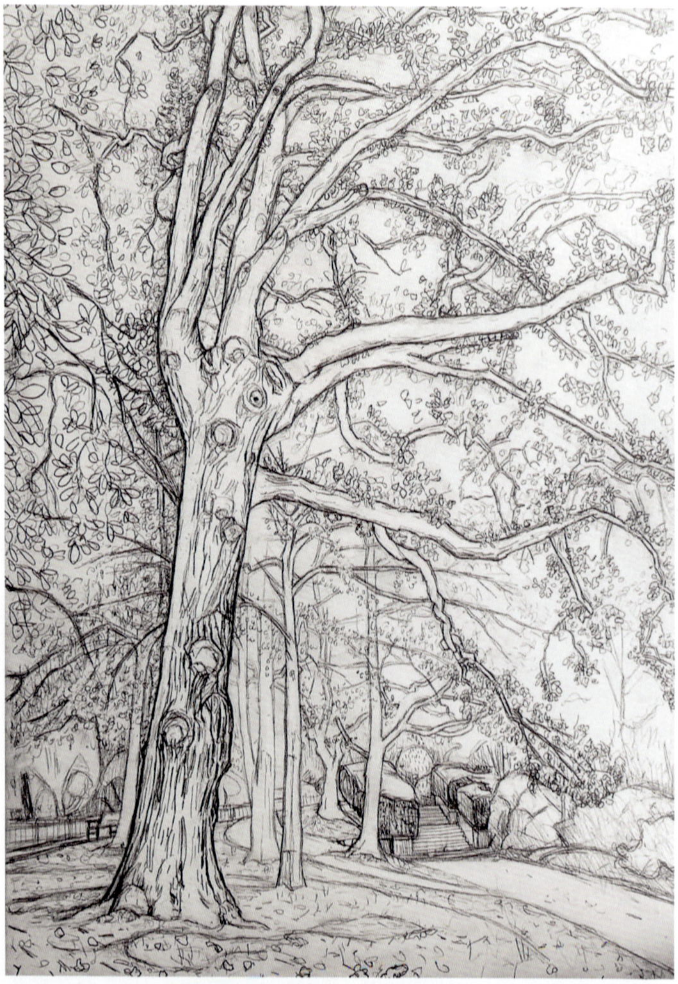

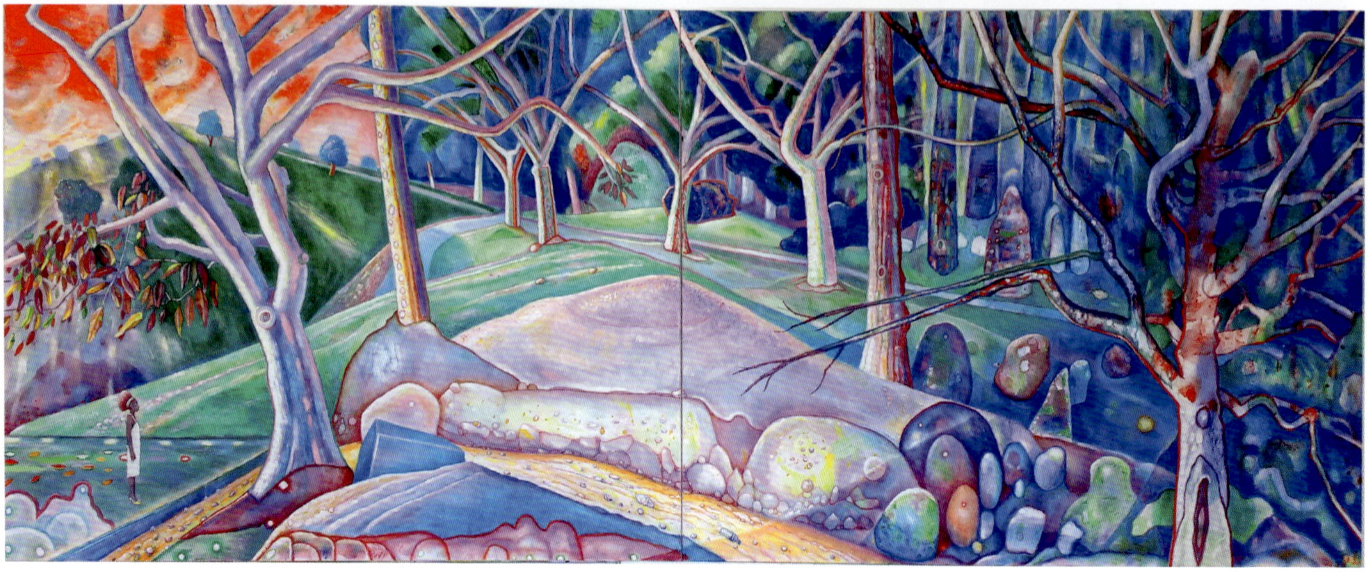

RIGHT *Seen And Unseen*, 2023

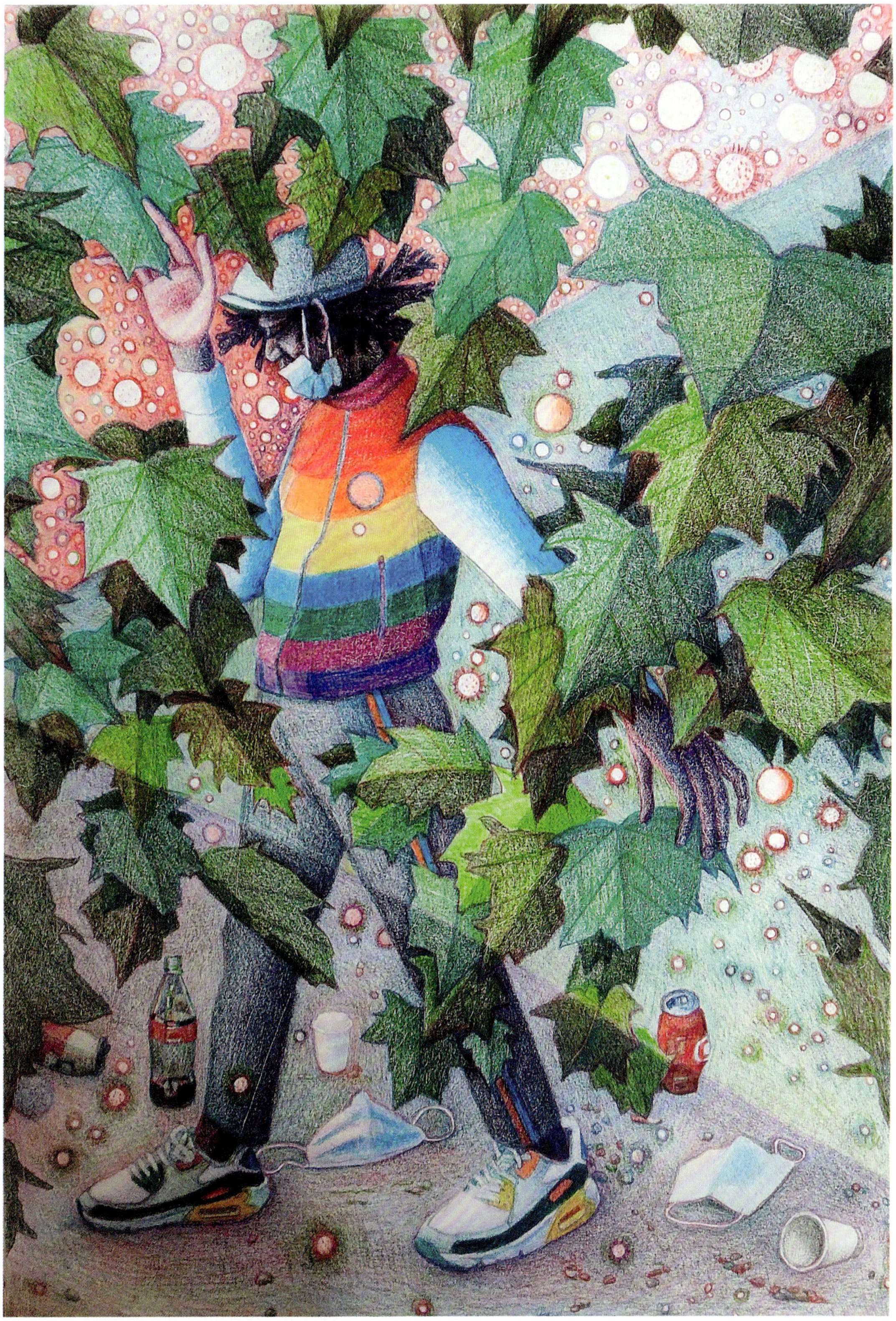

Kevin Tole

I have painted and drawn for as long as I've known. As a Directional Driller, my career has taken me around the world, living and working in many places. I returned to Plymouth to retire when made redundant. Redundancy made me concentrate on my art.

My painting is quite different from my drawing; however, seeing the work together shows the connections between the two. I'm not fond of rules. My work on trees has been primarily focused on large charcoal drawings, often handmade charcoal from the subject tree. I rarely work smaller than A1, because I want the feeling of drawing from the shoulder, not the fingers. A good drawing, like a good book, has to take you beyond the immediate expression into some contemplation, beyond the text or graphics. I am totally uninterested in the romantic view of trees and landscapes, though the images I end up with may capture (hopefully) some essence of beauty – or ugliness, or destruction, or death – whatever has drawn me to the subject. Thus, selecting a subject is as important as the drawing itself.

In recent work, I have used different materials and considered erasure as crucial as the mark. This is taking me away from the technical aspects of drawing, to a different realm where I feel the work has been leading for some time – towards what I like to call 'graphic painting'. The concept is as important as the image.

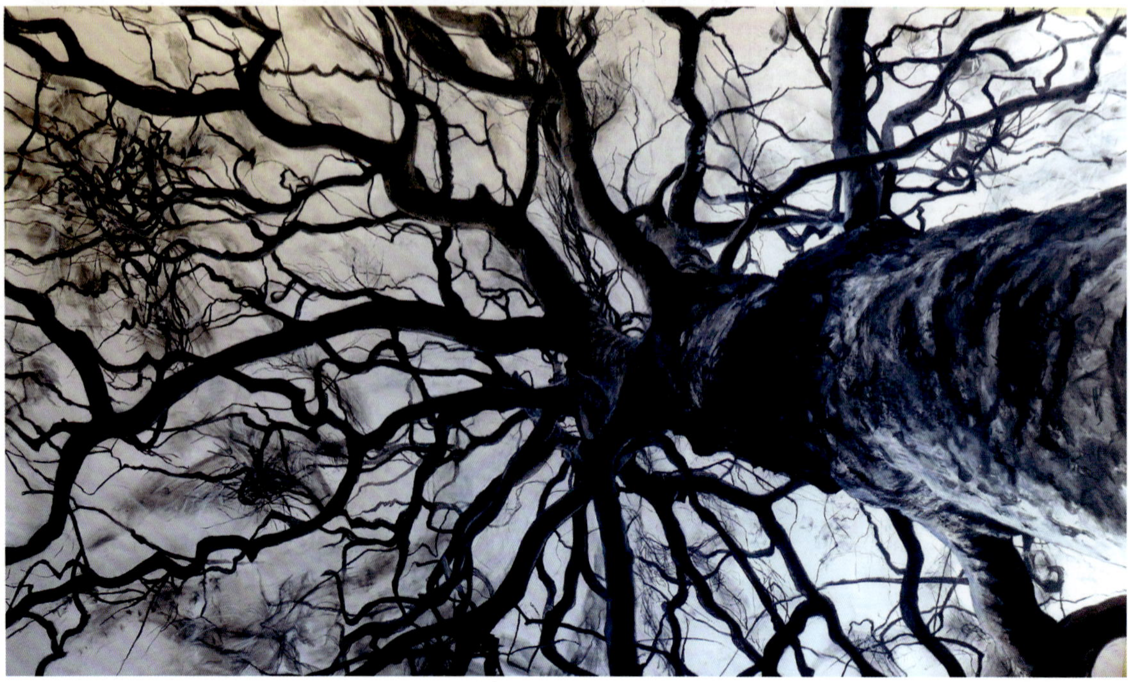

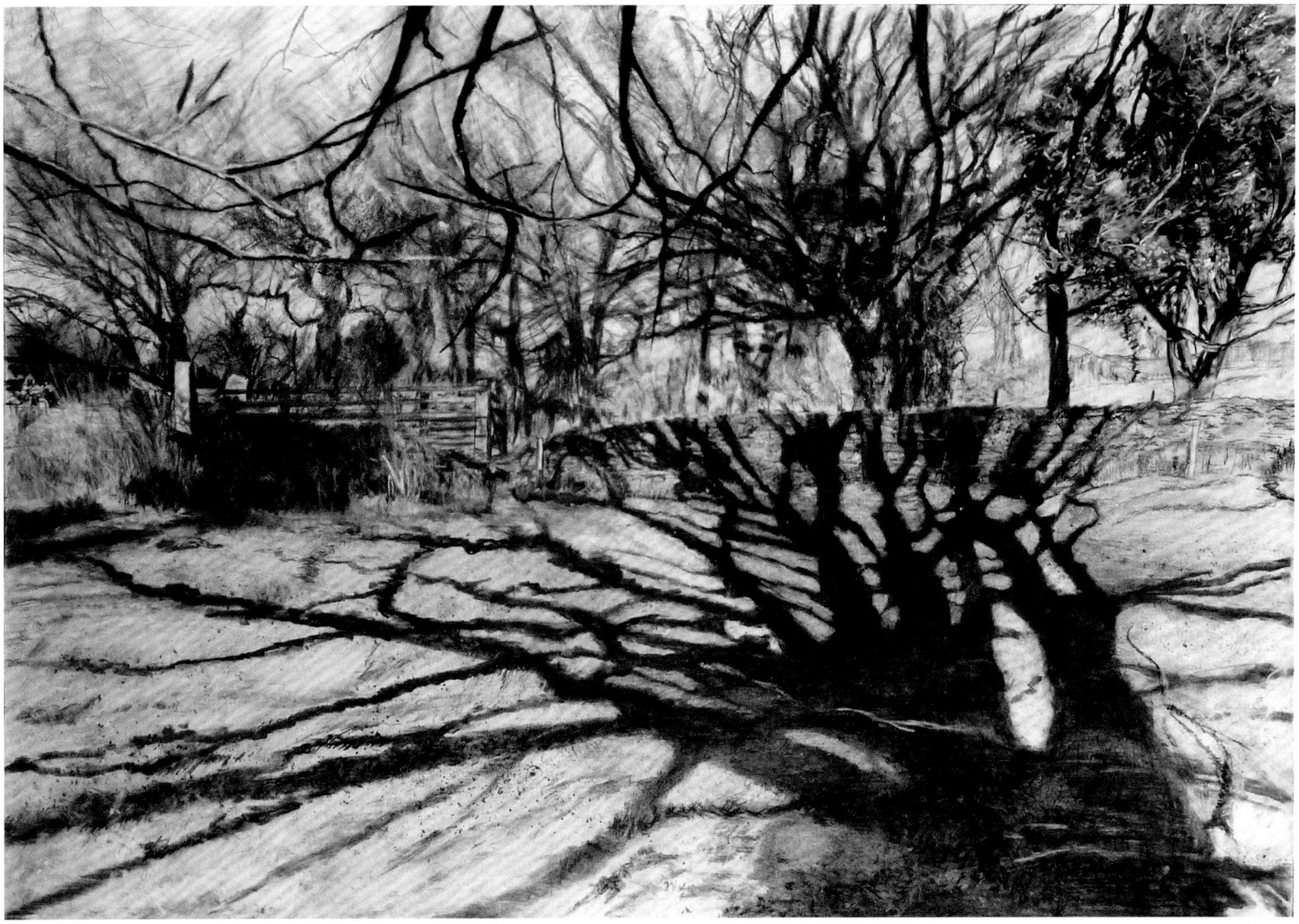

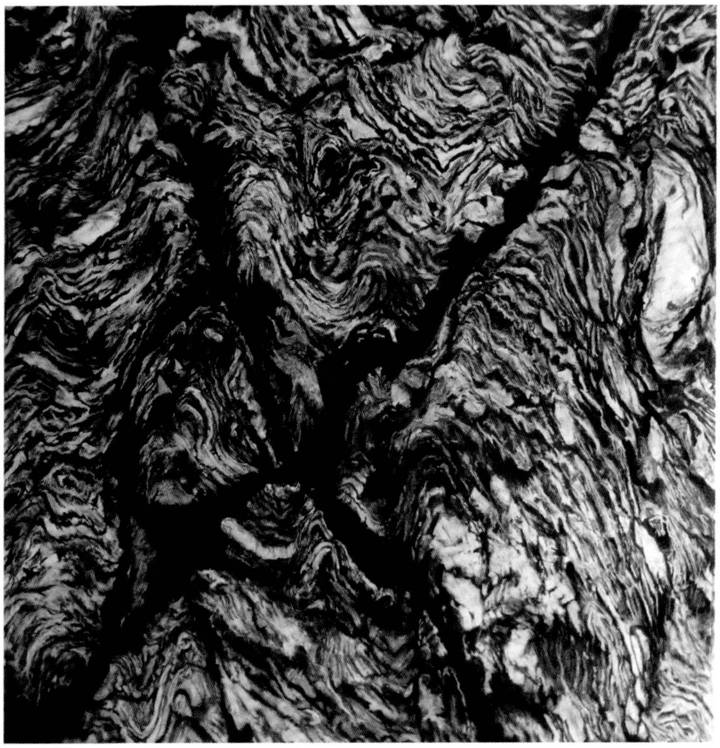

OPPOSITE *Antony Plane in Winter – The Kraken*

ABOVE *The Tree that's Not the Tree from the Tree*
RIGHT *The Important Difference Between Armorica and Avalonia*

Jacqueline Wedlake Hatton

Trees are frequent subjects in my work. I have long appreciated them as more than passive characteristics of the landscape; they express an acute response to the environment in which they grow. Their growth patterns are no less visible or telling than the postural habits and facial creases of any human being. My approach to both the selection and painting of a tree is similar to that of a portraitist, who seeks out an interesting face or a striking character to honour with careful attention. I approach my subjects close up and often do not reveal their entirety. In this way, the tree becomes the primary focus of the painting rather than being an adornment that punctuates an image of the wider landscape. My approach reflects the understanding that we are just part of a magnificent whole, and not separate from nature. Focusing on the intimate majesty of trees is, in its own way, paying romantic homage to that which is greater than ourselves. Still, it also turns that awe back on ourselves, for if we can recognise the majesty of nature in a tree, we can surely recognise it in ourselves.

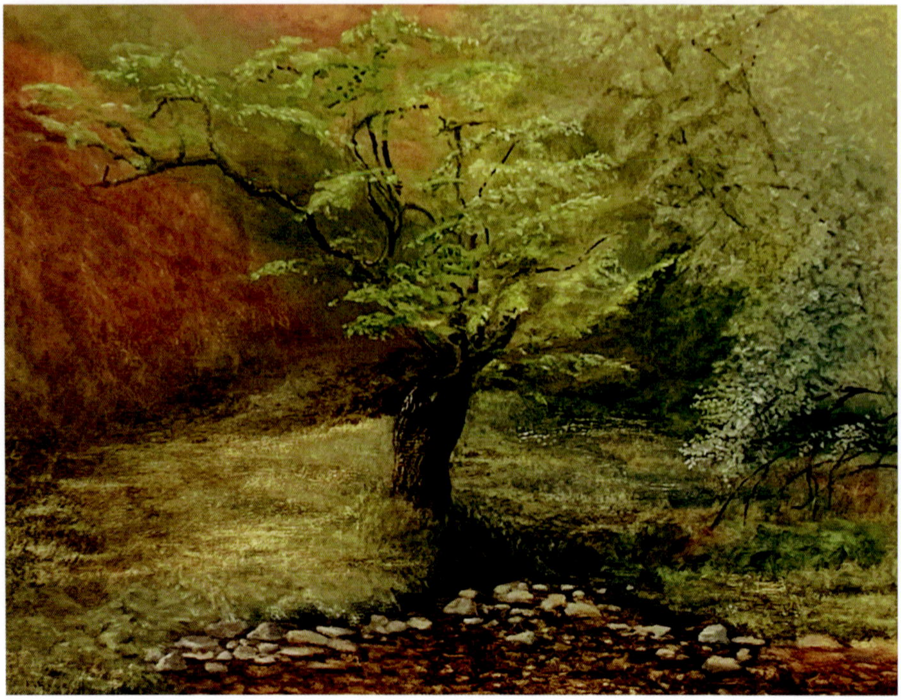

OPPOSITE *Dartmoor Oak*, 2020

LEFT *Holne Moor Oak*, 2020
BELOW *Shooting, Lady Park Wood*

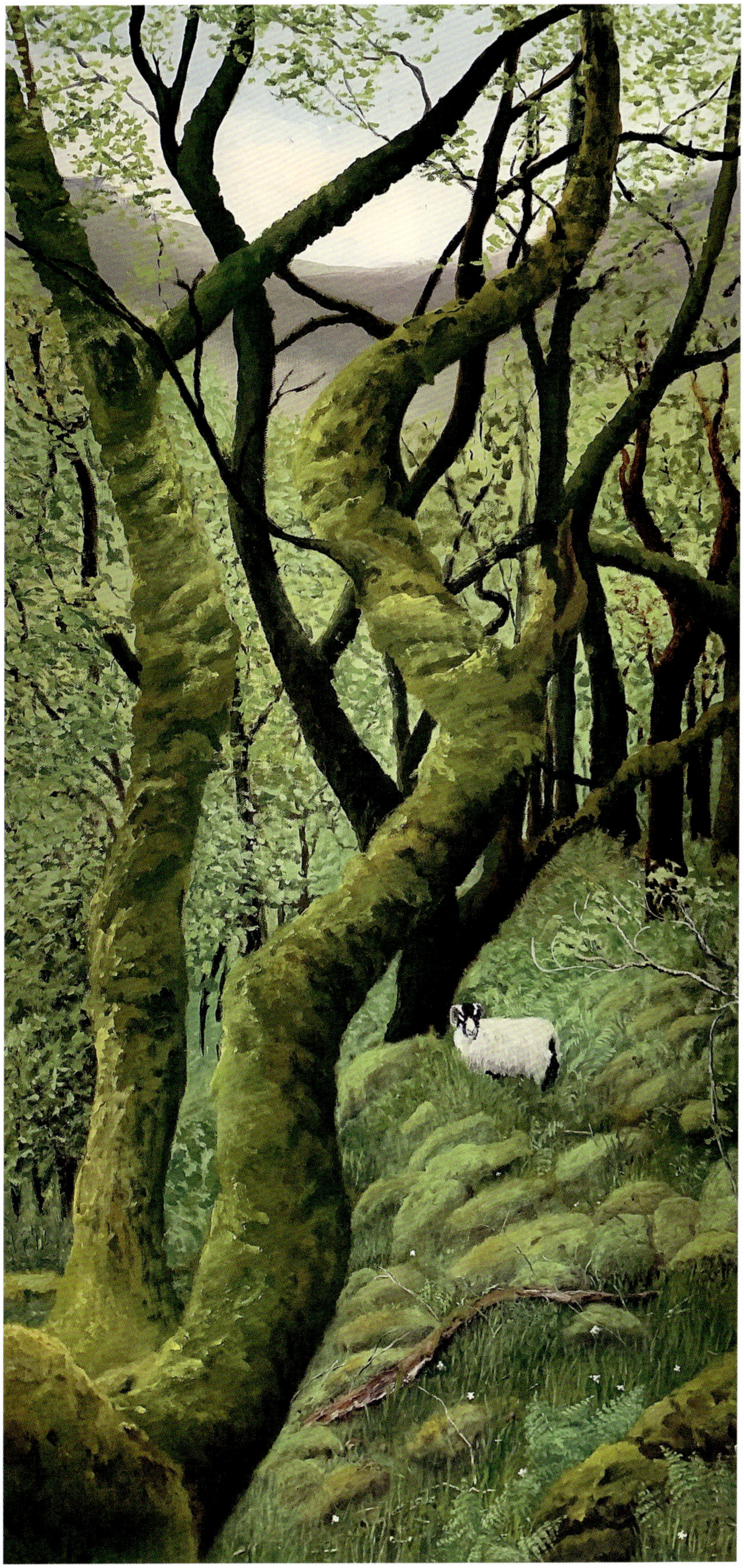

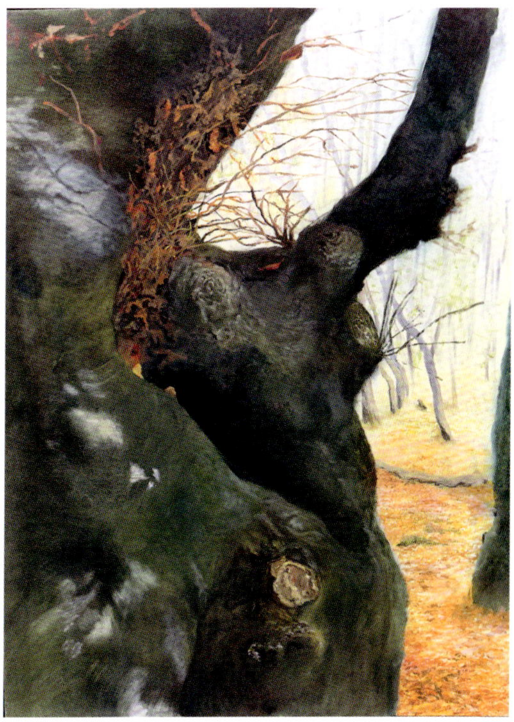

BELOW LEFT *Snake Dartmoor V*, 2017
BELOW RIGHT *Dartmoor IV*, 2016

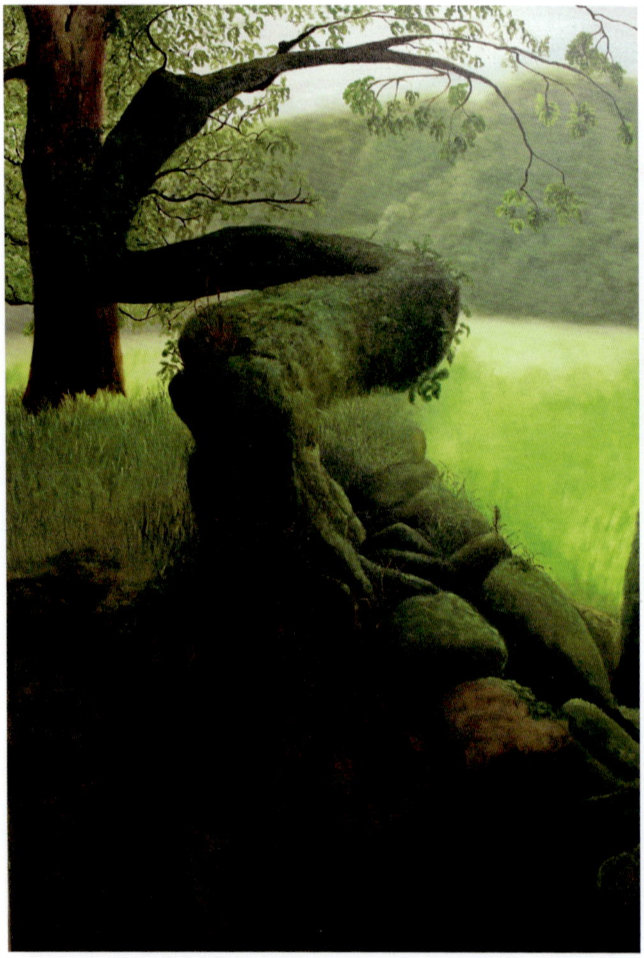

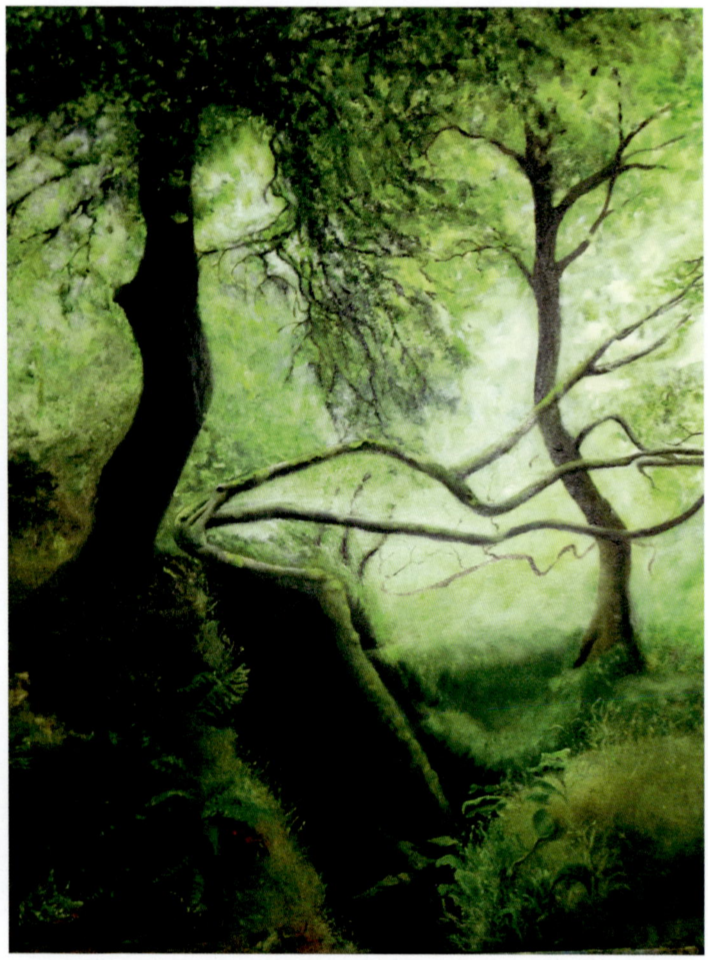

David Wiseman ARWS, LG

The canvas pieces and larger works on paper are made using acrylic in the studio, though I also work directly from the landscape using a variety of mediums. My paintings are not topographical but are inspired by particular places that are special to me. While I spend much time in Devon and the South Coast, I am equally inspired by the local tree-lined rivers and woods close to my Ealing home. My paintings are a playful, poetic response to the many contrasting elements of the landscape, such as the beautiful and complicated pattern of a tree trunk close-up, with a flash of distant light and colour. Calligraphic brush-marks, stains and shapes made with various brushes, rollers, sponges, etc. devise a landscape. The tree takes on many guises and is often used in contrast to the rivers and streams that have dominated my work. I want to instil a feeling of change and movement, as if we are passing through the landscape rather than depicting a static cut-out image. I want the paintings to be intriguing and ambiguous, held between all the wonderful qualities of paint and the celebration, illusion and evocation of the depiction of nature.

RIGHT *Rocky River Dartmoor*, 2020

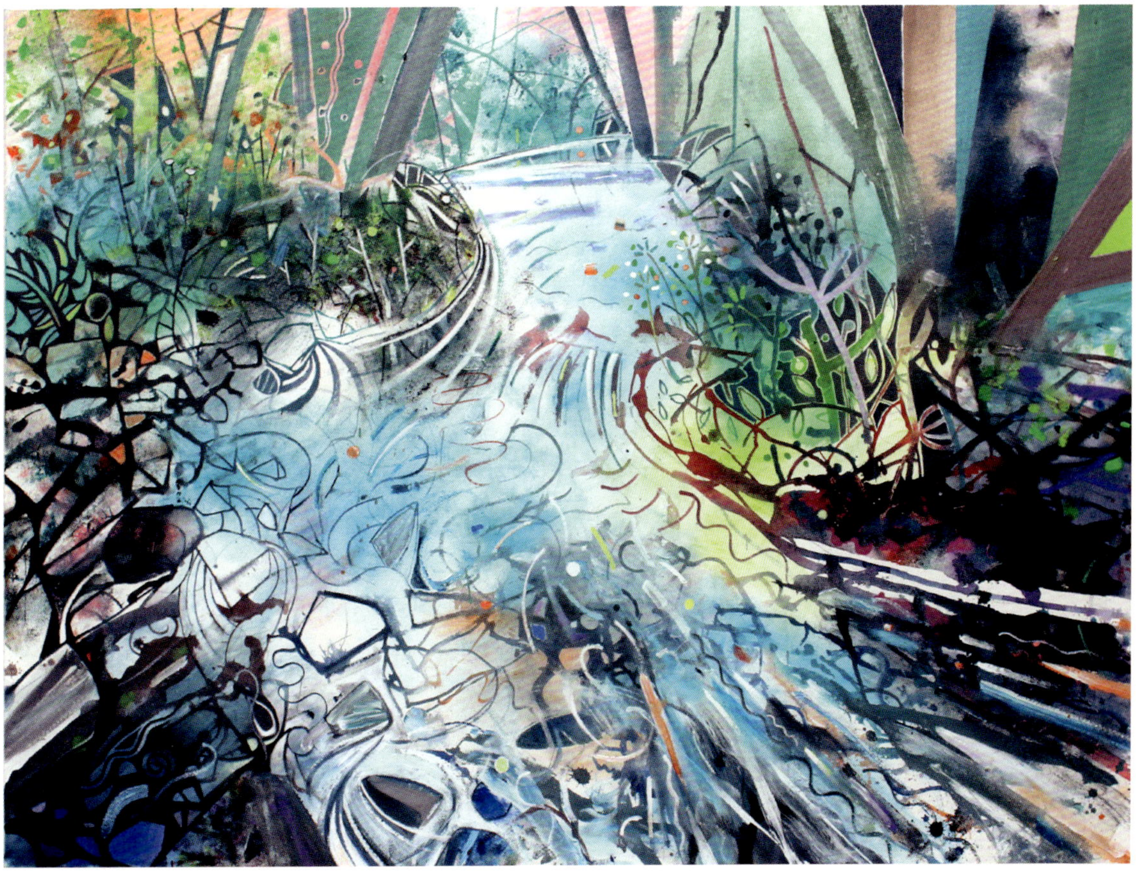

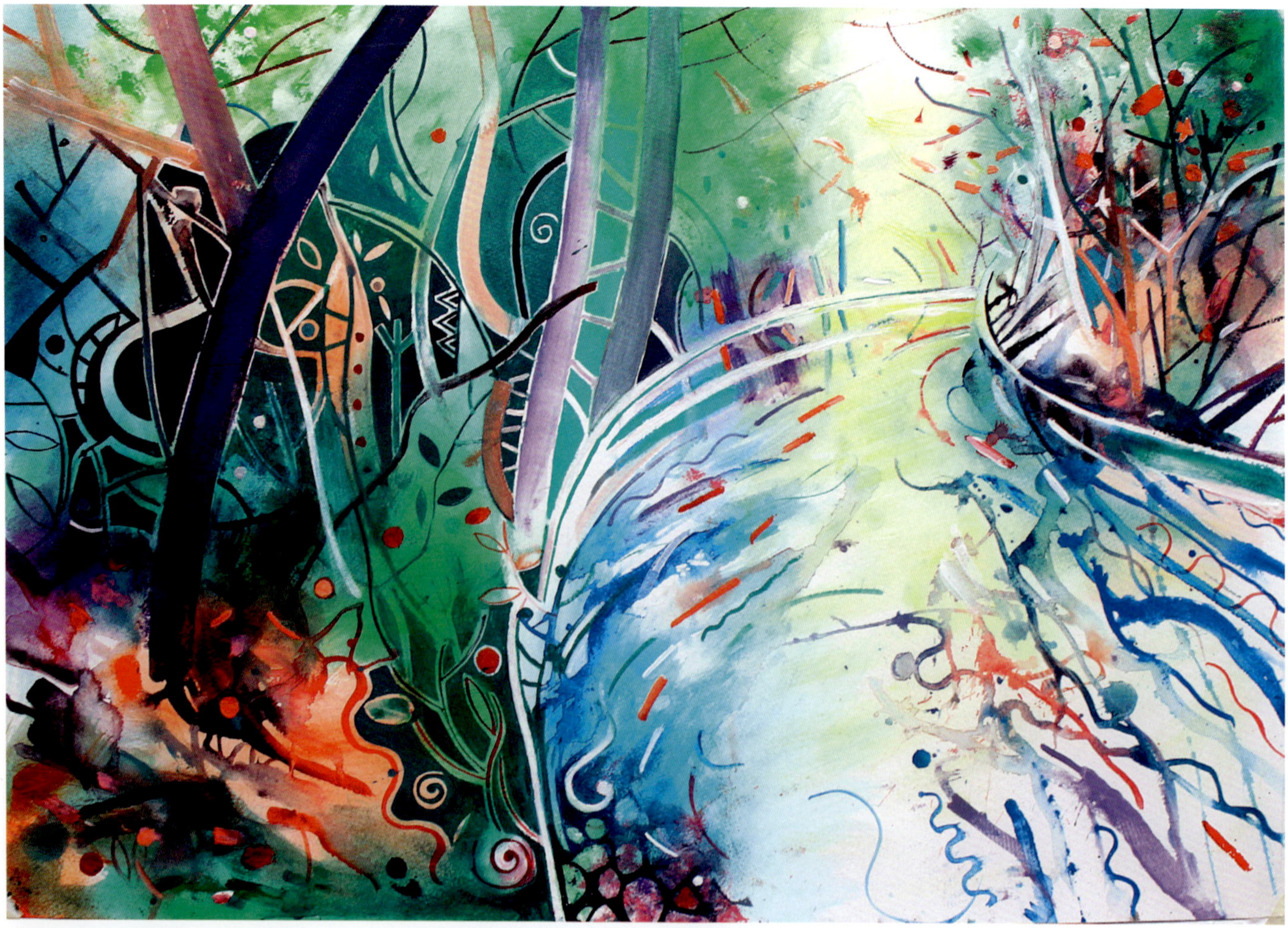

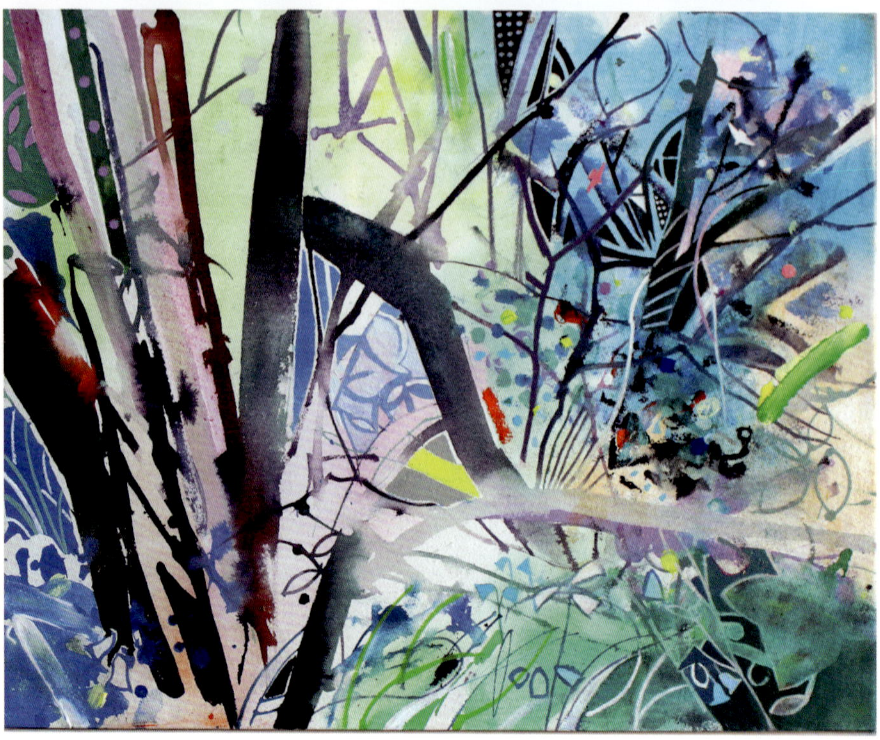

ABOVE *Tangled Bank, Autumn Light, Pitshanger Riverside*, 2023
LEFT *In the Bluebell Woods, Perivale*, 2022

OPPOSITE ABOVE *Woodland Water Brownsea Island*, 2024
OPPOSITE BELOW *River Brent, Autumn Light*, 2017

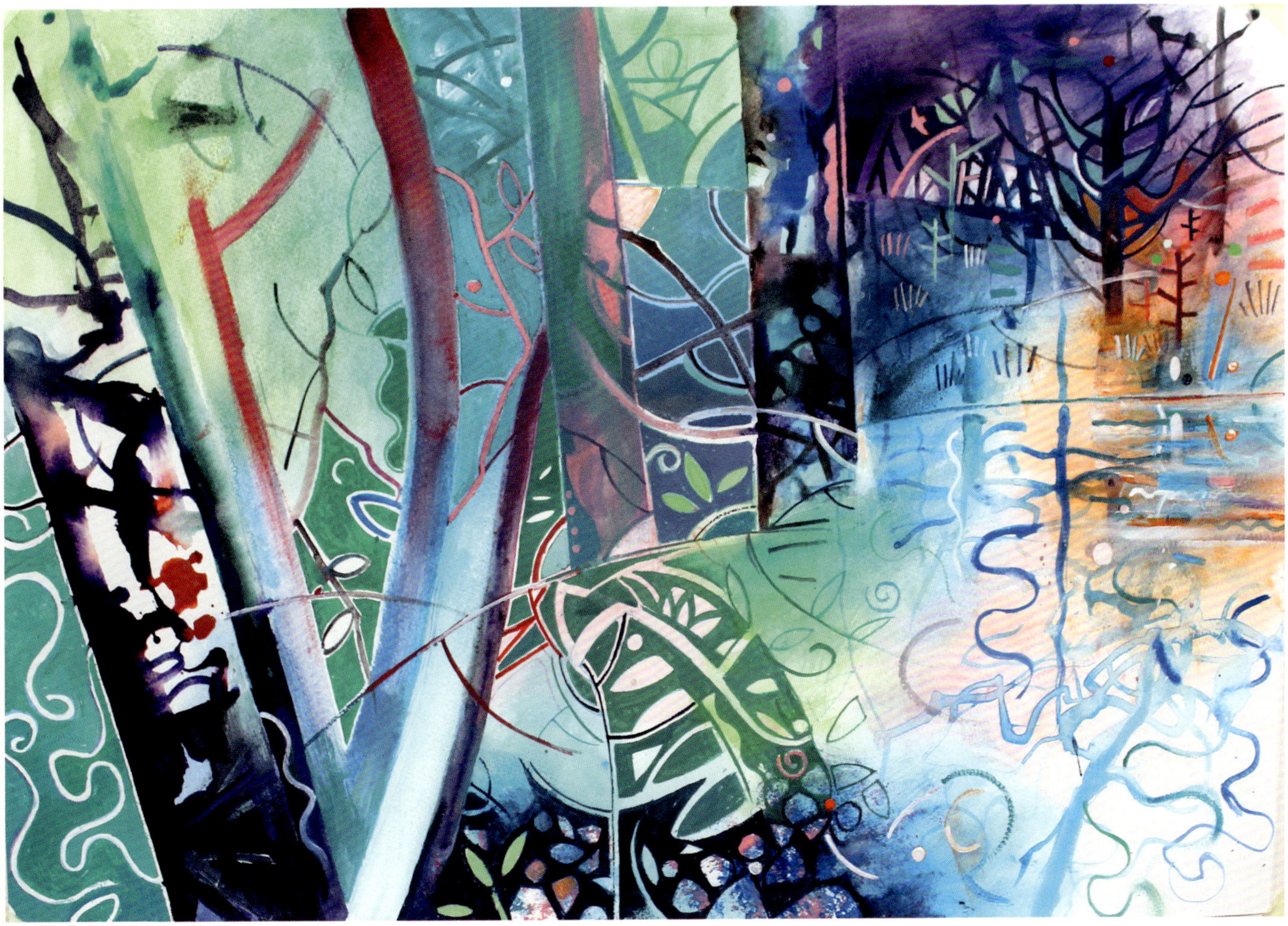

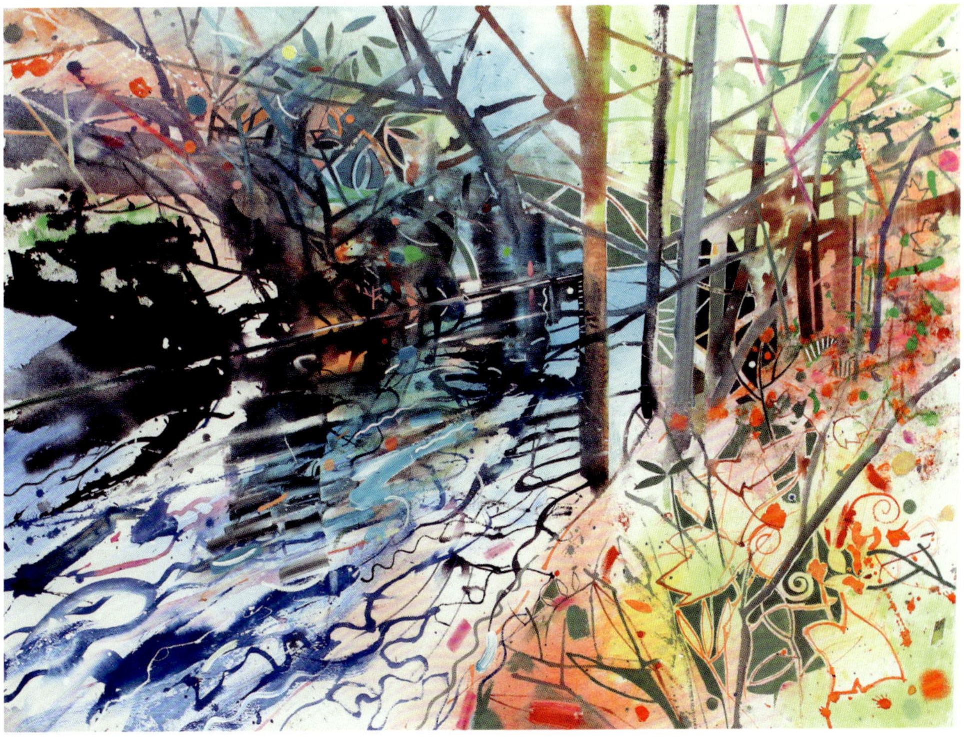

Artist biographies

Robert Amesbury Brooks
www.rabrooksfinearts.com
1964 – Born Bournemouth. Training: Slade School of Fine Art · Studied with full Scholarship under Euan Uglow, Patrick George and Norman Norris · Achieved 2:1 BA Degree in Fine Art. **1985** – Artist Award from Robert Burns Studies. Exhibited extensively across the UK and Europe, including Southampton City Art Gallery · The Euston Road Connection · Capture the Castle British Artists and the Castle from Turner to Le Brun · **2017** – Browse & Darby · **2010–2012** – The Mall Galleries London · **2015** – Landscape Annual Exhibition.

Jemma Appleby
www.jemmaappleby.com
Studied **2006/2009** – City and Guilds of London Art School · **2005/2006** – Byam Shaw School of Art. Public Collections: Royal Academy of Engineering · Macaulay Library, Babington House · Hartnett Holder & Co, Limewood · Lyndhurst and Whitley Ridge Brockenhurst. Prizes and Awards: The Academy Award at Royal West of England Academy · Shortlisted Drawing of the Year 2022, ArchiSource · Royal Society of British Artists residency award at The British School at Rome · Meantime Residency in Association with The Open West · The Arts Club Prize for Finest Drawing, National Open Art Competition · The Haworth Trust Award for Painting. Exhibitions: **2023** – The London Group Open · **2023** – 170th RWA Annual Open Exhibition Royal West of England Academy · **2023** – Royal Academy of Arts · **2023** – Pastel Society Annual Exhibition · **2023** – St Barbe Open St Barbe Museum and Gallery, Hampshire · Highly Commended: 193rd RHA Annual Exhibition, Royal Hibernian Academy of Arts, Dublin · **2023** – 197th RSA Annual Exhibition The Royal Scottish Academy · **2023** – Royal Cambrian Academy of Art Open, Conwy, Wales · Highly Commended: ING Discerning Eye Mall Galleries · Regeneration: The Queen's Green Canopy Nature in Art Museum and Gallery Gloucester · **2021** – 'Being With Trees', Gustavo Bacarisas Gallery Gibraltar.

Richard Bavin
www.richardbavin.com
Instagram @richardtreeart
BA (Hons) Fine Art, Cheltenham School of Art · Advanced Diploma in Fine Art, Hereford College of Arts · Masterclass on landscape painting tutored by David Tress. Herefordshire Wildlife Trust artist-in-residence · Drawing the Light residency, St Weonards Benefice, Herefordshire · Bleddfa Centre residencies · The PLACE Collective · The Methodist Modern Art Collection.

Philippa Beale
www.philippabeale.com
2006 – Fellow of Fine Art in Higher Education · Post Grad Cert Digital Image Making (Distinction) LCC University of the Arts · PhD Research Degree Supervision · MCIM Chartered Institute of Business and Management PG Dip Business and Management UAL · MA in Fine Art, Goldsmiths College, (MA Thesis: Semiotics and Cultural Forms) · Postgraduate Diploma in the Psychology and Philosophy University of Reading · BA (Hons) Goldsmiths College, University of London · Pre-Dip. Winchester School of Art · President the London Group · Founding Member the Arborealists. **Solo Exhibitions**: The Margate Gallery · Musee de Brux Vienne France · The Bermondsey Project Space · Retrospective 30 years of Conceptual Art Practice, LCC Galleries, London · Key London Ltd., Wimpole Street · video viewing Institute of Contemporary Art London · Les Cloitres Gallery, Poitiers France · Air Gallery, London · Southampton City Art Gallery · Angela Flowers Gallery, London · Akumulatory Galleria, Poznan Poland · Richard Demarco Gallery, Edinburgh · Acme Gallery, London · Park Square Gallery, Leeds · Camden Arts Centre · Chapel Gallery, Tisbury Wiltshire. **National Collections:** Tate Britain · ACGB – Southampton City Art Gallery · Bourg de Brux · Kraków Museum of Modern Art Poland.

John Blandy RCA
www.johnblandy.co.uk
Instagram @john2art
John Blandy has lived and worked in Queen's Park, London for over forty years. Blandy has been represented by the Francis Kyle Gallery and Cassian De Vere Cole, London · **2013** – He is a founder member of the Arborealists · The Arborealist exhibitions: 'Sante-Croix de Ludun', France · **2021** – The RWA in Bristol: 'Being with Trees' at The Bermondsey Project Space · The Gustavo Bacarisas Gallery in Gibraltar · 'Trees by the Water's Edge', Pie Factory Margate · **2021** – Solo shows: 'Pillars of the Forest', Portraits of Trees in Wytham Wood · **2023** – The Barn Gallery, St John's College, Oxford University.
Series of John's work are in the collections of Hammersmith Hospital and St George's Hospital, Tooting, and in various combinations of series in many private collections.

Ann Blockley
www.annblockley.com
BA (Hons) in Illustration from Brighton University.
Ann Blockley is a watercolour and mixed-media artist with an individual style developed over a lifetime of professional painting. Her pictures are evocative, atmospheric and intuitive, capturing an elusive air of mystery and magic within nature that lies tantalisingly between reality and the imagined. Her practice embraces a range of materials and techniques chosen to express the unique interpretations of nature that are her signature themes. Ann has written numerous books on her painting methods, including *Poetic Woods* (2023) published by Batsford.
Membership: The Royal Institute of Painters in Watercolour (RI) · The Society of Women artists (SWA) · The Arborealists: a diverse group of artists who value trees and a connection with nature.

Claire Cansick
www.clairecansick.com
Norwich University of the Arts BA Fine Art · **2024** – Jacksons Art Prize Shortlist, Bankside Gallery, London · **2023/2024** – Solo Exhibition: 'You and I Are Earth' · **2023** – Contemporary British Painting Prize Longlist.

Andrew Carnie
www.andrewcarnie.uk
1979/82 – Goldsmiths School of Art, London ·
1983–86 – Royal College of Art, London
Recent exhibitions: San Telmo Museum, San Sebastian · Fundación Telefónica, Madrid · The CCCB, Barcelona · Brain Observatory, San Diego · Kunsthall Charlottenborg, København · The RSU Anatomical Museum, Riga · Spencer Museum of Art, Kansas.

Stella Carr
www.stellacarr.co.uk
Instagram @stellacarr.artlandscape
1980 – Foundation in Art & Design Liverpool ·
1984 – Bachelor of Arts Print & Illustration from Kingston University, Surrey · **1984/1989** – Horticultural Internship The Grange & Balmoral Cottage, Benenden, Kent. Recent exhibitions: Bermondsey Project Space London · Gustavo Bacarisas Gallery, Gibraltar · Norwich Cathedral · The Pie Factory, Margate · Thelma Hubert Gallery Somerton. Recently awarded: **2024** – Artist in Residence and Curator at Valeni Manor, Cultural Centre and Dendrological Park, Romania · Arts Council England Grant.

Lara Cobden
www.laracobden.com
Instagram @laracobden
2023 – Artist Residency, Colstoun Estate, East Lothian Scotland · **2021** – Artist Residency, Cill Rialaig Project Kerry, Ireland · **2019/20** – Turps Correspondence Course – Turps Banana · **2016** – Artist Residency, Cill Rialaig Project Kerry, Ireland · **2016** – Art Residency, Lake

Kukkia, Finland August · **1992/95** – BA (Hons) Fine Art Painting, University of Brighton · **1989** – Foundation Art, Barnet Art College London · Selected Awards: **2021** – John Moores Painting Prize, Finalist, Walker Gallery Liverpool · **2020** – Castlegate Painting Prize, Finalist, Castlegate House Gallery Cockermouth · **2020** – BEEP Biennial · **2020** – Exhibited Shortlist, Elysium Gallery Swansea · **2019** – ING Discerning Eye · Chairman's Purchase Prize, Mall Galleries London · Westmorland Landscape Prize, Exhibited Shortlist, Rheged Centre Cumbria · 2nd Prize Winner, Lynn Painter-Stainers Prize, Mall Galleries London · **2016** – 1st Prize winner, Sir John Hurt Art Prize Holt Festival Art Prize, Norfolk. Solo exhibitions: **2022** – Incantations of Light, Irving Contemporary Oxford · **2022** – Falling Without Ever Landing, Liliya Art Gallery London · **2022** – The Shadows In Between, Cane & Davis London.

Tim Craven

1976 – BA (Hons) Fine Art Stourbridge College of Art · **1979** – Postgraduate Diploma in the Conservation of Easel Paintings Gateshead Technical College · Employment: **1980/2017** – Southampton City Art Gallery: Conservation, Collection Management, Curator · **2014** – Founder, the Arborealists · **2015** – Elected to The London Group · **2019** – Chair The Friends of Southampton's Museums Archives and Galleries · **2021** – Board member and regional co-ordinator SE/W The British Association of Friends of Museums · **2022** – Founder, Southern Exhibitions Group.

Annabel Cullen

www.annabelcullen.com

2009 – Tutor at Putney School of Art & Design · MA in Painting, Royal College of Art · BA in Fine Art, Camberwell School of Arts & Crafts.

Blaze Cyan RE SWE

www.blazecyan.com

Instagram @blazecyan

Studied at: **2013/2014** – MA Fine Art City & Guilds of London Art School · **1989/1992** – BA (Hons) Fashion Design University of Westminster · **2021** – Elected Member of the Society of Wood Engravers · **2017** – Elected Fellow of the Royal Society of Painter-Printmakers. Exhibitions: **2023/2021/2019** – Solo shows: *Eames Fine Art*, London · **2023** – Leith Hill Place NT Surrey · **2011** – Wellington College, Berkshire Collections Heilongjiang Museum of Printmaking, China. Collections: HRH Queen Elizabeth II · Ashmolean Museum · British Museum · Fitzwilliam Museum · Victoria & Albert Museum · Ashmolean Museum, RE Diploma Collection, Oxford · Wellington College, Crowthorne. Awards: ING Discerning Eye Collection Awards Eames Fine Art Purchase Prize · The Masters Exhibition, Bankside Gallery · First Time Exhibitor Prize, 81st Annual Exhibition, Society of Wood Engravers · Ashmolean / Vivian Leigh Purchase Prize, RE Exhibition, Bankside Gallery · Finalist ING Discerning Eye Drawing Bursary, Mall Galleries · Finalist RBA Rome Scholarship, Royal Society of British Artists, Mall Galleries · Norman Ackroyd, Prize for Etching, City & Guilds of London Art School.

Mike Dodd

www.mike-dodd.com

Studied at: Cardiff School of Art (UWIC) MA in Fine Art · Chelsea School of Art DipAD in Graphic Design. Residencies: Inverewe Gardens and Estate Wester Ross, Scotland · Outlandia Glen Nevis Fort William, Scotland. Exhibitions: 'At The Water's Edge', Pie Factory – Margate · 'Love Is The Meaning', St Stephen's Church – Norwich · 'Trees and the Sacred', The Hostry – Norwich Cathedral · 'Trees and Woodlands of Exmoor', Withypool – Somerset · 'Trees and Woodlands of Exmoor and Dartmoor' – Somerset Museum · 'L'Art des Arbres', Collégiale Sainte-Croix Loudun – France · 'Trees and Other Objects', Fairhurst Gallery – Norwich ·

'No Man's Land', St Peter Hungate Church – Norwich · 'Upstream Bickelhaupt Arboretum', Clinton Iowa – USA.

Alex Egan
www.alexegan.co.uk
Instagram @alexmdegan
Studied at: BA (Hons) Fine Art Bristol Polytechnic · Art Foundation Salisbury College of Art Artist and concept designer at Capco · Creating Adventurous Places www.wearecapco.com · **2018 to Present** – Tree artist in residence at the Somerleyton Estate in Suffolk · Devised and Leading Contemplative Drawing workshops among trees: including at Marchmont House www.marchmonthouse.com · **2017** – Arborealist member · 'Conversations with Trees' accompanied by Founder Arborealist members Tim Craven and Fiona McIntyre · Tree portrait commissions including: Houghton Hall estate, Norfolk – Sandringham for the King's 70th birthday – Daylesford, Oxfordshire – Aske Hall, North Yorkshire · Artist and Designer for Bewilderwood treehouse adventure playground · Designer at Riverside Screenprint, Bishop's Castle, Shropshire · Storyboard illustrator at Mike Rhodes studio, London.

Alex Faulkner
Studied at: **1979** – BA Fine Art, Bath Academy of Art, Corsham · **1979** – 'New Contemporaries', ICA London · **2003** – MA Creative Writing. Bath University College Exhibitions: **2015** – 'Dimitri & Wenlop', Riflemaker Gallery, Co-show with Christopher Bucklow · **2016** – Solo-show: 'Paintings and Drawings', Black Swan Gallery · **2018** – Print work acquired by the V&A Museum · **2019** – Group Show, 'Romantics' at St Barbe Museum & Gallery, Lymington · **2019** – Group Show, 'To the Fore' at Mount Art, Frome · **2020** – Group Show, 'Being With Trees' at Bermondsey Project Space · **2022** – Group Show, 'Trees & the Sacred' at Norwich Cathedral The Hostry · **2023** – Group Show, 'A Sense of Place' at Bermondsey Project Space · **2023** – 'The Alphabet of Dimitri & Wenlop', Antitaupe Gallery Bruton, with Christopher Bucklow · **2023** – Publication of the long poem, *Like Odysseus*, published by Ball-Press · **2023** – Publication of limited-edition deluxe Artists' Tarot cards, *The Tarot of Dimitri & Wenlop* · **2023** – Group Show, 'Regeneration' at Hansard Studio, Kensington · **2024** – Print work acquired by the Modern and Contemporary Collection and the Print Collection (The Golder Thompson Gift) · **2024** – Painting acquired by Contemporary Art Collection at Chippenham Museum.

Stephanie Fawbert
www.stephaniefawbert.com
Instagram @stephfawbertartist
1983/1984 – West Surrey College of Art and Design · **1984/1987** – University of Northumberland · **2022** – Shortlisted for Jacksons Painting Prize · **2022/2023** – Royal Academy Summer Exhibition.

Paul Finn
Instagram @paulfinn3
Brinkley Fellow University of the Arts Norwich · Slade School of Fine Art University College London · Ravensbourne School of Art.

Tom Genders
www.tomgenders.com
2003 – Foundation Diploma, Bournville College Birmingham · **2006** – BA (Hons) Illustration Portsmouth University · **2010** – PGCE Fine Art University of Brighton.

Crispin Heesom
www.crispinheesom.com
Studied painting and drawing at Norwich Arts school · Studied painting at the Byam Shaw School of Art in London · Studied etching at the City Lit and Morley Colleges · Resident at Acme art studios, Hackney · Winner of Collinson Landscape Prize · Exhibited London, Venice, throughout UK and France · Private collections include Oundle School and the Ealand / Warwick bequest.

Julie Held LG NEAC
www.julieheld.com
Instagram @julie.held
Attended Camberwell School of Art and The Royal Academy Schools, where she was appointed Picker Fellow. Exhibited widely in the UK and abroad. **Public Collections:** Nuffield College Oxford · New Hall Cambridge ·The Open University · Baker McKenzie · The Ben Uri Museum. **Membership**: The London Group · The New English Art Club · The Royal Water Colour Society · The Aborealists. Julie teaches at The Royal Drawing School, London.

Tilia Holmes
www.tiliaholmes.co.uk
2017 – Graduated from Arts University Bournemouth with a degree in visual communication · Tilia worked as a graphic designer and illustrator in the film poster industry while living in London · Now living in Dorset, her artwork is on display at Dansel Gallery among 200 makers producing high quality woodwork in the UK. Awards include: **2023** – Top Artist in Category by the CFA Artist of the Month · Solo exhibition at the Treehouse Hotel, London · **2023** – featured in *The Glossary* magazine for Earth Day · **2023** – selected to be in the final of 'Wildlife Artist of the Year'.

Abi Kremer
www.abikremer.com
Harrow College of Art Foundation · Bournemouth College of Art: Dip AD in Environmental Art · Licentiate of Designer Craftsmen. Work in public collections: Russell Cotes Art Gallery · Museum, RNLI, EC3 Legal · **2023** – 'Paradise Found' Thelma Hulbert Gallery · **2021** – 'Being with Trees' Gustavio Bacarisas Gallery, Gibraltar · **2020** 'The Arborealists' Somerset Museum · **2017** – 'The Arborealists: The Art of Trees' Poitiers, France · **2016** – 'The Arborealists' St Barbe Art Gallery and Museum · **2015** 'Arboretum' Royal West of England Academy · **2014** – 'Echoes of Woodland' solo show, Russell Cotes Art Gallery and Museum · **2013** – 'Under the Greenwood: Present' St Barbe Art Gallery and Museum · **2010** – 'Colour Rhythms' solo show, Lighthouse, Poole Centre for the Arts · **2009** – 'Abi Kremer: Painting' Kube Gallery, Poole (Book Launch) · **2006** – 'Works on Canvas' solo show, Highcliffe Castle · **2005** – 'Works on Paper' solo show, Russell Cotes Art Gallery and Museum.

Ursula Leach RE
Trained: Winchester School of Art · BA (Hons) Fine Art, R.E. · Wimbledon & West Surrey College of Art & Design. Selected solo exhibitions: The Art Stable from **2010–2020** – Oliver Contemporary · 2021 – The Art Stable Dorset · **2010** – Oliver Contemporary London · **2001** – The John Creasy Museum Salisbury · Dorset County Museum · **1994** – Southampton City Art Gallery. Selected group exhibitions: **2024** – London Original Print Fair, Somerset House · **2004** – International Original Print Exhibition, London · **2024** – Oliver Contemporary · The Art Stable · Nadia Waterfield Fine Art · Highgate Contemporary · Belgrave St Ives · Campden Gallery · Redfern Gallery · Dorset County Museum · Bankside Gallery.

Natasha Lien
www.natashalien.com
Studied at: **2005/2006** – The Royal Drawing School: Postgraduate Diploma · **1996/2000** – Central Saint Martins College of Art and Design. Residencies: **2008** – Tetbury Music Festival · **2002** – Students from The Royal Drawing School · The New York School of Art · The Forbes Chateau de Balleroy France. Private Collections: HRH King Charles III · Drawing of The Old Vic Theatre. Public Collections: Victoria & Albert Museum · Jordan National Gallery of Fine Arts.

Rosemary Mafrici
www.rosemarymafrici.com
Trained at: Dartington College, where she studied 'Art and Design in the Social Context' · **2014** – Collaboration with Nottingham University teaching art and painting a mural in South Korea · **2015** – Finished a 21-year career as an art teacher to focus on her own work · **2017** – Solo exhibition at The Sock Gallery, Loughborough · **2018** Winner of the annual open. Tarpey Gallery, Castle Donnington · **2018** – 'Can't See the Wood for the Trees' exhibition at the Ferrers Gallery, Staunton Harold · **2019** – Joint exhibition at the Ingleby Gallery, Derbyshire · **2021** – 'Into the Wild' international art competition **semi-finalist**, Stratford upon Avon · **2021–2022** Broadway Arts Festival **overall winner** · **2022/2023** – Joint exhibition at the Theatre Barn, Cotswolds · **2024** – Joint exhibition at Welsh Contemporary, waterfront gallery, Broadhaven.

Fiona McIntyre ARE
www.fionamcintyre.com
Elected Royal Society Painter-Printmakers (ARE) · Hosking Houses Trust Residency · Sidney Nolan Trust Residency · MA European Fine Art Winchester School of Art in Barcelona · Grafikskolan Forum Malmo, Sweden; mentored by Master Printmaker Bertil Lundberg · Fresco Techniques, KKV, Malmo; tutored by Domenico Inganni · Swedish Language, Kursverksamheten Malmo, Sweden · BA (Hons), Drawing & Painting Edinburgh College of Art · Diploma, West Surrey College of Art and Design · HNC Graphic Design, Farnborough College of Technology.

Władysław Mirecki
Collections include: Jiangsu Province Art Museum, People's Republic of China · Jiangsu Province Department of Culture, People's Republic of China · Chelmsford Museums Essex · Ipswich Borough Council Museums and Galleries, Suffolk · Colchester and Ipswich Museums (on behalf of Colchester Borough Council) · Beecroft Art Gallery/Southend on Sea Museum, Essex · Fitzwilliam Museum, Cambridge · National Railway Museum, York. Prizes include: 2nd and 3rd prizes Sunday Times Watercolour Competition, Mall Galleries, London · 1st prize Lynn Painter-Stainers, Mall Galleries, London.

Paul Newman
www.paulnewmanartist.com
With a degree in fine art from Falmouth University, Paul has worked extensively on producing large-scale regional arts events and has curated several exhibitions. He now works as the Creative Director for Dorset Visual Arts, which produces the biennial Dorset Art Weeks event. Paul is also the lead arts partner for Dorset Visual Arts, at a major new venue for Dorset and Wessex, The Sherborne. He has shown work at various galleries across the southwest: Bath Society of Artists · Messums Wiltshire · The Royal West of England Academy · The Society of Graphic Fine Art, London · The Arborealists, France.

Howard Phipps ARE RWA SWE
www.howardphipps.co.uk
1971/1975 – Fine Art (Painting and Printmaking) at the Gloucestershire College of Art, Cheltenham. Phipps has held numerous solo exhibitions, as well as illustrating over thirty books, including a series of his own fine press books.

Alan Rankle
www.alanrankle.co.uk
Studied at: **1968/70** – Rochdale College of Art · **1970/73** – Goldsmiths College London BA (Hons). Exhibitions: Alan Rankle: **1973** 'The Pardonner's Tale' Institute of Contemporary Arts, London · **1993** – 'Riverfall & Other Works' Southampton City Art Gallery · **1986/2006** 'Landscapes for the Turning Earth (Paintings)' · **2006** – Oldham Museum & Art Gallery ·

1996 'Landscapes for the North (touring)' · Maidstone Museum & Art Gallery · Radishchev Art Museum, Saratov, Russia · Tunbridge Wells Museum. Selected Works: **1992/2009** – Fondazione Stelline, Milan, Italy · Publication: **2017** – *Capture the Castle: British Artists and the Castle from Turner to Le Brun*, Southampton City Art Gallery.

Angela Rumble
www.angelarumble.co.uk
Instagram @angela_rumble
BDS University of London · BA Fine Art (first class) KIAD · MA Fine Art KIAD.

Celia de Serra
www.celiadeserra.com
1995 – Graduated: Exeter University: Fine Art · Collections: Somerset and Dorset NHS Trusts. Exhibitions: **2021** – Solo show: 'Run Deep', The Art Stable, Child Okeford, Dorset · **2023** – 'From the Mountains to the Sea', Beaux Arts, Bath · **2023** – 'Leave the Road, Take the Trails', Mrs Jones Art Gallery, Shrewsbury · Over fifty exhibitions since **1990s**.

Nahem Shoa
www.nahemshoa.co.uk
1968 – Nahem Shoa was born in London · **1991** – completed a degree at Manchester School of Art · **2004** – Postgraduate Study at the Royal Drawing School · Exhibited in The Royal Academy Summer Show · BP Portrait Awards · **1992** – Won The Royal Society of Portrait Painters · Four Major Museum exhibitions: The Walker, Liverpool · Southampton City Art Gallery · The Atkinson Art Gallery, Southport ·Ferens Art Gallery, Hull · Permanent Collections: V&A · The Walker · The Laing · The Graves · The Herbert · The Box · Southampton City Art Gallery · Manchester Art Gallery · RAMM · Hatton, Bury · Hartlepool · Ferens · Atkinson.

Kevin Tole
www.kevintole.com
1955 – Born in Plymouth
1974/77 – Studied Mining Geology at Imperial College
1983/88 – Cornwall College and Falmouth School of Art, studied Ceramics. Worked in theatre including the Royal Opera House and Stage Manager for Irish National Ballet. Art Education: **1988/89** – Bretton Hall College, PGCE Taught Art (3D) in Schools and Adult Ed for 2 years.

Jacqueline Wedlake Hatton
www.jacquiwedlakehatton.com
2011/2012 – University College London MSc Urban Studies · **1998/2001** – Falmouth University BA (Hons) Fine Art · **1994/1996** – Shrewsbury College of Art and Technology BTEC Art Foundation.

David Wiseman ARWS LG
www.davidwiseman.org.uk
1967/1969 – Colchester School of Art · **1969/1972** – St. Martins School of Art · **1972/1975** – Royal College of Art. Public collections: The Arts Council · Prudential · Bank of England · The Open University · Lewisham Hospital · Frimley Park · Large scale murals at Charing Cross · Royal London and Ealing Hospitals · **2016** – Winner of RWS Purchase Prize · **2016** – Winner Daler Rowney Prize · **2018** – Winner RWS Publicity Prize · **2013** – Elected to the London Group · **2016** – The Arborealists · **2021** – The Royal Watercolour Society · Exhibitions: New Contemporaries · John Moores · Hayward Annual · R.A Summer Exhibition · The Discerning Eye · London Group Open · Royal Watercolour Society · The Museum of Modern Art Oxford · Kettles Yard Gallery – Cambridge and the Camden Arts Centre · Solo show: Serpentine Gallery · Solo show: Rowley Gallery · Solo show: Water Street Gallery · Touring exhibitions: Germany, US, France and Spain.

About the authors

Philippa Beale is an artist and educator who has spent the last twenty-four years curating exhibitions in the United Kingdom, France and Gibraltar and was elected a Fellow in Fine Art for Higher Education in 2006. Her work is purposefully semiotic, employing non-specific images – reminding the viewer of a memory. She feels her role as an artist, drawing directly from specific tree and woodland sites is to bear witness to the greater environmental campaign and to provide visual experiences that enable people to feel connected to nature and their love of trees.

Tim Craven is an artist, freelance curator and lecturer. Through a career spanning 37 years at Southampton City Art Gallery (1980– 2017), Tim managed and developed the internationally renowned permanent collection centred on historic and modern British art, acquiring over 1,000 works. He also curated and co-curated various temporary exhibitions at Southampton and elsewhere. These included subjects such as the Euston Road School, the Camden Town Group, British Surrealism, St Ives, the Systems Group, Photorealism, cartoons and contemporary practice, for which he contributed essays and introductions to the accompanying exhibition catalogues.

George Peterken OBE worked with the Nature Conservancy and started the ancient woodland inventory, later working as a nature conservation adviser at the Forestry Commission. His research interests, which have centred on nature conservation, natural woodland and long-term and large-scale aspects of woodland ecology, benefited from a Bullard Fellowship at Harvard University. He is the author of innumerable books on both woodlands and meadows and was awarded an OBE for services to forestry in 1994.

Credits

Page 17 quote of 1898 taken from a Suffolk Institute of Archaeology publication.

Page 18 quotes from Blythe (2013), *The Time by the Sea*, Faber & Faber, 2013 (ISBN 9780571290956).

Page 18 quotes from Blythe (2016), *Stour Seasons*, Canterbury Press, Norwich (ISBN 9781848258846).

Page 19 quote from Macfarlane, *The Wild Places*, Granta, London (ISBN 1783744490).

Page 89–90 and **page 91** (top image) photographed by Mockingbird Press, Bristol.

Page 91 (bottom image) scanned by Advantage Digital Print Ltd, Dorchester.

Page 98–100, all photographs by Tony Hutchings.

Page 116–118, all photographs by Tim Nathan. Text and images previously appeared in *Mothland*, published by Bermondsey Project Space and Riverfall Press (2016). ISBN 97819161422718.

First published in the United Kingdom
in 2024 by
Batsford
43 Great Ormond Street
London
WC1N 3HZ

An imprint of B. T. Batsford Holdings Limited

ISBN 978 1 84994 978 1

A CIP catalogue record for this book is available from the British Library.

10 9 8 7 6 5 4 3 2 1

Reproduction by Rival Colour Ltd, UK
Printed by Elma Basim, Turkey

This book can be ordered direct from the publisher at
www.batsfordbooks.com, or try your local bookshop.

FSC www.fsc.org
MIX
Paper from
responsible sources
FSC® C164814